LATIN
AMERICAN
POLITICS

Chandler Publications in Political Science
Victor Jones, *Editor*

LATIN AMERICAN POLITICS

A FUNCTIONAL APPROACH

CHARLES F. DENTON
California State University, Fresno

PRESTON LEE LAWRENCE
Southwest Texas State University

CHANDLER PUBLISHING COMPANY
An Intext Publisher
SAN FRANCISCO • SCRANTON • LONDON • TORONTO

199410

JL
960
D47

Library of Congress Cataloging in Publication Data

Denton, Charles F
    Latin American politics.

    (Chandler publications in political science)
    Bibliography: p.
    1. Latin America—Politics—1948–   I. Lawrence,
Preston Lee, joint author.   II. Title.
JL960.D47   320.9'8'03   74–179035
ISBN 0–8102–0455–X

COPYRIGHT © 1972 BY CHANDLER PUBLISHING COMPANY
ALL RIGHTS RESERVED
INTERNATIONAL STANDARD BOOK NUMBER 0–8102–0455–X
LIBRARY OF CONGRESS CATALOG CARD NO. 74–179035
PRINTED IN THE UNITED STATES OF AMERICA

To Fred, Mark, Steve,
Jennifer, and Amy

Contents

vii

Tables and Figures

TABLES

ix

FIGURES

Preface

The need for a book such as this one became apparent to us when teaching introductory courses in the politics of the Latin American countries. We found it to be impossible to cover in a meaningful fashion all of the nations in a single quarter or semester. A much more useful teaching technique we find is to outline certain patterns in the politics of the area as a whole, using what has loosely become known in the discipline as functional analysis, and to encourage the students to research the individual countries as case studies. There are certain dangers inherent in such an approach: most importantly, if emphasis is placed on similarities in the politics of the countries, there is the possibility that certain important individual characteristics or less common attributes of one system or another, essential to the understanding of the political process in those countries, may be neglected.

This text is designed as a starting point for the study of Latin American politics, for no single volume can hope to survey the totality of political phenomena in the twenty countries. In each section or chapter, propositions are presented which the student can test in the light of data which he has obtained on the particular country of interest to him. In view of the state of development in the discipline of political science and especially in the work on the Latin American area, these propositions are tentative, very generally framed, and often based on fragmentary evidence. Nevertheless, they serve as directional guides for the beginning student, showing him where he ought to be looking and what it is that he should be analyzing.

This book received impetus from our mutual friend and mentor, Charles J. Parrish of Wayne State University. Through long discussion over a period of years, Professor Parrish outlined the need for an effort such as this one. We also wish to acknowledge an intellectual debt to Professor David V. Edwards, of the University of Texas, who taught us that the role of a teacher is to clarify rather than to obscure. Professor Karl Schmitt, of Texas as well, has been a source of considerable assistance in a variety of ways. Professor Max Mark, of the department of political science at Wayne State University, was sufficiently patient and cooperative with one young colleague to facilitate the completion of this manuscript. Thanks are due to Professor Francis Rich, chairman of the department of political science at Southwest Texas State University, for his consideration of the needs of a colleague completing a project of this magnitude. Jonathan Sharp, of Chandler Publishing Company, made a major contribution by encouraging us through some of the darker hours of the work.

It should go without saying that the fallacies, errors, misconceptions, and heresies of this book are exclusively those of the authors.

Fresno, California   *November 1971*

LATIN AMERICAN POLITICS

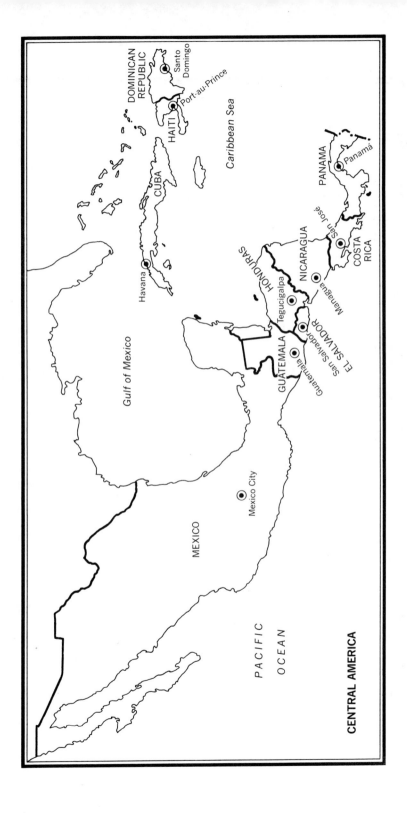

CENTRAL AMERICA

Caracas
VENEZUELA
Bogotá
COLOMBIA
Quito
ECUADOR
PERU
Lima
BOLIVIA
La Paz
BRAZIL
Brasília
PARAGUAY
Asunción
CHILE
PACIFIC
OCEAN
ARGENTINA
Santiago
Buenos Aires
URUGUAY
Montevideo
ATLANTIC
OCEAN

SOUTH AMERICA

THE STUDY OF POLITICS
AND LATIN AMERICA

The need to include countries such as those of the Latin American area in the comparative study of politics has led to major adjustments in the focus of political science as a whole in the last decade or so. Almond and Powell (1966) have labeled these changes an intellectual revolution. Until recently, very few political scientists concerned themselves with Latin American countries or others of the so-called developing areas, in large part because scholars in our discipline did not have the methodological equipment with which to carry out that sort of study. Until the late 1950's, political scientists primarily focused their attention on governmental institutions, studying how they functioned and why they were organized in certain ways. Although the study of institutions proved to be a reasonably relevant field of inquiry as far as the nations of Europe and North America were concerned, it became quite obvious that to restrict analysis to the governmental institutions of a Latin American nation was to explain very little about how politics really worked there. In fact until such nongovernmental phenomena as groups, political culture, and political so-

3

cialization became a legitimate field of inquiry for the political scientist, a book such as this one was not possible. Although this book does devote a chapter to the formal governmental structures of the Latin American countries, its primary focus is the *process* of politics—politics as activity rather than formal institutions.

The revolution in political science mentioned above involves a change not only in the focus of the discipline—what it is that we are going to study—but also in how we are to analyze our subject matter. The object of modern political science is the explanation of certain patterns of events or patterns of human behavior. In order to achieve maximum results from their research efforts, political scientists have adopted certain methods and commitments from the natural sciences. In some cases the scientific approach has meant the use of mathematical models, measurement, and scaling as complex as some of those used by physicists. But in general the scientific commitment in political science has implied a dedication to the systematic gathering and analysis of data, an effort to remove individual value preferences from research, and a desire to develop empirically testable generalizations about the phenomena under study.

In order to explain anything it is necessary first to clearly describe what it is that one desires to explain, then to compare it with objects or phenomena of a similar type, and from these comparisons to develop generalizations about the subject of study. The present volume is designed to examine our subject using this three-step approach. Major political phenomena in the Latin American countries are described in the broadest possible way, comparisons between the countries are made, and finally some generalizations about these phenomena are made. Further in-depth testing in one particular country may reveal that the generalizations provided about a particular phenomenon do not hold true in that case. It may be that the generalization will have to be modified or even totally discarded. The point is that we are moving in the right direction. Instead of being satisfied with mere description or data gathering in a nonselective fashion and remaining unable to distinguish what is important from what is not, we will be on the road to becoming worthy of the name political "scientists."

To survey all of the literature in political science which theorizes about the politics of the so-called developing areas would require a volume much larger than this one. Since the breakthrough in the discipline, analyses of that type have appeared in ever increasing quantities. This chapter is designed to fulfill two more limited functions. First, certain dominant themes in the literature of political science are outlined and a conceptual framework in which to place the material which follows is developed. The remainder of the chapter is devoted to a discussion of the pros and cons of viewing Latin America as a conceptual unit.

AUTHORITATIVE DECISION MAKING

A great deal of political-science literature today is concerned with the authoritative or the collective decision-making process of an entire society, as Mitchell and Mitchell (1969) point out. An important portion of this process may take place within the context of a governmental structure, but other important parts take place elsewhere. Thus while the formal governmental structure of a country must be analyzed in order to explain how decisions are made, a great deal of attention must also be paid to processes which take place in the society as a whole. Because the Latin American countries have been noted for their governmental instability, the lack of openness of their political processes (especially within the formal institutional context), and the importance of covert or half-hidden activities in public-policy making, these nations clearly deserve much attention to their noninstitutional political dimensions. The authoritative decisions in Latin American countries quite regularly appear to be either made or very strongly influenced by actors and processes far removed from the formal policy-making process.

Any reasonably adequate understanding of the politics of the Latin American area requires, then, some emphasis on the processes operating to produce the final public-policy outputs. The functional roles of the military, parties, public bureaucracy, and other actors must be considered; but also necessary to the examination are social-class structures, patterns of economic activity, extranational actors and influences, and socialization processes. This volume considers an inclusive list of processes and actors that play important political roles in the Latin American systems. While this inclusiveness may often require analysis which moves beyond the institutional-legal setting, such far-ranging inquiry is essential to an understanding of the subject—Latin American politics.

To speak of a *collective* decision-making process in any system is not to say that all or any of the decisions are made by the general community or for the benefit of the masses. As will be discussed, effective decision making is often carried out by a tiny minority of the population primarily for its own benefit. However, this form of decision making is still termed collective, in the sense that decisions made are for and binding on the general community. Thus, President François "Papa Doc" Duvalier of Haiti could make virtually all of the major decisions for his country with the participation of only the smallest coterie of advisers and still be engaged in collective decision making.

The Distribution of Resources

The most important issue decided by the authoritative decision-making process is how the resources of a society are distributed. While Latin Americans, at least partly as a result of their Iberian heritage, have traditionally looked to their political leaders for solutions to problems of distribution, people around the world are increasingly doing the same—a relatively recent phenomenon in many countries. Political decision makers have always accepted the responsibility for allocating certain goods and services, but in most countries this function encompasses an ever growing list. In addition to such services as police protection, hospitals, defense, and fire fighting—items which the Manchesterian school of economics would consider well within the responsibility of the political system—the list now embraces a major proportion of the economic goods and services of a society, political goods such as parks, schools, railroads, utilities, and socio-cultural values such as status, position, and influence. Naturally all of these factors are closely interrelated. In countries where resources are particularly scarce, their distribution is the most important and difficult task in the system and the individuals who assume the distributive roles possess tremendous power, particularly if they are members of a cohesive group, adhere to a similar ideological perspective, and share a basic outlook on life.

A major argument of this volume is that the politics of the Latin American countries are substantially shaped by a common scarcity of resources. In contrast to the United States and some other, mainly European industrialized states, where sizable elements of the population are relatively deprived and still receive some political goods and services, in most Latin American countries any deprivation results in exclusion from participation in political rewards. Scarcity reinforces the tendency of decision makers to take a restricted view of distribution of those resources which are available.

Decision makers in the Latin American countries do share basic attitudes and values, even though there may be some substantial differences in their more objective social characteristics, such as income and occupation. Thus while there is conflict among leadership groups, especially over means of achieving certain goals and protecting privileged social positions, there remains substantial consensus concerning basic values. The consensual base becomes especially apparent in the face of a perceived threat from any group or individual that does not receive a proportionate share of the available resources. That this shared ideological and value orientation may be and probably will be largely unarticulated as a cohesive, single system of ideas should not lead to an underestimation of its importance for the preservation of the national social and political systems. The common ideological ground does mean, however, that any "out-group" threat will be met by concerted action on the part of those having access to the society's resources.

Despite its importance, the study of distributive roles alone is insufficient for an in-depth and comprehensive explanation of politics in general. A series of other, closely related factors must be examined. If the political system assumes the task of deciding how a large proportion of the resources of a society are allocated, it will also be pressured to accept the responsibility for seeing to it that these resources are produced in quantities that will permit their distribution. Plans must be made, regulations issued, and varying proportions of the citizenry mobilized into the work force to produce what is needed. If resources are not produced in sufficient quantities to be allocated, then the expectations of both decision maker and populace must be restricted accordingly.

Furthermore, the actual pattern of outputs must be examined in some detail for an adequate understanding of political processes. To what purposes are government revenues actually put? What economic activities do decision makers subsidize, protect by tariff, rigorously regulate, completely bar, or allow to operate with neither restriction nor assistance? What groups find their incomes used to support what other groups? While none of these questions or others of similar relevance to this issue can be definitively answered in this volume, some general answers that at least can serve as guides for further inquiry in this important area will be presented.

The Distribution of Symbolic Values

Political decision makers also distribute what have been labeled by Almond and Powell (1966, p. 26) as symbolic outputs, which relate to the emotional expectations of a society. Many persons in the Latin American countries participate in the collective decision-making process largely because of the symbolic content of a particular issue or person. Since individuals, like the polity itself, possess only limited resources, including the resource of time, only a certain period can be devoted to the assessment of political issues. Therefore, decision makers must interpret issues to the citizenry. The easiest way of reaching the masses is to simplify the issue and to attach to it certain symbolic values which will trigger the emotional response of a large proportion of the population in a fairly predictable fashion.

Symbolic values also acquire importance in a system since decision makers, governmental or otherwise, can use symbolic outputs as substitutes for real, material rewards or deprivations. The worker can be told that social-security programs have been enacted to meet his demands while in fact little if anything may be done to implement such programs. Peasants can be told that land reform has been affirmed to them as a political right, but in the absence of any substantive action to further the program the statement means nothing in terms of tangible rewards such as land distribution and improvement of living conditions.

The Authoritative Decision-Making Process

An important pattern which emerges from the literature of political science concerning the collective decision-making process is that the decisions made are regarded as binding on the members of the society. If, for example, decision makers determine that all citizens must pay them tribute or must pay a new tax to support the system, those who do not comply are punished. It is for this reason that we have labeled the political decision-making process as the *authoritative* decision-making process for the society as a whole.

If a sufficient number of a population does not accept political decisions as binding on them, then the system as a whole loses its viability. In some societies, especially where resources are not relatively abundant, a group of decision makers who have lost their credibility will be replaced. In societies where resources are scarce, if the demands of some groups are not met and the system loses its credibility, not only are decision makers changed but the system itself may undergo major adjustments.

Mitchell and Mitchell (1969) state that each polity is in some respects like all other systems in the choices and processes it must employ; like some other polities in the nature of its resources, scarcities, and competing values; and finally like no other polity in its own solutions and their consequences. This book is oriented toward ascertaining the similarities in the collective decision-making processes of the Latin American nations; at the same time the differences between the countries will be pointed out.

POLITICAL SYSTEMS ANALYSIS

The word *system*, which has appeared several times in the foregoing discussion, requires some clarification. In this book the Latin American collective decision-making process will be regarded as a system of activity, a model of which appears in Figure I-1. It will be noted that the authoritative decision-making institutions represent only a small portion of the model; the system consists principally of a series of functions. Each of the functions is closely interrelated with all of the others, but if the model is to be useful all of the functions will have to be clearly identifiable as information about Latin American political processes are outlined.

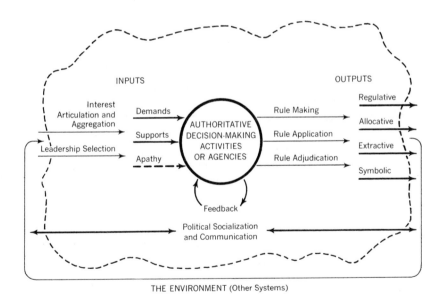

FIGURE I-1. A POLITICAL SYSTEM. *Source:* Marian D. Irish and James W. Prothro, *The Politics of American Democracy*, 3rd ed., © 1965, p. 15. Adapted by permission of Prentice-Hall, Inc., Englewood Cliffs, N.J.

Political Roles

The various functions outlined in the model are political activities which relate to the collective decision-making process. These activities are usually structured into political roles. Roles constitute the basic units of all social systems; political roles are those activities that form the basic units of the political system. Those performing political roles will almost surely have other, nonpolitical, social roles as well. The high-level Latin American army officer will probably be first and foremost a nonpolitical, career military man with no personal political ambitions or activities. At the same time the evidence indicates that in practically all of the countries of the region the high-level military figures also play political roles; that is, they engage in political activities of a significant, patterned, even predictable nature. Similarly, high-ranking clergymen perform distinctly religious roles and in a few countries now apparently play little if any political role at all in the system. But certainly in the past and even now in the vast majority of systems the ranking clergy play vital if often varying roles of clearly political relevance. Much of this book is dedicated to examining various political roles in the Latin American political systems and to assessing the sorts of functions which they perform.

System Characteristics

The very term system implies a discernible whole with clearly defined boundaries. In order to use this kind of a conceptual framework we will have to be able to distinguish between things political and things nonpolitical, a distinction given attention earlier in this chapter. Because of the central decision-making role assigned to the polity in the discussion above, an important consideration is the relationship between the political system and its environment—the society, the economy, and other countries.

In societies with scarce resources, like most of the Latin American nations, the boundaries between the political system on the one hand and the economic, social, and cultural systems (the environment) on the other hand are often indistinct. In noting this overlap between the various systems in a less developed country, Riggs (1964, pp. 52–54) has called for a "pan-disciplinarian" approach to the analysis of social phenomena in nations such as those of the Latin American area. Although the approach taken in this book is definitely derived from political science, considerable attention is given to the environments of the political system. A chapter is devoted to each of the two major portions of this environment in the Latin American countries—the society and the economy. And since there not only is considerable functional overlap between the various domestic systems—political, economic, and social—in the society with limited resources but also less distinct boundaries between the total system and its international environment, a separate chapter is devoted to the latter.

There is, however, a sharp difference in a country with scarce resources between the relationship of the polity with its socioeconomic environments and the relationship between political decision making and the international environment. For while the political system represents the central locus of decision making for the various domestic systems, this is not the case in its relationship with other countries. Rosenau (1966) has defined a "penetrated" society as one in which nonmembers of that system participate directly and authoritatively in either the allocation of its resources or the mobilization of support to obtain those resources. Rosenau notes further that the degree of penetration is directly related to the amount of resources a particular country possesses; the poorer a country is, the more citizens of other countries, officially or unofficially, participate in the political decision-making process. The Latin American nations are not exceptions to Rosenau's hypotheses; this phenomenon is considered in the chapter on the international environment of the Latin American systems.

To recapitulate briefly, although this book regards the collective decision-making process of the Latin American nations as a system of political activity, the great deal of overlap between the polity and its environments requires that these relationships be reconsidered. The sort of collective and authoritative decision-making process which emerges in a particular country and even the types of governmental structures which are designed by its leaders are as much a product of the nation's society, economy, and culture and of the interactions these men have had with other countries as they are of an on-going and semiautonomous system of activity.

We should note another general characteristic of systems that is especially relevant to the discussion at this point—the interdependence of the various elements that make up the system itself. In Almond and Powell's view (1966, p. 19), interdependence means that "when the properties of one component in a system change, all the other components as a whole are affected." For example, the decision of one political party to organize and mobilize the peasantry can have a profound impact on the structure of political influence, increasing the pressure for certain kinds of political outputs, forcing other parties to compete for peasant support, and restructuring the nature of sociopolitical relations in the countryside.

The fragility of some of the political institutions of Latin American countries, the pressure from some sources for significant political change, and the scarcity of resources make the interdependence of component parts even more apparent and consequential. While a consistent argument of this volume is the strongly rooted basic stability of the Latin American societies and political patterns, at the same time there is clearly present the potential for significant change in important elements of the systems. The introduction of forces causing changes in some key system components will mean transformation of a significant nature in the systems affected. One of the most important potential sources of change is the large proportion of nonmobilized, and presently politically irrelevant, peoples in all of these countries.

Systemic Change and the Developing Nations

Whatever the model selected by a social scientist, it will inevitably contain biases of a remarkable variety. The systems model in Figure I-1, besides bearing a close resemblance to the political system of the United States, contains another innate bias: it is basically static in nature. Any system naturally tends to be homeostatic; when it undergoes significant change, it ceases to be the same system. A lengthy and occasionally heated debate has taken place within the discipline of political science over this problem of change. Some analysts, for example, Almond and Powell (1966), realize the problem and have attempted to modify their systems model to account for change. Others avoid it completely for a variety of reasons, including the belief that the systems model will tend to distort the analysis of politics of the "developing" areas.

Since political scientists are also unable to agree on a definition of the term "development," it should be noted that in this volume the word refers exclusively to economic development.[1] Political change will be discussed, assessed, and explained at least partly, but no unidimensional or historically inevitable movements will be introduced into the term "change" as has occurred with the term "development."

Since the amount of change which is occurring or will occur in any of the Latin American political systems lies somewhere between the revolutionary model and the conformity model, and for reasons to be outlined in this book probably closer to the latter one, the systems model with its static bias may be more adequate for the comparative analysis of the twenty nations south of the Rio Grande than for the politics of the United States. Latin American political systems will be assessed throughout this volume, then, within the conceptual framework outlined in Figure I-1. And regardless of the direction in which the systems are moving, the movement will be labeled change rather than development, decay, or some other similar term.

INPUTS TO THE POLITICAL SYSTEM

Interest Articulation and Aggregation

Irish and Prothro (1965) state that every political system must somehow identify the basic interests that unite and divide its citizens. The interest-articulation and -aggregation function, depicted in Figure I–1, permits decision makers to identify the problems and conditions in the environment which require action. Or, viewed from another perspective, this function is the manner in which the population of a country lets its political decision makers know what it is that they want. The manner in which the articulation-and-aggregation function is performed is also dependent on the pattern of social and economic relations of a particular system. The nature of the stratification system, the degree of concentration of land, business, and corporate wealth, and the general levels of education and income are only the more important features of a society that will structure the performance of this function. The issue of which social structures in the Latin American systems perform the function of articulation and aggregation is also important in terms of what kinds of demands are made on decision makers and by what means they are made. In Chapters VII, VIII, and IX this issue is examined in some detail. In general, however, the theme of this volume in regard to articulation and aggregation is that the performance of this function is sharply limited in an economically underdeveloped country to the very few—the educated and wealthy individuals and the groups into which they are organized—whose social and economic power relative to the rest of the population provides them with rarely challenged access to decision-making positions. In other words, in countries with scarce resources it is probable that only a small group of citizens will have access to the decision makers, will be recognized by the system, and will let their interests be known to decision makers.

Leadership Selection

The leadership-selection function of the political system is the manner in which a country chooses and grooms the individuals who will play the authoritative decision-making roles at a particular period in time. The persons selected will probably be those who have accumulated a certain minimal number of economic- and social-status resources prior to attaining decision-making positions. The criteria for selection vary from system to system and could involve anything from a person's kinship relations to his acquired managerial and political skills. Methods of recruitment vary as well, from rising through the ranks of a political-party apparatus to high rank in an interventionist military organization. Students of Latin American politics have made little systematic effort to study the background of leaders and patterns of recruitment to leadership positions, perhaps a result of the frequent change of formal governments in a number of countries and the political importance of figures and groups not holding formal positions. However, by focusing on the social and economic groups from which decision makers are largely chosen, the relevant values which predominate among members of these groups, and the policies pursued by these leaders, we can at least partly overcome the problems arising from the lack of empirical data on recruitment patterns.

Political Socialization

Although interest articulation and aggregation and leadership selection are the only two functions in the model in Figure I-1 which can be described specifically and exclusively as inputs, there is no doubt that these functions are influenced by the patterns of political socialization in the society and types of political communication which have become established. "Political socialization" refers to the process by which a person's attitudes and expectations about the authoritative decision-making process in his country are formed. Essentially this is the process of learning what kind of role one is supposed to play relative to the political system. "Learning to be a good citizen" would be a more colloquial expression for one of the results of this function, although the implication that all socialization processes are positive in terms of building support for the prevailing system should be avoided. As a matter of fact, all systems are characterized by strong efforts by dominant elites to maintain socialization processes that build or reinforce support, but at the same time none is ever completely successful. The degrees of success vary sharply from system to system, with the differences having significant impact on how important sectors of the society view their political roles and in turn defining the context within which decision makers are chosen and interests are presented.

The sum of the attitudes and expectations of the population of a country toward their political decision-making process is labeled by Almond and Verba (1963) as the political culture of the society. Thus, in countries such as those of Latin America it can be expected that only individuals with certain very specific characteristics will expect or be expected to assume political decision-making responsibilities or to identify their interests with the polity.

The working classes of Latin American societies are normally so cut off from the decision-making process that they are provided with little basis for any kind of reaction to the political system. These groups are in effect not socialized politically; there is a lack of learning of political attitudes and expectations. It should be remembered that the working-class population in economically underdeveloped societies is characterized by extreme poverty, very low levels of education, long hours of labor, and little if any contact with organized groups, especially groups with political content or positions. Recent findings in the study of socialization processes indicate that even in the most economically advanced countries the segment of the population on the lower end of the social ladder does not usually learn a pattern of expected political behavior, and those few political attitudes and roles that are learned are fragmentary and disorganized.[2] In general, no identification with or rejection of the political system is generated. If this is true in countries of Western Europe and the United States, how much more true it must be in Latin American nations—where a substantial portion of the population, even in some major urban areas, is even outside the money economy. Education in particular seems to be a vital factor in enabling an individual to acquire sufficient knowledge of the political world for functioning effectively or even protesting effectively against disagreeable aspects of a regime. And education is not a characteristic of the mass of Latin Americans.

The kind of socialization individuals receive is also dependent on the media of socialization. These media include newspapers, television, radio, political parties, interest associations, the authoritative decision makers themselves, as well as family, schools, churches, and other social institutions of importance to an individual. At this point it is sufficient to note that the working-class population is not significantly affected by the first set of factors—except possibly radio, which serves to disseminate nothing more than the most general political knowledge. Furthermore, among the working-class population the latter media—family, church, and so forth—do not generate any significant interest in things political. What few politically relevant values are transmitted by the family are values that contribute to a passive role. Education is usually so limited that little effective learning of political roles takes place. And the church and clergy, when affecting the lower-class individual, have traditionally been used by the elites (or have been in agreement with the elites) in teaching values which perpetuate the existing order and justify an obedient subservience rather than effective participation from the masses. To be sure, the traditional patterns are undergoing some change. In some countries, the clergy, even at higher levels, is beginning to engage in teaching and leading lower-class groups in recognizing and articulating grievances. Moreover, a few political parties in countries such as Chile and Venezuela have initiated efforts to mobilize working-class elements, even the long-forgotten peasants. Nevertheless, it can still be safely argued that the vast majority of the working class is unaffected by major socialization media and remains politically illiterate in the most literal sense.

Particular attention is paid in this volume to the political-socialization process in the Latin American countries because of its importance in influencing the way the system performs. In a society with more resources, a wealthier nation, the political-socialization process is a relatively smooth one, beginning at childhood and continuing throughout an individual's lifetime with few interruptions. The agencies or institutions which carry out the function convey much the same values to the population; there is not a great deal of disparity among the values they proclaim. Whether at home, in school, or on the job, the citizens of a wealthier country encounter much the same set of values and beliefs; differences are found only from one social class to another and these tend to be minimal. In the countries with scarce resources, the poorer nations, the political-socialization process is smooth and uninterrupted only for the lower classes, simply because so few contacts with socializing media are made. For the small group at the top there are rude shocks and incongruities built into the process, particularly during the years when education in the formal sense is being acquired. This situation has important and often peculiar results, especially for the leadership-selection function; for example, those who protest the loudest about the incongruities in the value systems with which they are presented, university students particularly, are often the authoritative decision makers of the future in the Latin American countries.

Political Communication

The political-communication function is also closely interrelated with all functions of the system. It relates not only to how an individual is socialized politically, but also to how he is able to communicate his interests to the decision makers and vice versa. Political communication also has an influence on the relationship of the authoritative and collective decision-making process to its socio-economic and international environments. Because of such factors as rigid class stratification, illiteracy, and lack of party organization and activity in the countryside and in many lower-class urban areas, an absence of communication may exist between decision makers and much of the population. On the other hand, a rapid extension of the mass media may lead to augmented communications and an increase in the interests articulated or the demands made by the population, demands which often cannot be met and which result in powerful strains being placed on the system, ultimately resulting in system change.

The nature of the communications process also determines to what extent and by what means interests and demands can be made known to decision makers. A major problem with the political-communications network in most Latin American countries is the lack of media for transmission of lower-class demands and interests to those in decision-making positions. As will be discussed in some detail, political parties do not normally try to present for policy consideration the demands of the working-class groups. Interest associations that might represent them politically are virtually nonexistent. Even in economically advanced nations, newspapers, radio, and television are not effective means of communicating demands from the lower classes. The ballot, a crude and uncertain tool of communication, is denied in most Latin American countries through legal requirements such as literacy tests, informal barriers such as physical isolation from voting places and coercion from the upper class, or simply lack of free elections. For example, in 1971, nearly 65 per cent of Latin America's population lived in countries without even the veneer of democratic elections. Quite regularly, political communication for the working classes consists only of a one-way flow—from leaders to masses. Clearly, then, political communication, or lack of it, has considerable impact on the way the authoritative decision-making institutions of a system are able to perform.

Demands

The way in which these functions, interest articulation and aggregation and leadership selection as well as political socialization and communication, are performed leads to a series of different demands and supports being placed on collective decision makers. Almond and Powell (1966) provide a particularly useful breakdown of the sorts of demands and supports which are normally applied to a system. The first category is for goods and services, for scarce resources. Some of these have already been listed, and what follows is not an exhaustive list: education, health care, banking and insurance facilities, electricity, water, refined petroleum, land, housing, transportation, concerts, summer camps, sports facilities, pensions, white- and blue-collar positions, and status. The better a system establishes itself as an adequate supplier of goods and services to the population, the more the population comes to expect from its decision makers. This is just one illustration of feedback in a system, in this case different inputs generated by past outputs of a system.

Almond and Powell also describe a demand for the regulation of behavior. People living in a society must have their behavior circumscribed in order to restrict the chances for one group to infringe upon the behavior of another. This demand often results in the creation of military and police forces and of courts, and in the issuance of legal restrictions on behavior. In any society, but especially in societies with scarce resources, it is not unusual for one group to insure, through the manipulation of the political decision-making process, that they receive a larger share of the resources available than that of other groups. To guarantee the continued favorable distribution, close regulation of the behavior of certain classes is maintained.

The third type of demand input outlined by Almond and Powell is for participation in the collective decision-making process: the rights to vote, hold office, petition government bodies and officials, and organize. Largely as a result of pressure from the international environment, most Latin American countries now permit participation in voting by all adult citizens. However, other kinds of participation are more restricted, and even voting is subject to a number of significant informal restraints. While these restrictions will be examined in more detail later in the text, it may be safe to propose that in a society with limited resources, such as any one of those in Latin America, to extend participation to any great extent is also to paralyze the decision-making capabilities of the system. Time and time again abrupt increases in participation have led to political stalemates and subsequent restrictions.

One more type of demand input is the demand for symbolic display. In a country with a deep sense of national consciousness, collective decision makers are expected to pay deference to certain symbols and to use these symbols for mobilizing or demobilizing the citizenry as certain issues are considered. Since decision makers can usually determine the form which a significant part of the political-socialization process will take, it is not overly difficult for them to manipulate certain symbols when and if they perceive it necessary to do so. In societies with scarce resources, more symbolic outputs are required than in societies with more resources, simply because some outputs are demanded by the citizenry and it is often much easier to substitute symbolic for substantive rewards. Since other resources are not available, decision makers use symbolic outputs to placate certain groups in the political system.

Supports

Equally important to the collective decision-making process are the supports which decision makers receive from the society, economy, and other sections of the political environment. Clearly, nothing can be achieved in terms of allocating scarce resources if the system is not first capable of obtaining them. In a society where resources are particularly scarce, decision makers may take great steps to avoid redistributing political values as they solicit support. As a result, material supports may come primarily from one particular sector of the society. It should be added here that supports also include services rendered to the political system and may include everything from leadership provided to manpower obtained through a military conscription.

Unless most members of a society automatically abide by the decisions of the political system, those decisions quickly become invalidated. Thus it is necessary for most persons to lend at least tacit support to decision makers in order to permit them to perform; even if decisions are adverse, obedience supports must be provided. In societies with scarce resources it is necessary for a large proportion of the population to be apathetic to the system in order to maintain systemic equilibrium. Although apathy is depicted as a third type of input to the political-system model in Figure I-1, it can actually be a kind of support. Apathetic persons are affected by decisions made in their political system if in no other way than by being deprived of certain resources. Virtually every allocative decision involves taking from one group and giving to another or perhaps giving back to one group a particular resource which had been taken earlier. If a great percentage

of the members of any society were not apathetic, upon being deprived
of resources with seemingly little in return they would make demands
for a major revision in the system.

Lipset (1959a) provides an interesting commentary on the apathy of
the working classes of several countries. According to Lipset, people
who are deprived of economic goods and services over long periods of
time do not clamor ever more loudly for them to their authoritative
decision makers, but instead come to accept the idea that they will
never have them. This relationship is illustrated in Figure I-2. For

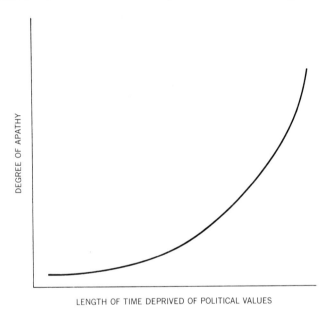

FIGURE I-2. THE TIME-APATHY RELATIONSHIP.

example, in the United States, roughly 15–20 per cent of the potential
electorate never votes, and about 40 per cent fails to participate in any
given presidential election. Not coincidentally, the percentage of the
population considered below the poverty line falls within these same
boundaries, depending on the criteria used. In the Latin American
countries, where a large proportion of the population has never shared
in the resources, the result has not been demands for an increased
share or for a drastic change in the collective decision-making process,
but rather almost complete apathy on the part of the underprivileged.

A different situation emerges when an upper-status group in a society is deprived of its customary share of values. Rather than becom-

ing apathetic, a group of this type can become disenchanted with or alienated from the system, and attempt to change or destroy the prevailing arrangements. This is more or less what occurred in Cuba prior to 1959, and when a similar group was deprived of its share of the resources after 1959, it too became alienated. Unable to easily oust the new decision makers or to destroy the Castro-formed system, this group chose to leave and take up residence in nearby Florida. Thus certain kinds of apathy at its earliest stages lead to neither supports nor demands but to alienation. In societies with scarce resources, more obedience supports will be expected from the underprivileged elements of the population than from others.

Still another type of support input takes the form of participation. While it is probably functional for certain groups in the population, for example, those with significant grievances and demands for government-produced goods and services, to remain apathetic to the collective decision-making process, if members of other groups, especially the upper socioeconomic groups, choose not to become involved the result can be dysfunctional. In every system enough support must be acquired from one source or another to balance or counteract the apathy and sometimes hostility that much of the population will express toward its operation. The amount of support necessary depends for continued stability on the degree of apathy and hostility present, which is directly dependent on the amount of resources available and the equity of their distribution, among other things. In short, while apathy may be widespread, portions of the population, and most particularly the well-educated, high-income, high-prestige groups, must share a certain positive and emotional sentiment toward their leaders and the system in which they operate in order for decision makers to carry out their task.

OUTPUTS OF THE POLITICAL SYSTEM

Essentially, political outputs take three forms, although they perform several functions. Collective decision makers either make rules relating to inputs received, apply rules already in existence, or modify or eliminate old rules.

The output function which receives the most attention throughout this volume is the allocative one. This function includes the process whereby demands and supports on the systemic decision makers are transformed into goods and services. It is almost a universal characteristic of political systems that resources are allocated to individuals and groups in the society which are capable of making the strongest demands and supports on decision makers. Not to allocate resources in this way could alienate precisely those groups capable of causing severe disruptions in the system. However, it is also feasible and a common practice in some systems, especially those where the base of support for the incumbent set of decision makers is weak, to allocate resources where there is no overt demand in order to create support for a particular policy or for a specific group of decision makers. Once a group is brought into the system in this fashion, depriving it of its share of resources at a later date may lead to antagonizing that group and creating negative feedbacks. This was the case in the republic of Argentina throughout the 1950's and early 1960's.

Equally important is the extractive output. Since it can be assumed that many necessary resources will not come voluntarily to collective decision makers, it may be necessary to exert authority to obtain them. It is possible that systemic decision makers may attempt to influence the political culture of the society—through the use of symbolic outputs, for example—so that most resources will be offered without the need to extract them forcibly. However, in societies with few resources those persons possessing status or wealth or commanding certain services may be more loath to relinquish them.

The regulative and symbolic outputs usually occur in response to specific demands for them. As a consequence, these outputs, especially the regulative ones, tend even more than others to be favorable to those who are most capable of applying pressure to decision makers, of clearly and forcefully making their demands known. By judiciously combining the two functions, decision makers can usually assure compliance with their decisions. The symbolic output is particularly important because it has been through its use that many nations with scarce resources, such as those of Latin America, have attempted to mobilize the population into support for a concerted drive toward the creation of more political and economic values. Symbols have been utilized to elicit a sentiment which has been labeled nationalism.

THE COMPARATIVE STUDY OF
LATIN AMERICAN POLITICS

The basic premise of this book is that the politics of each Latin American country comprises a system of activities leading to the collective and authoritative decision-making process for the society as a whole. The emphasis will be on which processes in the various countries influence this system and why. We shall examine the various environments of the Latin American political processes in succeeding chapters. However, it is first necessary to provide a justification for combining the countries for analysis.

Methodological Problems

A principal problem in the comparative study of political processes is the selection of a model to be used. It is quite possible that the model which an analyst chooses could have an influence on the data which he gathers and how he analyzes the data, in some cases such an influence that distortion occurs. There is no doubt, for example, that the model for a conceptual framework presented in Figure I-1 contains biases, both cultural and personal as they relate to its designers. The point is whether these values and prejudices can be recognized and isolated so that their influence on data analysis can be minimized. The political scientist studying a foreign country, while recognizing that it is impossible to be completely impartial, must attempt to isolate his personal values from his work as much as is humanly possible. The model in Figure I-1 bears a close resemblance to political patterns in the United States; yet it still can be employed if the North American biases are recognized and isolated.

Studies of Latin American politics by North Americans have usually been unconcerned with objective analysis and at times have been openly normative in nature. This state of affairs led Braibanti (1968) to note that political scientists working in the Latin American area seem to be the furthest removed from the methodological mainstream of the discipline of all area specialists. Kling (1964) states that research in the Latin American area by political scientists somewhat resembles the area which they are researching; both are underdeveloped. The biases of various analysts as they study the politics of Latin America have resulted in some almost spectacular misinterpretations. For example, North Americans traditionally have viewed Latin American countries as unstable and perpetually on the verge of a revolutionary uprising. The advent of Fidel Castro stimulated these ideas and led to a great outpouring of articles, newscasts, and books purporting to predict a massive outbreak of violence in the area momentarily. Apparently, many social scientists did not question some of the fundamental assumptions of the press and others in using a revolutionary model and adopted it for their own. The result has been a sizable number of books and professional articles which have employed this particular model. Titles such as *Evolution or Chaos?* (Schmitt and Burks, 1963), *The Winds of Revolution* (Szulc, 1965), and *Latin America: Reform or Revolution?* (Petras and Zeitlin, 1968) underscore the concerns of some writers with the possibility of violent change in the countries. Some analysts have gone so far as to suggest methods for averting the revolutions which they regard as imminent in Latin America. As Castro remained in power in Cuba and none of the other nations of the hemisphere seemed to be following his lead, and, in many cases, seemed to be moving in a conservative direction in the late 1960's and early 1970's, some analysts began to question the revolutionary model as the basis for analyzing Latin American politics. Interestingly enough, most of the political scientists who rejected the North American model were Latin Americans. One of the most influential pieces suggesting that some other model be employed was written by the Argentine José Nun (1965), who suggests that frequent coups by the military forces of the area may represent efforts by the middle social classes to maintain or retain the traditional power relationships and basic stability of their systems. Véliz (1967) and others have questioned whether there will be a revolution in Latin America at all and suggest "conformity" and other static or immobilist models as a basis for studying the politics of the twenty nations.

Latin America as a Conceptual Unit

The Uruguayan political philosopher José Enrique Rodó, writing in the early part of this century, stated in his widely read *Ariel* (in Davis, 1963, pp. 319–320):

> Perhaps there lacks in our South American character the definite contour of a personality. But even so, we Latin Americans have an inheritance of Race, a great ethnic tradition to maintain, a sacred bond which unites us to immortal pages of history and . . . the genius of our race must avail itself in the fusing of the elements that shall constitute the American of the future.

While intellectuals such as Rodó dreamed of a united Latin America, it has only been in recent times that the countries have communicated with each other on a regular basis. Since independence, which came for all except Panama and Cuba in the first decades of the nineteenth century, nations of Latin America have traveled on different paths, in many cases maintaining closer ties with Europe than with other nations of this hemisphere.

Latin American intellectuals and political leaders who have written and spoken of the need for unity in the Western Hemisphere have usually been unwilling to consider the United States as a candidate for membership in this union, at least until recently. The first Pan American conference held on the isthmus of Panama in 1826 and hosted by Simón Bolívar did not include representatives from the United States. While Great Britain was invited to send participating conferees, the government in Washington was asked to send only nonvocal observers. This occurred despite the fact that the Monroe doctrine had been issued only a few years earlier as a unilateral expression of American foreign policy toward the area. Toward the beginning of this century, when many of the Latin Americans were more willing to accept the idea of total hemispheric unity and invited the United States to participate in some form of alliance, decision makers in Washington were willing to accept the idea of special commercial ties, but rejected efforts to establish a special hemispheric political relationship.

Interestingly, it has only been with the founding of the Organization of American States (OAS) with the United States as a charter member that any movement toward unity among the Latin Americans themselves has occurred. Since World War II, at the behest of the OAS, the United States, and various United Nations agencies, Latin Americans have commenced to communicate with one another and the idea of a racial bond as described by Rodó has become more widespread. However, the chances for the establishment of some form of political unity among the countries are as remote as they are for the members of the European Common Market. While Latin Americans are beginning to perceive themselves as more than members of a single national group, as having ties with their neighbors, these sentiments probably have not led to significant changes in the international politics of the area and little evidence exists to indicate imminent changes in loyalties, from the national to regional level.

Latin America was originally settled and conquered by the leading nations of the late fifteenth and sixteenth centuries. After independence the colonies splintered into many nations and it has only been with the encouragement of the leading nations of the late twentieth century that the area is being recreated as an international political unit. In his study of Latin American voting patterns in the United Nations, Cornelius (1961) has noted that the twenty countries vote as a bloc only on specific issues of a narrow range: (1) when the United States requests their support in some Cold War cause, or (2) when certain kinds of development issues arise either for the consideration of the General Assembly or as the result of a study made by one or another of the regional commissions.

Country-by-Country Studies

The issue of whether or not Latin America is or will be an international political unit someday is only marginal to the problem of
whether or not the twenty nations can be considered a conceptual
unit. Because of the many differences between the countries certain
political scientists who have specialized in studying one or several of
the countries have argued that the nations are so different there is no
justification for the use of the term "Latin America." Actually this
position is based on another factor as much as on differences between
countries; analysts who have insisted on the uniqueness of each of the
Latin American nations have displayed a considerable lack of understanding of comparative methodology. To cite one example, Kantor
(1969) assesses each country separately and makes no effort to discern
similarities or patterns in the political processes. This approach is no
more disadvantageous than the one taken by other analysts where no
differences between the countries are discerned at all.

The primary difficulty involved in writing a book with a chapter
devoted to each of the Latin American nations is that none of the
countries receives in-depth analysis. Little more than a description of
some of the most important political structures and processes of each
country can be included. The reader then becomes very superficially
acquainted with all twenty countries. At the same time there is so
much information offered about each of the countries that comparisons and generalizations, so vital to social-science explanation, are
difficult to make. It is preferable to develop preliminary ideas and
hypotheses about the area as a whole and then gather data from one
or two countries to see how they apply to those cases.

In order to explain how the politics of any country works, a number
of steps have to be followed:

First, a *description* of the basic variables must be made.

Second, the descriptive data must be *compared* with data gathered in
similar or dissimilar countries.

Third, *generalizations* can be made about the politics of one or several
countries, generalizations which can then be tested with data gathered
from all of the countries of the world and modified if necessary.

Eventually a series of laws can be developed, based on rigorously
tested, systematically analyzed, and carefully selected political data.
This book presents the student with preliminary data from all of the
countries of Latin America, some comparisons between them, and

some very tentative generalizations. The student, it is hoped, will gather more extensive data about the one or two countries which particularly interest him and will test the generalizations in this book. The authors readily concede that some of the generalizations are tentative, but we present them on the basis of a lack of strongly conflicting evidence and as a heuristic guide, rather than for more scientific reasons. Hopefully, the near future will see further development of empirical and comparative analyses of important aspects of Latin American politics.

Similarities among the Countries

All of the Latin American nations are characterized by economic underdevelopment. Resources are more scarce than in certain other portions of the world, although potentially more could be generated. The vast majority of the populations of the countries spend their time growing crops to feed themselves, and their farming is conducted inefficiently. At the same time urban areas are mushrooming, growing several times faster than the countries as wholes. This situation is not wholly dissimilar to that of the nations of Africa, the Middle East, and Asia, commonly labeled as "the developing nations" along with Latin American countries. If economic underdevelopment were the sole determining factor, then there would be little justification for establishing conceptual boundaries around Latin America, separating it from other areas of the world with similar problems.

However, there is a series of factors which serve to distinguish the economically underdeveloped nations of this hemisphere from those of other areas of the world. With few exceptions, the Latin American nations have experienced over 125 years of independent existence in their economically underdeveloped state, so that the pattern of scarcity and accompanying sociopolitical systems has become institutionalized. In contrast, the nations of Africa and Asia, for example, which are just emerging from a colonial status, have generally not had sufficient time to institutionalize practices and processes which block the development of their resources.

The Latin American nations display similar social structures, varying yet significant degrees of social disintegration, a lack of social infrastructure, and other variables which serve to continue their economically underdeveloped status. In a sense it might be said that the nations of Latin America, which were once colonies of the leading powers of the international system, have now developed systems of internal colonization.[3] To the working classes of Latin America freedom from Spain, Portugal, or France has not changed their lot.

During the formal colonial period the peoples of the area learned to expect their political decision makers to resolve their most serious difficulties. Participation by any considerable number of people was not expected, and this situation has remained relatively unchanged. At the same time it might be pointed out that informal, external colonization did not cease in Latin America after national independence.

The colonial heritage reveals itself in the political culture of the twenty nations in more than the perspectives held by the Latin Americans on the role of the government as decision maker and the amount of participation in political processes expected of the members of the societies. There has long been an undercurrent of both personalism and authoritarianism in the area's political culture. Simón Bolívar, the great liberator, recognized these traits, and in one of his writings described the type of executive power which he believed was the best for any or all of the Latin American nations (in Davis, 1963, p. 34): "The President of the Republic, in our Constitution becomes the sun, which, fixed in its orbit, imparts life to the universe. This supreme authority must be perpetual." Although at times in their histories certain Latin American countries have been able to limit the powers of their chief executives, in general the efforts have not been long-lived. Neither have efforts, notably the one in Uruguay, to depersonalize the presidency been any more successful.

The cultural traits held in common, often inherited from the Iberian peninsula, and the social structures which also are remarkably similar, have had effects on patterns of behavior in the various nations. The average Latin American, while expecting much from his political decision makers, does little or nothing if the political system does not live up to his expectations. Apathy and inaction are the keynotes to the political behavior of most of the peoples south of the Rio Grande. Most Latin Americans cannot conceive of a political system as being of their own creation. This is equally true of all classes of society. The personalist nature of their cultures means that most of the population can retain loyalties only to those immediately connected to them by kinship or long friendship. At the same time a mysticism, which could have been inherited from either the Iberian peninsula or the indigenous cultures of pre-Colombian times, permits the people to be loyal to concepts such as liberty, democracy, and so forth. Intermediate and somewhat distant groups such as political parties, the government, or courts are not as susceptible to receiving loyalty or allegiance. The upper classes regard obedience to systemic regulations as required only if heavy sanctions are uniformly applied to those who do not obey. They have not been socialized into immediate and unquestioning obedience. At the same time the upper classes expect total compliance from the lower classes, foreigners, or those unrelated to them.

SUMMARY

The behavior of the people of Latin America is the central theme of this volume. Because the emphasis is on political behavior, largely in its aggregate form, behavior which is oriented toward authoritative decision making, particular attention will be paid to the major problems, those issues causing conflict in the Latin American societies. Structures affecting behavior and determinants of political culture will be examined.

Hopefully the individual Latin American, his life, loves, and expectations, will not be totally absent from the analysis. As Shively (1969) has pointed out, the use of aggregate data often produces different results and correlations from the ones obtained when individual data are utilized. Considering the fact that the aggregate data available about Latin America is often spotty, a major effort has been made here to modify distortions as they apply to the individual living in Brasília, Port-au-Prince, or in the *altiplano*.

NOTES

1. Economists have in the main agreed that if a country has a real per-capita income of less than $500, it is underdeveloped. A country experiencing economic development would be one where real per-capita income is increasing.

2. For a critical analysis and summary of mass-elite differences in one of the wealthier, highly educated, and socially "open" societies in the world, see Dye and Zeigler (1970), esp. Chaps. 5, 6, 8.

3. For a more detailed explanation of the term *internal colonization*, see Chapter III.

SUGGESTED READINGS

Almond, Gabriel A., and G. Bingham Powell, Jr. *Comparative Politics: A Developmental Approach.* Boston: Little, Brown, 1966.

Almond, Gabriel A., and Sidney Verba. *The Civic Culture.* Princeton, N.J.: Princeton University Press, 1963.

Blondel, Jean. *Comparative Government.* Garden City, N.Y.: Doubleday, 1969.

Dahl, Robert A. *Modern Political Analysis.* Englewood Cliffs, N.J.: Prentice-Hall, 1963.

Easton, David. *The Political System.* New York: Knopf, 1953.

Huntington, Samuel P. *Political Order in Changing Societies.* New Haven: Yale University Press, 1968.

Langton, Kenneth P. *Political Socialization.* New York: Oxford University Press, 1969.

Masannat, George S., and Thomas W. Madron. *The Political Arena.* New York: Scribner's, 1969.

Mitchell, Joyce N., and William C. Mitchell. *Political Analysis and Public Policy: An Introduction to Political Science.* Chicago: Rand McNally, 1969.

Pye, Lucian W. *Aspects of Political Development.* Boston: Little, Brown, 1966.

Rasmussen, Jorgen. *The Process of Politics.* New York: Atherton, 1969.

Scarrow, Howard A. *Comparative Political Analysis.* New York: Harper and Row, 1969.

Strickland, D. A., L. L. Wade, and R. E. Johnston. *A Primer of Political Analysis.* Chicago: Markham, 1969.

Wasby, Stephen L. *Political Science: The Discipline and Its Dimensions.* New York: Scribner's, 1970.

Wiseman, H. V. *Political Systems: Some Sociological Approaches.* New York: Praeger, 1966.

Young, Oran R. *Systems of Political Science.* Englewood Cliffs, N.J.: Prentice-Hall, 1967.

THE SOCIOCULTURAL
ENVIRONMENT

Each of the twenty Latin American countries displays a wide variety of cultural and social traits. As mentioned in Chapter I, the many diversities among Latin American countries have led some analysts to doubt the possibility of discerning similar traits and patterns throughout the area. The contrast between the large Argentine nation, with its predominantly European-descent, literate, and Spanish-speaking population, and tiny Haiti, with its predominantly black, illiterate, and French-speaking people, can lead to serious questions about areawide generalizations. Some of the Latin American nations contain large indigenous populations while others have virtually none. Some have substantial sectors of middle-level incomes and occupations while others have few so characterized. Some are semi-industrialized while others are little changed, especially economically, from the agrarian states of the eighteenth and early nineteenth centuries.

Most of the countries, as former colonies of Spain, are primarily Spanish-speaking. However, Brazil, which contains approximately one-third of the entire population of Latin America, is a Portuguese-speaking nation. All of the other non-Spanish-speaking countries are small in both population and size. Haitians are French-speaking, while Paraguay's population is bilingual in Spanish and the indigenous Guaraní language. In at least three of the countries, a significant percentage of the population does not speak the predominant language (Russet et al., 1964). In Peru, 63 per cent of the population speak Spanish, while the remainder speak several Indian languages. In Guatemala, only 59.5 per cent speak Spanish, while in Bolivia the figure drops to 36.5. In other words, two-thirds of the population of Bolivia do not speak the language of their government and school system. Since language can have a tremendous impact, not only on the way individuals conceptualize about themselves, but also on political-integration efforts and the conduct of politics in general, these differences are anything but insignificant. The "race" issue will be discussed later in this chapter.

It is not only in language and race that differences among the peoples of Latin America are noticeable, but also in food, dress, musical tastes, family relationships, and courtship patterns. Taking food as an example, it is interesting to note that Argentina is one of the world's great beef-eating countries. Cattle-slaughtering rates in that country range around 28 per cent a year. Not only is beef available to all but the very poorest Argentinian on a daily basis, but a tourist can obtain filet mignon, a salad, and a bottle of the local wine for approximately $1.50 at a good restaurant in Buenos Aires. In contrast, cattle-slaughtering rates in the rest of Latin America range around 12 per cent a year, and beef is a luxury afforded only to the very rich. Besides varying in beef consumption, each of the nations has a national dish or dishes, and staple foodstuffs vary widely from region to region. The Mexican food now available throughout most of the United States is an example of the food from one country only. Colombia boasts of the *sancocho*, a savory soup which contains a wide variety of meats and local vegetables and seasonings, while the *lechón asado*, a delicious pork roast, is found in the nations of the Caribbean area.

As for folk music, the mambo, the samba, the tango, and the boogaloo each originated in a different country. Dress, traditions, and folklore are often unique to each country. Even the tiny Central American republics, which formed a single country for two decades of the nineteenth century, boast what can be termed nothing less than their own culture and social makeup.

THE CULTURE OF SCARCITY

As discussed in the previous chapter, the underlying theme of this book is that politics are the processes involved in the authoritative allocation of certain types of scarce resources. One of the principal patterns shared by all of the countries of Latin America is the scarcity of political goods and services, status, and other values found in more abundance in North America and Europe. The scarcity of economic resources, which are allocated to an ever increasing degree by the political systems of Latin America, is discussed in detail in Chapter III.

Population Growth

In terms of available habitable space, Latin America is probably underpopulated. The habitable living area is estimated as being capable of supporting 2 billion people, compared to the 232 million presently found in the area. Only the small Central American republics, excluding Honduras, can be said to have the overpopulation problems characteristic of certain Asian areas. At the same time it can be argued that one of the principal factors contributing to the general scarcity of resources in the Latin American area is overpopulation. It is a selective overpopulation problem, however. There are basically two issues involved: very high birth rates, and even higher rates of movement into large urban complexes.

High birth rates in nearly all of the countries, coupled with ever decreasing death rates, have led to startlingly rapid population increases. The republic of Costa Rica, with its 48 births per 1,000 of the population and only 10 deaths per 1,000, is usually considered to have the fastest-growing population of any country in the world. As can be noted in Table II-1, with few exceptions all of the countries have mushrooming populations. To a great extent these growth figures can be explained by improved medical facilities and treatment and to a lesser extent by dietary improvements and religious preferences.

The principal short-run effect of these high birth rates has been to place the burden of supporting a large number of nonworkers on a small percentage of the population of the twenty nations. As data in Table II-2 reveal, on the average one-third of all Latin Americans are supporting the nonworking two-thirds of the population. Those who do not work either are too young to do so or are women, who must devote their time to caring for their many offspring. At a time when rapid economic growth is desirable—a phenomenon which would undoubtedly be aided by each increment of effort allocated to production

TABLE II-1. Total Population, Population Growth Rate, Percentage of Population in Major Cities, Percentage Urban, and Urban Growth Rate.

Country	Total Population (millions) 1970[a]	Population Growth Rate (per cent) 1968-1969	Percentage of Population in Cities over 100,000	Per Cent Urban[b]	Annual Urban Growth (per cent) 1969-1970[a]
Argentina	24.4	1.5	47.5 (1960)	74 (1960)	2.4
Bolivia	4.9	2.4	N.A.	35 (1969)[a]	2.4
Brazil	93.5	3.0	18.8 (1960)	46 (1960)	4.6
Chile	9.8	1.9	33.3 (1960)	68 (1960)	3.4
Colombia	21.1	3.2	27.5 (1964)	52 (1964)	5.0
Costa Rica	1.8	3.4	24.0 (1963)	35 (1963)	4.3
Cuba	8.3 (1967)	2.6 (1967)	N.A.	N.A.	N.A.
Dominican Republic	4.3	3.4	12.1 (1960)	30 (1960)	5.7
Ecuador	6.1	3.4	18.9 (1962)	36 (1962)	4.7
El Salvador	3.4	3.4	10.2 (1961)	39 (1961)	4.0
Guatemala	5.2	2.9	13.4 (1964)	35 (1964)	4.9
Haiti	4.9	2.4	N.A.	12 (1967)	3.8
Honduras	2.6	3.4	7.1 (1961)	23 (1961)	5.2
Mexico	50.7	3.5	18.6 (1960)	53 (1960)	5.2
Nicaragua	2.0	3.2	15.3 (1963)	44 (1963)	4.6
Panama	1.5	3.3	25.4 (1960)	47 (1960)	4.4
Paraguay	2.4	3.1	15.9 (1962)	36 (1962)	3.5
Peru	13.6	3.1	18.4 (1961)	47 (1961)	1.2
Uruguay	2.9 (1969)	1.3	44.7 (1963)	80 (1963)	2.9
Venezuela	10.4	3.5	30.0 (1961)	72 (1963)	5.6
Total	273.8				
Average		2.9			4.7
Canada	21.1 (1969)	1.5		74	
United States	203.2 (1969)	1.0		70	

a. Estimates.
b. From most recent census data; also definitions of "urban" vary considerably from country to country and are not strictly comparable.

Source: "Total Population" and "Annual Urban Growth," *América en Cifras* (Washington, D.C.: Pan American Union, 1970), pp. 6-7, 42-43. "Population Growth Rate," "Per Cent Urban," and figures for United States and Canada, *The Statistical Abstract of Latin America, 1969,* Kenneth Ruddle and Mukhtar Hamour (eds.), Publ. by the Latin American Center, University of California at Los Angeles (1971), pp. 65, 74-75, 84-85. Reproduced by permission. "Percentage of Population in Cities over 100,000," *Economic Survey of Latin America, 1968* (New York: United Nations Commission for Latin America, 1970), pp. 41-42.

—the large number of nonworkers in Latin America is a decided liability.

Urban Growth

As the data in Table II-1 reveal, urban growth has outstripped population increases in almost all of the Latin American nations. The

TABLE II-2.   Wage and Salary Earners as Percentage of Working-Age
Population, in Rank Order, excluding the Dominican
Republic, Guatemala, and Uruguay.

Country	Per Cent
Argentina	43.4
Chile	42.5
Costa Rica	42.2
Cuba	40.7
Ecuador	36.8
El Salvador	34.8
Venezuela	33.5
Nicaragua	32.0
Colombia	31.3
Brazil	30.0
Mexico	28.0
Peru	27.2
Panama	24.7
Honduras	22.9
Bolivia	19.0
Paraguay	18.4
Haiti	12.0

Source: Bruce Russet *et al.*, *World Handbook of Social and Political Indicators*
(New Haven: Yale University Press, 1964),
pp. 29-30. Reproduced by permission of
Yale University Press.

result has been the rather curious spectacle of primarily agrarian societies with predominantly urban populations. More than half of all
Latin Americans now reside in cities. It is in the cities where the great
political battles are fought, where decisions are made, and where major
proportions of the resources are allocated. Yet without a continuous
influx of wealth, resources, and personnel from the rural areas the
cities could not survive.[1] This situation constitutes a major difference
from the causes of urban growth in North America and Europe, where
people flock to the cities to obtain industrial jobs. In Latin America,
jobs in industry have not even begun to match increases in over-all
population, much less in the rate of urban growth.

If there are not great numbers of industrial jobs, a reasonable inquiry would be why the residents of rural Latin America are moving
into the cities, where housing shortages are so acute that even slums
are often not available. A number of factors seems to have led to this
state of affairs. The peasant, unable to obtain his own land (a problem
discussed in Chapter III) and faced with the challenge of not only
making a living but subsisting in the face of adverse health and housing
conditions and a shortage of educational opportunities, finds life in a

city slum more attractive than in a rural area. The mass media, especially through the transistor radio, are making rural residents aware of the urban amenities of life despite the fact that they are not available to most of the urban population. Mechanization in certain rural areas has made large numbers of peasants jobless. Finally, since it is in the cities where political decisions are made, it is not surprising to find that urban areas are receiving the principal attention of national problem solvers, often to the neglect of the rural regions. Rural residents are increasingly aware of this lack of attention to their needs. In other words, the city is "where the action is" and the pull of the urban areas is great, even if it means the breaking of familial, friendship, and other ties.

Educational Facilities

The scarcity of sociocultural and other kinds of resources in Latin America is supported by a wide variety of data. As the data in Table II-3 reveal, the scarcity of resources has meant that schooling has not been offered to all Latin Americans. In only one of the countries is more than 80 per cent of the school-age population in attendance at any one time, and the average, considering that approximately one-third of all Latin Americans live in Brazil, is still less than 60 per cent.

As a direct result of the paucity of educational opportunities, literacy is considerably limited in the Latin American area. As the data in Table II-3 reveal, there is some relationship between the number of children in primary school and the rate of illiteracy in each of the countries. For example, the top five countries are the same in both categories except Peru; of the bottom seven only Colombia is out of place. The language problem in those countries with large indigenous populations has influenced the literacy statistics. Despite the fact that not a few of the indigenous peoples now have written languages, official statistics include only those who are literate in the predominant language of the country, which in all of Latin America, with the exception of Paraguay, is a European-derived tongue. In countries where literacy is a prerequisite for voting and other forms of political participation, literacy rates are of particular importance to this analysis and the problem is assessed in a later chapter.

As expected, economic status is a very good indicator of the amount and quality of education an individual is likely to receive. In the poor urban sectors and especially in the rural areas not only are there economic pressures working against completion of more than 3–4 years of schooling, but there are equally important political and social

TABLE II-3. Percentage of Population 5-14 Years of Age in Primary School, in Rank Order, and Illiteracy Rate, excluding Cuba.

Country	Pupils		Per Cent Change, 1960-1970	Illiteracy	1970[i]
	1960	1970			
Chile (3)[a]	66.9	93.8	40.2	11.8 (1960)[b]	10
Argentina (2)	74.4	83.0	11.5	10.5 (1960)[c]	6
Uruguay (1) .	70.3	80.6	14.6	8.9 (1963)[b]	7
Peru (12)	54.5	78.1	43.3	39.4 (1961)[b]	29
Costa Rica (4)	58.4	69.0	18.0	16.0 (1963)[d]	11
Paraguay (9)	62.0	65.6	5.8	32.0 (1965)[c]	22
Mexico (7)	51.8	65.5	26.4	29.0 (1964)[e]	27
Dominican Republic (11)	59.6	65.0	9.0	36.0 (1962)[f]	30
Venezuela (6)	62.8	62.0	-1.2	22.5 (1961)[b]	30
Panama (5)	58.0	66.1	13.9	22.2[g] (1960)[b]	17
El Salvador (13)	48.5	56.0	15.5	41.9 (1961)[e]	42
Ecuador (10)	51.1	57.0	11.4	35.1 (1962)[e]	27
Bolivia (18)	43.0	57.4	33.7	68.0 (1965)[e]	53
Brazil (16)	40.7	57.3	41.0	39.0 (1960)[h]	29
Honduras (15)	36.8	52.5	42.6	55.0 (1961)[d]	43
Colombia (8)	39.4	50.0	27.0	30.6 (1963)[b]	22
Nicaragua (14)	38.7	50.6	30.9	50.0 (1963)[f]	40
Guatemala (17)	26.7	36.9	38.5	67.7 (1964)[b]	55
Haiti (19)	N.A.	N.A.	N.A.	89.5[i]	76
Average	49.0	62.9	27.8		27

a. Figures in parentheses are ranks by illiteracy rate.
b. 7 years and over.
c. 5 years and over.
d. 15 years and over.
e. 6 years and over.
f. 10 years and over.
g. Does not include Indian population.
h. 9 years and over.
i. Estimates.

Source: Office of Development Programs, Bureau for Latin America, Agency for International Development, *Summary Economic and Social Indicators 18 Latin American Countries: 1960-1970* (Washington, D.C.: Government Printing Office, April 1971), pp. 67, 84. Illiteracy estimates for 1970, *Socio-Economic Progress in Latin America: Social Progress Trust Fund Ninth Annual Report, 1969* (Washington, D.C.: Inter-American Development Bank, 1970), p. 137.

factors. The paucity of schools in poor regions, especially in the countryside, often denies or at least reduces access to education for substantial numbers. Also, the quality of urban-slum and rural schools is often so poor that students in those areas are not effectively educated. For example, in Chile, a country that ranks in the top five on practically any education criterion and which has made definite efforts to provide widespread educational opportunities, only 1 of 25 provinces has a higher percentage of noncertified teachers in urban areas than in rural areas. In 22 of 25 provinces 30 per cent or more of the rural teachers are not certified. In nearly half of the 25, the figure rises above 40 per cent, and these are the most rural provinces (Mattelart and Garreton, 1969, Table XIX, p. 190). This pattern is repeated virtually without exception in those countries where data are available. In 1938 a coalition of center and leftist parties won the presidency in Chile, with one of their major goals being expansion and improvement of the educational system. Yet two decades later, 27 per cent of the population finished only one year of school, 50 per cent of working-class children did not finish the third grade, 85 per cent completed no more than six, and less than 2 per cent went on to universities (Hamuy *et al.*, 1960).

One must also note the access of higher socioeconomic groups to private schools. These institutions are almost always significantly better financed and staffed than their public counterparts and are usually subsidized by public funds. In the countries for which data are available it can be noted in Table II-4 that a very large percentage of high-school students attend private schools. In general, public high schools in Latin American countries are vocational in orientation and the chance of getting from one of these establishments into the university is relatively remote. Thus, although university education is free

TABLE II-4. Number of Students in Public and Private High Schools, excluding the Dominican Republic and Honduras (thousands).

Country	Total	Public	Private
Argentina (1967)	848	567	281
Bolivia (1966)	109	71	38
Brazil (1967)	2,816	1,466	1,350
Chile (1967)	184	129	55
Colombia (1966)	514	223	291
Costa Rica (1965)	52	38	15
Cuba (1966-1967)	241	241	-
Ecuador (1965-1966)	117	70	48
El Salvador (1967)	69	29	40
Guatemala (1967)	60	31	29
Haiti (1965-1966)	25	18	7
Mexico (1967)	1,087	732	355
Nicaragua (1967-1968)	34	21	13
Panama (1967)	64	37	27
Paraguay (1966)	41	22	20
Peru (1965)	380	300	80
Uruguay (1957)	77	66	11
Venezuela (1967-1968)	367	286	81

Source: *América en Cifras* (Washington, D.C.: Pan American Union, 1967), Vol. 5, pp. 133-157.

in most of the countries, the high cost of obtaining the credentials to gain entrance into the university excludes most lower-class children from achieving the ultimate in social credentials—a college degree. It is undoubtedly for this reason, as the data in Table II-5 reveal, that such a small portion of all Latin Americans receive any university education at all.

As we will note in detail later, educational level is a significant

TABLE II-5. Number of University Students, in Rank Order, and Growth and Rate of Growth in Enrollments and Graduates.

Country	Students per 100,000 Population, 1960	Growth, 1960-1969 (thousands) 1960 Enrol.	Grad.	1969 Enrol.	Grad.	Average Rate of Growth, 1960-1970[a] (per cent) Enrol.	Grad.
Argentina	827	173.9	8.83	271.5	22.10	4.7	10.2
Uruguay	541	15.0	0.51	19.7	1.04	3.0	7.8
Panama	371	3.6	0.22	7.9	0.50	9.2	7.3
Venezuela	355	26.5	1.88	72.6	2.30	11.4	2.3[b]
Costa Rica	326	6.8	0.45	14.2	1.13	8.9	10.6
Colombia	296	24.6	1.90	72.2	4.89	12.4	10.9
Cuba	258	N.A.	N.A.	N.A.	N.A.	N.A.	N.A.
Mexico	258	78.0	6.00	188.0	12.50	9.5	11.6
Chile	257	24.7	2.38	71.0	5.50	12.3	9.7
Peru	253	35.0	2.85	118.0	8.43	13.1	12.6
Ecuador	193	9.4	0.49	22.6	1.54	13.6	-[c]
Paraguay	188	3.4	0.24	7.6	0.81	8.8	13.9
Bolivia	166	9.6	0.47	16.0	0.77	5.4	5.4
Dominican Republic	149	3.4	0.53	18.0	0.73	19.7	6.5
Guatemala	135	5.2	0.12	14.3	0.43	12.2	15.8
Brazil	132	95.7	19.46	349.6	49.76	15.6	11.5
Nicaragua	110	1.3	0.06	7.7	0.40	19.5	22.0
El Salvador	89	2.2	0.06	7.5	0.30	15.2	18.0
Honduras	78	1.8	0.12	3.8	0.30	8.7	12.8
Haiti	29	N.A.	N.A.	N.A.	N.A.	N.A.	N.A.
Total Average		520.2	46.58	1,282.3	113.43	10.4	11.0[d]

a. Based on projections for 1970.
b. For 1960-1969.
c. Government closed schools for entirety of 1970.
d. Excludes Venezuela and Ecuador.

Source: Office of Development Programs, Bureau for Latin America, Agency for International Development, Summary Economic and Social Indicators 18 Latin American Countries: 1960-1970 (Washington, D.C.: Government Printing Office, April 1971), pp. 74, 80. "Students per 100,000 Population," Bruce Russet, et al., World Handbook of Social and Political Indicators (New Haven: Yale University Press, 1964), pp. 214-216. Reproduced by permission of Yale University Press.

determinant of political participation, perhaps the most important variable (Inkeles, 1969). It is of significance, then, that in almost all the countries of Latin America the poor—rural and urban—are notably absent from school at the higher levels and while in school receive the lowest quality of education. Equally important, since the uneducated poor do not participate, they are not likely to be included among those who will receive future allocations of resources, such as more schools, better equipment, and adequate staffs.

Another important aspect of the educational system in most of Latin America is the type of education emphasized at the higher levels, especially in the private, better-financed, and well-staffed institutions. Students are routed through certain preferred professional disciplines that are largely irrelevant to economic development or political change and often serve to effectively coopt the brightest young people of the society into the value system of the dominant elite.[2]

At the same time the educational system may polarize youth politically by broadening the chasm between aspirations generated by the educational process and possible achievements by using that education. This effect seems to be especially true for those students from the lower sectors who do manage to reach the higher levels of education. In most countries, for example, the faculties with the highest percentage of students with lower social status are clearly the most radicalized.

Health Care

Despite the large increases in the populations of the various nations, health conditions are often poor. Since adverse health conditions can have retarding effects on thought processes as well as on the ability of an individual to perform the various roles assigned to him by society, these factors must be considered here.

Evidence of the shortage of health facilities and medical-care resources is presented in Table II-6. As can be noted, there is a sizable deficit both in the number of medical practitioners and in the number of hospital beds available to most Latin Americans. What the data do not show is that the shortages are most acute in the rural areas of these countries. In the areas outside of the cities, diseases long since eradicated, controlled, or isolated in North America and in Europe still run rampant. Tuberculosis, diphtheria, leprosy, and other diseases now unfamiliar in certain parts of the world are still common in certain rural sectors of Latin America. In Peru, 60 per cent of all doctors practice in one city, Lima; 40 per cent of Bolivian doctors practice in La Paz; 60 per cent of Ecuador's doctors and facilities are found in Quito and Guayaquil, which account for only 20 per cent of Ecuador's

TABLE II-6. Number of Inhabitants per Doctor, in Rank Order, and per Hospital Bed, and Per Cent Change.

	Doctors		Hospital Beds	
Country	1 per, 1969	Per Cent Change, 1960-1970[c]	1 per, 1969	Per Cent Change, 1960-1970[c]
Argentina (1)[a]	545	-32.6[d]	147	-5.7[d]
Uruguay (2)	814	-17.7	165	-20.5
Cuba (7)	1,000 (1967)	N.A.	330 (1967)	N.A.
Venezuela (5)	1,101	-25.0	307	10.0
Chile (3)	1,502	-10.5	226	-12.9[h]
Paraguay (15)	1,612	-7.5	492	-11.7
Dominican Republic (16)	1,697	10.9	614	-2.5[i]
Costa Rica (4)	1,701	-37.2	237	13.2
Panama (6)	1,777	-34.4	312	30.9
Mexico (18)	1,850	5.6	752	-56.7
Brazil (8)	1,896	-39.5	350	-4.3
Nicaragua (N.A.)	2,034	-24.4	N.A.[g]	-4.8
Peru (10)	2,026	-4.1[e]	422	-0.1
Colombia (11)	2,293	-10.9	444	22.2[e]
Ecuador (12)	2,560	-10.8	460	-3.3
Bolivia (14)	3,636	-3.0	478	-19.5
El Salvador (13)	4,265	-5.6	475	27.7
Honduras (17)	4,296	-67.3	617	11.2
Guatemala (9)	4,725	4.4	415	12.9
Haiti (19)	10,000 (1967)	N.A.	1,600 (1967)	N.A.
Average	1,538[b]	-21.7[f]	350[b]	-11.0[j]

a. Figures in parentheses are ranks by bed per unit of population.
b. Excludes Cuba and Haiti.
c. Negative indicates improvement.
d. Per cent change 1958-1969.
e. Per cent change 1964-1970.
f. Excludes Argentina, Nicaragua, Peru, Cuba, and Haiti.
g. Estimate for 1970 is 403.
h. Per cent change 1960-1969.
i. Per cent change 1969-1970.
j. Excludes Argentina, Colombia, Dominican Republic, Chile, Cuba, and Haiti.
Source: Office of Development Programs, Bureau for Latin America, Agency for International Development, Summary Economic and Social Indicators 18 Latin American Countries: 1960-1970 (Washington, D.C.: Government Printing Office, April 1971), pp. 101, 105.

population. While sketchy for other countries, data suggest similar if not worse concentration, especially in the more populous countries, such as Brazil, Colombia, Venezuela, and Chile. Furthermore, even in the cities the data suggest that the lower-class population has less access to health facilities than is apparent. For example, the number of beds available in general hospitals, those available to the lower classes in most of the countries, is from one-half to one-third lower than the total-beds figure presented here (Inter-American Development Bank, 1970, p. 121).

THE CLASS STRUCTURE

Latin American societies are no exception to the general rule that certain groups of people within a country receive disproportionate shares of the sociocultural and economic resources available. Social analysts generally have classified members of a society according to how many of the various kinds of resources they have in their possession. Depending on the criteria used by the analyst in making his classifications will be the types of people in each group and how large the groups will be.

Class and society in Latin American nations are different from those of other countries of the so-called underdeveloped world and of Western Europe and North America. Economic criteria, so often considered as causal factors in social analyses, may not be as important in the Latin American countries. Social patterns in the twenty nations have much longer traditions of autonomous existence than are found in other economically underdeveloped countries and, as a result, are much more difficult to change. In fact, this longevity in the patterns of Latin American societies and the similarities in the class structures of all of the countries may be a key factor in making relevant a discussion of the various nations as an "area."

There are various criteria within the broad outlines above which can be utilized for establishing boundaries and determining the class structures of a society. In the Latin American countries, depending on which criteria are used, a social structure of two, three, or more classes can be defined. As in any country or group of countries, the upper classes consume and enjoy a larger share of the sociocultural resources than their numbers alone would warrant. In Latin America, where resources are particularly scarce, this distribution situation has meant that the lower classes, whatever their number, but certainly the largest percentage of the population, consume or enjoy very few of the resources, whether economic, educational, status, or simply government services.

Race as a Criterion

Race is a criterion which has been used with some frequency for drawing class boundaries in Latin America. Analysts who use this criterion, such as Stokes (1959, pp. 1–9, 13–25), have noted that in most of the countries the upper class is almost exclusively white while the lower class is almost entirely nonwhite. Table II-7 provides data on the racial composition of the Latin American nations. Undoubtedly, some

TABLE II-7. Racial Composition (percentages).

Country	White	Mestizo	Indian	Negroid
Argentina	89	9	2	-
Bolivia	12	31	57	-
Brazil	39	20	3	37
Chile	25	66	9	-
Colombia	20	59	12	9
Costa Rica	48	47	2	3
Cuba	30	20	-	49
Dominican Republic	5	14	-	81
Ecuador	7	32	58	3
El Salvador	8	52	40	-
Guatemala	3	30	67	-
Haiti	-	-	-	100
Honduras	10	50	40	-
Mexico	9	61	29	1
Nicaragua	10	76	14	-
Panama	8	50	10	31
Paraguay	5	30	65	-
Peru	13	37	49	-
Uruguay	90	8	-	2
Venezuela	12	68	10	10

Source: *Racial Composition of Latin American Nations* (University of Texas at Austin, Population Research Center, Mimeograph, 1968).

relationship exists between a person's race and his occupation, economic status, or social role; but the data on such correlations are extremely scarce and unsystematic.

There are several considerations that should be taken into account in assessing the validity of race as a criterion for determining social status. First, in nations such as Argentina, Uruguay, and Haiti, where the populations are almost exclusively of one race, it would seem apparent that distinctions cannot be made on this basis. Second, there is some doubt as to whether the *mestizo*, or mixed, group does indeed form a middle sector of any Latin American society. In predominantly *mestizo* nations like Mexico or Chile it seems unrealistic to call the mixed group a middle sector or class in any meaningful sense. Neither does the Indian (or Negro) consistently occupy the bottom rung of the social ladder.

In the recent heated presidential campaign of 1970 in Chile, all three candidates were European with virtually no physical traces of Indian ancestry. In fact, all were upper-class by practically any standard; yet an observer would need to look no farther than the nearest campaign posters to see what groups and classes were being courted by each candidate. Allende, candidate of the Marxist Socialist party, had posters dominated by figures with distinctively Indian features—in a country where the descendants of Europeans dominate the sociocultural life and even *mestizos* are quite fair in complexion. On the other hand, the rightist candidate's campaign literature pictured figures who could have walked the streets of any city in the United States as white-collar, professional, or executive types.

In a similar vein, Zeitlin (1967) argues that a principal recipient of the Cuban revolution has been the Negro, after many long years of deprivation at the hands of white and *mestizo* governments. The Mexican and Bolivian revolutions have had strong racial overtones. The abortive Arbenz reforms in Guatemala in the early 1950's were characterized by their efforts to raise the status of the Indian, even in that country where being Indian is so clearly culturally, rather than physically, defined.

While one can make the general comment that descent on the social ladder is marked by progressively darker skin in countries such as Chile, Venezuela, Bolivia, Costa Rica, the Dominican Republic, Ecuador, and Mexico, the generalization may confuse the situation rather than clarify it because of the numerous exceptions and qualifications that must be added. In the southern regions of Chile the Indian may be a local notable. He still is not likely to carry weight in national affairs, however. Particularly in countries less dominated by European racial (and cultural) influences, such as Brazil, Mexico, Venezuela, and Colombia, race does not seem to be the most useful criterion for making class distinctions, at least in any reasonably sophisticated manner. Certainly, if one is looking for causal factors in class differences, the racial criterion must be supplemented if not supplanted by other factors.

This is not to deny the importance of race. It plays too obvious a role in some systems to be ignored. Particularly if the observer wishes only to draw a line between those who control most of the social-economic resources of a system—and thereby exercise the greatest access to the instruments of decision making—and those who do not, then race may be of some considerable assistance. But even in this situation, considerable care must be exercised and other criteria are probably more useful.

Racial prejudice is quite strong in many of the countries. Racist attitudes are evinced by both the white and indigenous populations toward each other and toward the blacks.

Economic Status as a Criterion

Economic position has been one of the most widely used criteria for determining boundaries of Latin American class structures, particularly in analyses by North Americans. Unfortunately, income-distribution figures are unavailable for most of the countries. For those countries for which data exist, they seem too misleading and unreliable to use very seriously.

Some of the data are of more than passing interest, however. In 1960, the average income per person in Peru was $250. In 1961, 65 per cent of the economically active population received 19 per cent of the national income, while 2 per cent received 41.4 per cent (Quijano Obregón, 1968). Quijano Obregón argues that concentration of *wealth* would be even higher than distribution of *income*. Wage workers and salaried employees (83 per cent of the employed) received 47 per cent. Entrepreneurs, businessmen, and property owners (2 per cent of the active population) received 45 per cent. The underemployed or "casual workers" (32.3 per cent of the active population) received 5.6 per cent. In Mexico, 66 per cent of income goes to 1 per cent of the economically active (Navarrete, 1960, p. 75). This figure may be an exaggeration but it indicates an incredible concentration, nevertheless.

Delgado (1962, p. 350) argues that of the approximately one-half of the Latin American population that lives in the countryside, nearly 50 per cent is economically active. Of this 30 million economically active, about 63 per cent are landless peasants. Nearly 20 per cent more have amounts of land insufficient to make a living.

It is estimated by the authors that perhaps as much as one-third of the population of Latin America is not within the money economies of the various nations. Horowitz (1970, p. 6) argues that even in countries like Brazil and Mexico between 40 and 60 per cent of the population "exist as total dependents excluded from political, economic, or educational institutions." In the absence of extensive data in this area, only a rough approximation of income distinctions can be made. It does seem clear that close to 90 per cent of the population in the region have a monthly income below $100. Another 8 per cent have monthly incomes between $100 and $600, while probably no more than 2 per cent have monthly incomes above $600. However, there is now considerable doubt among many Latin Americanists that the social element earning between $100 and $600 monthly shares the same behavior patterns allegedly evinced by a European or North American middle class.

Occupation as a Criterion

Basing his arguments on occupational criteria, anthropologist Richard N. Adams has asserted that in general most Latin American societies can be divided into two classes for analytic purposes (Heath and Adams, 1965, pp. 266–270).[3] According to Adams, the factor which distinguishes the upper group from the lower is that the former do "mental" work and the latter "physical" work. Thus the prestige, or upper, sector is made up of those who do white-collar work. The lowest reaches of this group encompass those who are only barely included by virtue of their minor clerical or administrative jobs. Major goals of the upper sector include joining the proper clubs, making the right contacts, receiving invitations to prestigious functions, and so forth.

It is probable that some Latin Americans located in the upper reaches of the blue-collar class enjoy incomes larger than those of some members of the prestige class. There are also innumerable and involved variations within each class. But doing work with one's hands is an automatically excluding factor in the determination and allocation of scarce status resources in the various Latin American societies.

The two classes also vary in the methods available to members for the achievement of upward social mobility. In the working class the chief method of getting ahead (without moving into the prestige class, of course) is through the acquisition and accumulation of scarce economic resources. Wealth determines the position of a member of the working class within his own group. In the prestige class, on the other hand, the way to move upward is through the acquisition and accumulation of scarce status resources. Wealth and status do not necessarily complement each other; status in only limited fashion can be bought.

The differences between the two classes have major effects in the way that their members make demands and provide supports to their political systems and in the sorts of things they demand. The occupational criterion for drawing class boundaries seems to be more adequate than either the racial or economic criterion.

Adams has also noted that the individuals whose economic and occupational situation has relegated them to a middle level in the social structure tend to emulate the behavior of those above them to the extent that is reasonable, given their access to resources.[4] This well-documented phenomenon tends to cast some doubt on the status of this middle level as a third force in the political and social spheres. The idea that the middle sector can in some way become a stabilizing and democratizing factor in the political decision-making process appears to be contradicted by anthropologist Adams and by other Latin Americanists from various social-science disciplines.[5]

Kinship as a Criterion

Kinship ties may be important factors in determining behavior in the various countries and in placing a person within a particular class. The study of the Latin American family is in its primitive stages, with the exception of basic anthropological work usually on the working class (see Lewis, 1961 and 1965). One analyst (Smith, 1956) has pro-

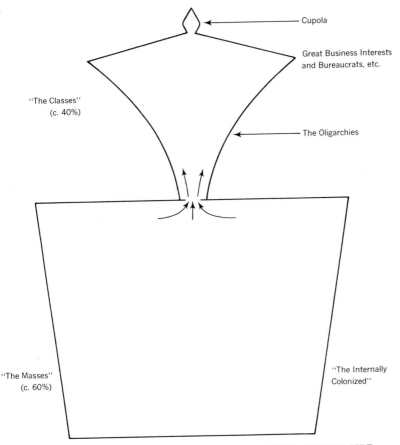

FIGURE II-1. BRAZILIAN CAREERS AND SOCIAL STRUCTURE.
Source: Anthony Leeds, "Brazilian Careers and Social Structure: A Case History and Model," *American Anthropologist,* 66 (1964), p. 397. Adapted by permission of the American Anthropological Association and Anthony Leeds.

posed that the role of the husband in many Caribbean homes is directly related to his role in the occupational structure. However, in general, it has been found that in many countries there seem to be essentially two very large kinship clusters: one which more or less relates to the prestige or upper sector, and another which relates to the nonprestige sector.

Figure II-1 has been adapted from an analysis by anthropologist Anthony Leeds (1964) of the class structure of Brazil, where he noted the relationship between family and occupational criteria. It would appear that in the upper sector family relationships are another way of acquiring status and getting ahead. Members of the lower class cannot move into the higher class in one generation, a factor which will be further assessed.

Political Attitudes as a Criterion

Only in recent years have political attitudes been studied in a few of the Latin American countries and then used as still another criterion for drawing class boundaries. In conjunction with these studies the political-socialization process has also been examined. One of the broadest-scale studies was conducted as part of the research for a book written by Almond and Verba (1963). Unfortunately the data gathered for this study were obtained only in population centers of at least 10,000 in Mexico, thereby excluding the large percentage of rural inhabitants of the country. Almond and Verba identify three broad classes of political attitudes in the countries they study, including Mexico: (1) the "participant" or upper group, (2) the "subject" or middle group, and (3) the "parochial" or lower group. The participant group, made up of about 10 per cent of the Mexican sample, was capable of making demands and providing supports to the decision makers of the country as well as perceiving the outputs of the system. Members of the subject group, which comprised 65 per cent of the sample, were capable of perceiving the outputs but did not or could not make demands or provide supports. The parochial group was either not aware of the system or ignored it because of apathy or alienation. It seems doubtful that this subject group in Mexico can be considered a middle class in the sense that the term might be applied to other countries which Almond and Verba studied, such as the United States and Great Britain. Until more comprehensive studies are conducted, it is difficult to assess their worth or to use the data which they have generated as a basis for drawing Latin American class boundaries.

Social Mobility

Whatever criteria are used and whether or not a two- or a three-class social structure is distinguished, there is a definite concentration of values—political, social, and economic—in the hands of a very few throughout Latin America. Even in Costa Rica, which is usually considered to be one of the most egalitarian societies of Latin America, only 62 per cent of a group of high-school students polled by Goldrich (1966) agreed with the statement, "One can succeed in this country with ability and effort."

The key to upward social mobility within each major social sector of the Latin American societies has already been discussed. In the lower sector the acquisition of economic values is the keynote to getting ahead, while in the upper sector it is the acquisition of status values, both of which are primarily allocated by the political systems. There is generally only one way to move from the lower social sectors into the prestige sectors, and that is through the educational system. However, access to education largely depends on the economic wealth of the family and on urban residence. The small percentage of lower-income students in the higher levels of even the high schools indicates how difficult it is to attain education. The low quality and vocational nature of the public schools accentuate the problem. The fact that the prestige sectors continue to receive public support for maintaining private institutions, which train and socialize most future university students, provides strong insight into the nature of political relationships, especially in terms of whose demands are met by the decision makers.

SUMMARY

There are some patterns which emerge from the foregoing. First, there is a scarcity of sociocultural resources in all of the countries of the area, a scarcity so pronounced that many Latin Americans do not receive a proportionate share. Second, all of the countries have relatively similar class structures, although the number or percentage of the population in each varies according to the criteria used for drawing class boundaries. Third, sociocultural patterns in Latin America have demonstrated a remarkable longevity, which retards any efforts at alteration.

NOTES

1. See Andreski (1969) for an enlightening account of this situation and its results.

2. For a discussion of the situation in one country, Chile, see Glazer (1966).

3. An expansion and sophistication of this argument is in Adams (1967).

4. The position that these middle sectors are a progressive and clearly identifiable group in some of the Latin American nations is presented in various writings; for example, Johnson (1964) and Kling (1956).

5. See Nun (1965) and articles by Frederick Pike, Maurice Zeitlin, Aníbal Quijano Obregón, and Gustavo Polit in Petras and Zeitlin (1968).

SUGGESTED READINGS

Adams, Richard N. *The Second Sowing*. Scranton: Chandler, 1967.

Adams, Richard N., et al. *Social Change in Latin America Today*. New York: Random House, 1960.

Bonilla, Frank. *The Failure of Elites*. Vol. 2 of *The Politics of Change in Venezuela*. Cambridge: M.I.T. Press, 1970.

Germani, Gino. *Política y Sociedad en una Época de Transición*. Buenos Aires: Editorial Paidos, 1966.

Heath, Dwight, and Richard N. Adams, eds. *Contemporary Cultures and Societies of Latin America*. New York: Random House, 1965.

Hirschman, Albert O. *Journeys Toward Progress*. Garden City, N.Y.: Doubleday, 1965.

Hirschman, Albert O., ed. *Latin American Issues*. New York: Twentieth Century Fund, 1961.

Horowitz, Irving Louis, ed. *Masses in Latin America*. New York: Oxford University Press, 1970.

Lewis, Oscar. *The Children of Sanchez*. New York: Random House, 1961.

Lipset, Seymour Martin, and Aldo Solari, eds. *Elites in Latin America*. New York: Oxford University Press, 1967.

Petras, James, and Maurice Zeitlin, eds. *Latin America: Reform or Revolution?* Greenwich, Conn.: Fawcett, 1968.

Tannenbaum, Frank. *Ten Keys to Latin America*. New York: Knopf, 1962.

Vega, Luis Mercier. *Roads to Power in Latin America*. New York: Praeger, 1969.

THE ECONOMIC CONTEXT

Resources of all varieties are more scarce in Latin America than in North America and Western Europe. The twenty nations can be labeled economically underdeveloped regardless of the criteria used in making such an assessment—per-capita income, gross national product, productivity per worker, or balance-of-trade figures.

There are very wide differences between the economic positions of the various countries, however. As the data in Table III-1 demonstrate, per-capita income varies considerably within the area. With the exception of Argentina and Venezuela, all of the nations had per-capita incomes of less than $600 in 1967, which, despite doubts as to the value of per-capita income as a measure, economists seem to agree is a fairly accurate sign of an underdeveloped economy.[1] Venezuela's high per-capita income can be attributed to its vast petroleum reservoirs, which have largely benefited only a tiny fraction of the population. The per-capita figures become more meaningful when we bear in mind that 5 per cent of all Latin Americans receive 33 per cent of the total income and the lower 50 per cent of the populations share only 16–20 per cent of the national income (United Nations, 1964, p. 53).

TABLE III-1.   Per-Capita Gross National Product, excluding Cuba and
Haiti (U.S. dollars).

Country	1950	1960	1967	1968 (pre-liminary)	Current Growth Rate (per cent)[a]
Argentina	539	596	643	663	0.3
Bolivia	N.A.	138	164	171	2.4
Brazil	242	316	347	359	2.9
Chile	459	510	599	607	0.4
Colombia	230	268	288	296	1.2
Costa Rica	300	373	421	439	3.2
Dominican Republic	230	292	278	280	0.4
Ecuador	190	229	245	249	1.6
El Salvador	211	242	287	288	1.0
Guatemala	250	259	291	297	1.4
Honduras	183	222	236	239	0.8
Mexico	331	436	528	546	3.2
Nicaragua	224	279	367	375	1.6
Panama	341	420	582	594	2.4
Paraguay	196	204	221	223	1.2
Peru	187	261	321	317	0.2
Uruguay	N.A.	580	533	526	-3.6
Venezuela	567	843	911	927	1.7
Average	310	384	429	441	2.1

Note: GNP data are unadjusted for inequalities in purchasing power among
countries.
a. Arithmetic average of per cent change for 1968 over 1967 and 1967 over
1966.

Source: Adapted from Office of Program and Policy Coordination, Agency for
International Development, *Latin America: Economic Growth Trends* (Washington,
D.C.: Government Printing Office, December 1969), p. 14.

Since this volume is devoted primarily to political processes, a concerted effort has been made to emphasize those aspects of Latin American economics which call for attention from political problem solvers. The negative tone which characterizes this discussion is understandable if it is remembered that the orientation of this chapter is toward economic problems rather than a comprehensive description of the Latin American economies.

MONOCULTURALISM

All of the Latin American economic systems are characterized by an extreme overconcentration of capital and labor in the production of one or two crops or raw-material commodities which are sold on the international market. Diversification has been introduced in some of the countries, but not to the extent of removing monoculturalism as a serious problem. For example, from 1965 to 1968, primary products —food, fuels, ores, and agricultural raw materials—averaged 87 per cent of Latin American exports.[2] As can be seen from Table III-2,

TABLE III-2. Principal Exports, 1965-1968, excluding Cuba.

Country	Products (Per Cent of Total Exports)
Argentina	wheat and corn 30, meat and meat products 24, wool 8
Bolivia	tin 62, lead and zinc 7
Brazil	coffee 44, cotton 6
Chile	copper 74, iron ore 9
Colombia	coffee 62, petroleum 15
Costa Rica	coffee 39, bananas 24
Dominican Republic	sugar 55, coffee 14, cocoa 7
Ecuador	bananas 54, coffee 19, cocoa 11
El Salvador	coffee 49, cotton 14
Guatemala	coffee 43, cotton 18
Haiti	coffee 49, bauxite 10, sugar 9
Honduras	bananas 47, coffee 14, wood 8
Mexico	cotton 17, coffee 6
Nicaragua	cotton 42, coffee 16
Panama	bananas 51, refined petroleum 28
Paraguay	meat 32, lumber 18, cotton 6, quebracho 6
Peru	fish and fish products 27, copper 23, cotton 10, sugar 6
Uruguay	wool 47, meat 27, hides 9
Venezuela	petroleum and petroleum products 92, iron ore 5

Source: Adapted from data compiled by the International Monetary Fund, reprinted in International Financial Statistics, 23, No. 12 (December 1969).

fourteen of the Latin American countries depended on the export of one product for more than 40 per cent of their export earnings. Mexico, Argentina, and Peru have the highest degree of export diversification; but even of these, Peru and Argentina derive a high percentage of their export earnings from only three commodities. Primary commodities (agricultural products and mineral wealth) have constituted 85–90 per cent of Latin American exports over the past decade (Inter-American Development Bank, 1970, p. 29).

The effects of overconcentration are at times disastrous. International commodity markets are highly unstable, and the over-all price structure has deteriorated since World War II. The Latin American nations have been producing ever larger quantities of their one crop or raw material, selling for a lower price, and at the same time paying more for imports. The countries have a chronic balance-of-payments problem, as shown in Table III-3, which currency devaluation and international loans have only partially offset. Because of their specialization in the production of primary products in a monocultural fash-

TABLE III-3. Balance of Payments, excluding Cuba (millions of dollars).

Country	Average for 1960–1962	1963	1966	1968
Argentina	-355.0	+231.8	+257.0	-17.0
Bolivia	-35.9	-46.2	-31.7	-55.9
Brazil	-431.7	-204.0	-67.0	-520.0
Chile	-227.4	-204.1	-87.0	-133.0
Colombia	-132.2	-137.1	-290.0	-188.0
Costa Rica	-19.6	-29.0	-47.5	-47.7
Dominican Republic	+20.1	-38.1	-67.6	-76.3
Ecuador	-17.6	-8.1	-20.3	-75.0
El Salvador	-10.1	-13.6	-110.6	-43.2
Guatemala	-23.9	-19.7	-17.1	-48.3
Haiti	-12.3	-6.5	-51.0	-7.7
Honduras	-0.3	-17.4	-46.0	-55.8
Mexico	-255.1	-217.0	-396.0	-738.0
Nicaragua	-10.2	-7.4	-54.2	-42.9
Panama	-32.5	-35.0	-48.2	-20.8
Paraguay	-10.3	-8.8	-16.6	-28.8
Peru	-12.4	-84.0	-239.0	-23.0
Uruguay	-56.9	-4.9	+49.6	+15.6 (1969)
Venezuela	+418.2	+476.0	-45.0	-221.0

Source: Adapted from *Balance of Payments Yearbook*, Vols. 17, 18, 19, and 21 (Washington, D.C.: International Monetary Fund, 1966, 1967, 1968, 1970).

ion, there is often little opportunity for offsetting losses suffered in the sale of one product by selling more of another.

Position in the international market is only one facet of the problem faced by the Latin American nations as a result of their monocultural economies. In order to produce the few primary commodities which they export, the countries often place their best farmlands or most skilled and modern labor force and technology to the task, neglecting many other activities in the process. The result has been that although the majority of the nations are primarily agricultural, they have often been forced to import staple foodstuffs. The best farmlands, which could be employed to grow rice, beans, and corn, are used instead to produce bananas, coffee, or sugar. The most capable and productive of the labor force, the best entrepreneurial and administrative talent, all are employed in the export-producing trades, to the neglect of other enterprises.

THE AGRICULTURAL SECTOR

Regardless of the crop or commodity which each of the Latin American countries has oriented itself to produce, all of the nations can be labeled as either agrarian or preindustrial.

In some of the countries, such as Paraguay, Honduras, Colombia, Nicaragua, and perhaps Brazil, agriculture is so predominant that discussing economic development without considering the agricultural sector is to introduce insurmountable distortions. The experience of Cuba, Mexico, Chile, and Argentina would indicate that even where agriculture does not dominate the economy the development of this sector is at least necessary to general economic development[3]

In 1965 of all economically active Latin Americans 46.1 per cent were engaged in the production of foodstuffs, livestock, and related agricultural pursuits (United Nations Economic Commission for Latin America, 1966, p. 31). The figures vary from country to country, but agriculture is the principal economic activity of the largest group of workers in all of the countries. Despite the large percentage engaged in agriculture, in none of the countries does the level of production match the large labor investment. As the data in Table III-4 demonstrate, in only one country does agriculture contribute 35 per cent or more of the gross national product.

One of the reasons for the low levels of production has already been discussed: the most fertile and accessible lands are used for cash-commodity production despite the fact that the earnings of these internationally marketable products have dropped. Much more important for understanding the problem of low production are the effects which the social-class structures of each country have had on agricultural productivity. This is true of all of the countries except Cuba, where it is safe to assume that since 1959 social classes of a postrevolutionary variety have not gelled to the point where they would have a bearing on production problems. In the rest of the countries social class is so tightly interrelated with the agricultural sector, with landholding patterns, and with social and economic status as well as political influence that the entire syndrome deserves considerable attention.

Land-Tenure Patterns

With the exception of Cuba, all of the Latin American nations are characterized by extreme inequity in land ownership. Members of the prestige classes often possess large, undercapitalized, underproductive tracts of land which they have inherited or accumulated; members of the lower class rent and sometimes own tiny plots of land which barely provide them with a subsistence for their families. The large plots of land are commonly referred to as *latifundios*, while the tiny plots are known as *minifundios*. The *latifundio* should not be confused with the plantation, either foreign or domestically owned, which is characterized by heavy capitalization and large inputs of labor often to produce

TABLE III-4.   Agriculture and Manufacturing: Percentage Population
Engaged and Contribution to Gross Domestic Product,
excluding Cuba.

Country	Agriculture		Manufacturing (Value Added)	
	Population Engaged, 1967	Contribution to GDP, 1967	Population Engaged, 1967	Contribution to GDP, 1968
Argentina	18	15.4	36[a]	35.2
Bolivia	48	19.8	7	13.8
Brazil	52	28.3	13[a]	25.1
Chile	28	8.2	28[a]	25.6
Colombia	47	30.5	15	18.9[b]
Costa Rica	49	23.0	11	19.3
Dominican Republic	61	22.9	7	15.9
Ecuador	53	33.4	14	16.8
El Salvador	60	26.4	13	19.6
Guatemala	65	27.3	13	14.9
Haiti	83	N.A.	N.A.	13.7
Honduras	67	38.4	9	14.9
Mexico	47	15.9	17	21.2
Nicaragua	60	28.7	10	15.4
Panama	46	21.7 (1966)	12	16.9
Paraguay	54	33.0	15	14.9
Peru	50	19.9 (1966)	13	20.2
Uruguay	18	15.0 (1966)	23	23.2[b]
Venezuela	32	7.4	12	14.9
Average	46	20.2	13.8[c]	23.4

a. Includes mining and construction.
b. Includes mining.
c. Estimate for 1969 from United Nations Economic Commission for Latin
America, *Economic Survey of Latin America* (New York: United Nations,
1968), p. 24.

Source: Agricultural statistics are from Statistics and Reports Division, Of-
fice of Program and Policy Coordination, Agency for International Development,
Latin America: Economic Growth Trends (Washington, D.C.: Government Printing
Office, December 1969), pp. 10, 11, and 16.   "Manufacturing: Contribution to
GDP, 1968," *Socio-Economic Progress in Latin America: Social Progress Trust
Fund Ninth Annual Report, 1969* (Washington, D.C.: Inter-American Development
Bank, 1970), p. 16.

export crops. Despite these advantages, the plantation pattern of
agriculture results in even greater "dehumanization" of the laborer
and even greater concentration of land, wealth, status, and ultimately
political power than in the *latifundio* system. As Stavenhagen (1970, p.
x) notes, "the crudest forms of exploitation have historically taken
place on the plantations and estates most closely linked to the world
export market."

The term *latifundio* encompasses the self-sufficient, minimally productive holdings which bear different names in different countries.
They are referred to as *fazendas* in Brazil, *haciendas* in Mexico, *fundos*
in Chile, *estancias* and *fundaciones* in Argentina. A certain amount of

the land in a *latifundio* may be used for the production of cash crops, but a sizable portion is used by sharecroppers, for cattle grazing or for no purpose at all.

The degree to which large landholdings conform to this pattern varies from country to country. In Colombia it is not uncommon to find lush green and fertile valleys used to raise a few head of cattle, while crops are scratched out of the rocky hillsides by sharecropping peasants. In certain sections of Brazil, Peru, and a few other nations, debt peonage is still prevalent in the *latifundios*, which proportionately produce very little in the way of cash commodities for export or the staple foodstuffs required by a rapidly growing nation.

For many years, perhaps because they lacked an entrepreneurial orientation, members of the Latin American upper classes were content to live on the cash returns from their holdings, selling none of the land and making few efforts to improve production. Capitalization was regarded as an unnecessary expenditure as long as plentiful and cheap labor was available. Some landowners have assumed new concerns, however, and these are discussed under the general heading of industrialization.

Land still bestows status on its owners. Members of what is sometimes referred to as the "middle class" invest in it just as soon as they are financially able. Members of the upper class hold onto it, using the freedom their holdings provide to engage in, among other things, the political decision-making process. The extent to which there is lack of interest in production for the market may be indicated by the fact that agricultural production per head is lower today than in the prewar period and since 1960 has not improved (Pearse, 1966).

The situation of the owners of *minifundios* is in stark contrast to that of the *latifundistas*. The *minifundista*, who often holds disputed title to his lands, usually does not farm in the better and more productive areas of a particular country. These holdings—and they are the vast majority of all farms in Latin America—are located far from farm-to-market roads, on hillsides, on the less fertile lands, and in the jungles and forests. Many *minifundistas*, especially in tropical areas, are not landowners at all, but squatters who engage in slash-and-burn agricultural methods. These people occupy a piece of unused land, burn off the covering brush and trees, grow crops on the soil until it becomes exhausted, and then move on.

Minifundio ownership or operation does not bestow status on the farmer. Scratching out a subsistence by the most primitive agricultural methods, at times tying themselves to trees as they work a plot of steep hillside land, sleeping with their handful of precious livestock, and growing little or nothing in the way of cash crops, the people engaged in this kind of production are usually not in the money economies of their respective nations. If they require cash to acquire some form of commodity, they usually must accept employment on a neighboring *latifundio* or travel to an area where there are many of these larger farms—a risky venture which could lead to debt peonage or the loss of their meager holdings.

Many workers in the agricultural sector do not own either a *latifundio* or a *minifundio*, but are simply migrant laborers. It is estimated that in Chile approximately 40 per cent of the agrarian labor force is landless.[4] Other countries, with more thoroughgoing *latifundio* tenure systems, probably have higher percentages of landless workers, the "proletarianized" farm workers.

The entensiveness of the concentration of land resources is shown in Table III-5 for the seven countries for which comparable and valid data are available. The situation may be even more serious than is indicated by these data, however. If one combines landless workers and "sub-family-sized" operators, the percentage totals for the same countries, minus Peru, are 56, 68, 54, 60, 87, and 88 per cent of the respective farm populations (Barraclough, in Horowitz, 1970, p. 117). There can be little wonder that the society and most particularly the class structure are affected, and the effect which the Latin American class structure has on political processes is a theme which will recur throughout this volume. Land tenure has a profound effect on other economic sectors as well. The large number of *minifundistas*—outside the money economy, possessing little hope of upward social mobility, and outside the political decision-making arena—insures that industrialization is severely limited in its growth potential, for anything manufactured will be unpurchasable for as many as half the population.

Proposals for Reform

The solutions which have been proposed for the problems of the Latin American agricultural sector are many and varied. Several of them have been economically feasible, but politically impossible. Since we are most interested in what is both practical and political, we will note those proposals that have been seriously broached or attempted in one form or another.

One solution which views the problem as exclusively economic proposes that at a time when the world is experiencing rapid population growth, when the number of people is outgrowing the food supply, the future of Latin America with its vast stretches of unused land should

TABLE III-5. Number and Area (in hectares) of Farm Units by Size Groups in Selected Countries.

Country	Subfamily[a]	Family[b]	Multifamily Medium[c]	Multifamily Large[d]
Argentina				
Number	43.2	48.7	7.3	0.8
Area	3.4	44.7	15.0	36.9
Brazil				
Number	22.5	39.1	33.7	4.7
Area	0.5	6.0	34.0	59.5
Chile				
Number	36.9	40.0	16.2	6.9
Area	0.2	7.1	11.4	81.3
Colombia				
Number	64.0	30.2	4.5	1.3
Area	4.9	22.3	23.3	49.5
Ecuador				
Number	89.9	8.0	1.7	0.4
Area	16.6	19.0	19.3	45.1
Guatemala				
Number	88.4	9.5	2.0	0.1
Area	14.3	13.4	31.5	40.8
Peru				
Number	88.0	8.5	2.4	1.1
Area	7.4	4.5	5.7	82.4

a. Subfamily: Employment for less than 2 people with the typical incomes, markets, and levels of technology and capital now prevailing in each nation.
b. Family: Employment for 2 to 3.9 people on the assumption that most of the farmwork is carried out by the members of the farm family.
c. Multifamily Medium: Employment for 4 to 12 people.
d. Multifamily Large: Employment for over 12 people.

Source: Adapted from Solon L. Barraclough and Arthur L. Domike, "Agrarian Structure in Seven Latin American Countries," *Journal of Land Economics*, Volume XLII, Number 4 © 1966 by the Regents of the University of Wisconsin), pp. 391-424, at p. 395.

be a promising one. If the production of foodstuffs could be improved to the point where the countries could feed not only themselves but also people in the industrial nations, then there is no reason why the over-all price, market, and development situation of the countries could not improve. Argentina, one of the world's principal beef producers, has managed this to a certain extent. However, that nation, like so many others in the Latin American area, has been neglecting agricultural production in an attempt to become industrialized. Rapid and indiscriminate industrialization has not been a panacea.

The extent to which deterioration has taken place in the agricultural sector in a number of countries is indicated in Table III-6. Only Guatemala, Panama, and Nicaragua, all small in both population and size, and Venezuela show significant increases. The majority show decreases in production per capita over the decade. Only Guatemala, Nicaragua, and Venezuela show increases of more than 10 per cent. Translated into more practical terms, given the distribution of resources, including food resources, it seems reasonable to assume that

TABLE III-6.   Index of Per-Capita Agricultural Production, excluding
Cuba and Haiti (1957-1959 = 100).

Country	1960	1961	1962	1963	1964	1965	1966	1967	1968	1969 (pre-liminary)
Argentina	87	96	96	106	103	91	97	101	93	98
Bolivia	100	100	96	99	97	95	94	89	89	88
Brazil	100	104	101	103	91	115	100	104	101	101
Chile	96	95	90	96	97	95	94	94	96	87
Colombia	99	96	98	95	94	95	92	93	93	92
Costa Rica	109	106	102	99	88	90	99	103	104	101
Dominican Republic	100	95	93	89	85	75	75	75	69	77
Ecuador	108	111	108	105	105	107	107	111	102	101
El Salvador	96	112	111	118	118	99	101	107	95	101
Guatemala	102	107	119	120	117	129	114	120	118	111
Honduras	92	102	103	100	106	109	107	107	104	98
Mexico	100	100	102	105	109	114	111	108	108	98
Nicaragua	97	113	129	136	165	147	149	145	138	120
Panama	87	94	90	92	98	107	104	107	109	109
Paraguay	96	98	101	100	95	95	89	95	90	92
Peru	109	114	111	106	109	103	100	96	88	85
Uruguay	104	105	104	107	114	109	99	86	98	98
Venezuela	109	99	103	112	113	115	116	119	121	120
Average	98	102	101	104	99	107	101	103	100	99

Source: Office of Development Programs, Bureau for Latin America, Agency for International Development, *Summary Economic and Social Indicators 18 Latin American Countries: 1960-1969* (Washington, D.C.: Government Printing Office, June 1970), p. 42.

most of the population in Latin America has suffered an absolute decline (at best, no improvement) in food intake.

The lesson learned by the revolutionary leaders of Cuba should not be lost on decision makers in other parts of the hemisphere. After assuming power in Cuba, the Castro government through INRA (National Institute of Agrarian Reform) plowed thousands of acres of sugar cane under the ground and commenced to plant other crops.[5] Great emphasis was simultaneously placed on industrialization. In a short time, Cuba became deficient in foodstuffs, cash crops for export, and manufactured commodities. Since that period the emphasis has been placed again primarily on the production of agricultural commodities with an eye to very long-term industrialization.

Many proponents of reform have refused to consider the harsh reality that it will not be possible in countries other than Cuba to increase agricultural production until patterns of land ownership are changed, perhaps even radically. A Mexican sociologist, Rodolfo Stavenhagen (1970, p. ix) concludes:

Rural underdevelopment is the result of a number of economic, social, and political institutions which over the centuries have created and maintained rigid stratification systems and a bipolar class structure. The low-status peasant groups . . . have been permanently and ruthlessly kept at the fringes of survival for the greater benefit and glory of small but well-organized and politically powerful ruling groups.

He is emphatic in denying that the introduction of technology into the countryside will eliminate the poverty and backwardness of the peasantry. Edmundo Flores (1963, esp. pp. 7–9), Jacques Chonchol (1964, esp. Chap VI), and many other serious Latin American observers have long argued the same point.

In order to change land-tenure patterns, however, reformers must enter the political arena. Most of the traditionally dominant groups do not propose voluntarily to change the social system of the countryside, a system that has allowed them to maintain and even increase their social status and political power. Change in the land-tenure system means change in the entire fabric of social relations—the end of a captive, cheap labor force; the end of a monopoly of the productive land; and the end of economic and political dependence of the laboring mass of peasants on the landowner. Since the ownership of land is a principal factor underpinning the entire economic, political, and social system in each of the countries, the importance of the land-tenure system is evident.

Considerable evidence exists that genuine reform in the agrarian sector, with the attendant consequences in the rest of the society, does not occur without intervention from some source outside the countryside. In Chile, where reform in a moderately democratic setting is being attempted, it appears clear that the rebellion of the peasants, as evidenced in their seizure of *fundos*, labor strikes, and support of radical issues and candidates, was precipitated by organization and agitation from urban-led parties and movements, urban-based mass media, and urban intellectuals.[6] We will discuss a number of other alternatives and issues related to land reform in Chapter VI.

THE INDUSTRIAL SECTOR

For many years the leaders of the Latin American nations opposed industrialization. Writers like Rodó argued that the introduction of industry would purge the essentially spiritual aspects of agrarian life and convert the people into the emotionless semihumans that he believed abounded in the United States as the result of its technological advancements. However, as increasing numbers of upper-class Latin Americans went not to Europe but to the United States for higher education, the attitude represented by Rodó changed. Other, equally important factors influenced this change in attitude, such as the effects of the mass media and foreign-currency problems. But the change in locus of education of the intellectual leadership, from France and other European nations to the United States, seems to have been a major variable. Since World War II, the young people returning to their countries have been filled with a desire to emulate the industrial productivity of the United States and to provide themselves with a capital city where it would be possible to live on a modern American economic standard.

Two important factors must be assessed in any discussion of Latin American industry. The first is the form industry has taken, and the second is the effects it has had on the social structure and political processes.

Import Substitution

As of the early 1970's a very large portion of Latin America's industrialization has been of the import-substitution variety. In 1929, imports accounted for 20–29 per cent of total production; in 1963, for about 10 per cent. According to Petras, "About 36% of the expansion of the industrial product (for Brazil, Argentina, Chile, Colombia, and Mexico) was directly related to import substitution incentive between 1929–1960" (Petras, 1970, p. 9). Lured by protectionist tariff barriers, foreign and domestic entrepreneurs have established industries within the countries despite their small money economies. High costs per unit, low labor productivity, and the need to import a large percentage of the raw materials used in this kind of manufacturing have led to anything but an ideal industrial situation. The sole reason for the survival of many Latin American enterprises is that the high tariffs make imported commodities more expensive than articles produced domestically.

Import-substituting industries produce a wide variety of articles, ranging from soap flakes, clothing, and transistor radios to assembled automobiles. Very often these enterprises include both foreign and local capital. The obstacles to economic development presented by these kinds of enterprises are varied. If they are not labor-intensive and they produce at a cost as high as the same commodity produced abroad, there is some doubt as to the amount of foreign exchange saved by having the enterprise locate in a particular country, particularly if a high percentage of the raw materials must be imported. If, on the other hand, the industries are labor-intensive, then there is some question as to their ability to export their products, in competition with industries of more economically developed nations, because of their inefficiency. At best, import substitution has represented a mixed blessing to the countries of the Latin American area.

Ownership Patterns

As a result of a traditional mistrust of all persons not related by kinship or close friendship, the mass ownership of private enterprise engineered through a publicly regulated stock market has not occurred in Latin America. Ownership is usually of one of three patterns. The first is foreign ownership, perhaps with one or two local partners of a non-policy-making variety. It was largely foreign enterprise which introduced the plantation type of agricultural operation, and it is also foreign enterprise which has taken a leading role in the creation of much of the Latin American industrial plant. Protective barriers serve to make it economical to venture into the markets, but high tariffs alone would be insufficient to attract foreign investment. Making this kind of investment attractive is the rate of return commonly experienced on capital by entrepreneurs. Average yearly profits on private investments in the nations of Latin America are difficult to estimate, since in many cases deliberate efforts are made to keep this kind of information private. However, it is reasonable to estimate that average profits probably range around 12 per cent and might run much higher. No one in Latin America is surprised at a 20 per cent return on annual investment, while many native entrepreneurs will abandon a business which does not provide an annual return of 30–40 per cent. In comparison, the average annual rate of return on investments in the nations which comprise the European Economic Community has been unofficially estimated at about 8 per cent.

A second form of industrial enterprise is the wholly locally owned family type of operation. Petras (1970, p. 41) found that in Chile the small industrial firms tended "to be almost completely closed family-controlled operations," but that the large firms (500 or more employees) were more corporate in structure. But even in the large firms Petras (1970, p. 44) found 70 per cent either family-owned or owned by a very small group. Lauterbach's analysis (1965, p. 203) is even more interesting since it relates more generally to Latin America. On the

basis of interviews with 324 managers from companies of more than
100 employees, he notes that "actual ownership of the shares typically
still remains in the hands of a small or large family group, perhaps
with the participation of some close friends of the family." The most
significant feature of this type of enterprise is that it is often held in
conjunction with large tracts of land. The *latifundista*, in contrast to
his forebears in Europe in the nineteenth century and earlier, has
moved into the industrial sector of the economy of his country, bringing the same business practices and attitudes toward labor that he
traditionally used on the farm. Thus industrialists and businessmen
purchase land for status reasons and to guard against inflation, but in
addition in a number of countries "most enterprises had their roots in
agriculture holdings which under a suitable stimulus or market threat
were expanded into processing, commerce, banking, and eventually
non-related industrial activities" (Lauterbach, 1965, p. 205). Petras's
(1970, p. 40) figures for Chile show that nearly one-quarter of the
industrial managers had grandfathers who were landowners. Almost
half of the large businessmen in Chile either own large farms or are
closely related to owners. Most of the wholly owned Latin American
businesses are of the labor-intensive variety, dependent on plentiful
and inexpensive labor plus high tariff barriers to make them economical. The result, as Adams (in Véliz, 1965) has noted, is that the process
of industrialization in Latin America, rather than establishing a new
entrepreneurial class which brings major social changes, has served to
reinforce the socioeconomic and political position of the traditional
elites. The immigrant entrepreneur often used his gains to purchase
land and to acquire status with the traditional oligarchy. The spectacle
of countries embarking on an industrial revolution, as in Argentina
and Brazil, without a concomitant social revolution as predicted by so
many, reveals the tremendous resiliency of Latin American social
structures, especially the ability of the middle and upper reaches of the
prestige sector to adapt to new situations without losing their socioeconomic advantage.

The third pattern of industrial ownership is the result of active
government intervention in the economies of the countries. Utilities in Mexico and Brazil, oil refineries in Peru, Bolivia, and Costa
Rica, and steel mills in several of the countries are just a few examples of the industrial operations of Latin American governments.
Sometimes ownership is achieved through expropriation; other
times it is the result of public entrepreneurship. The governmental
sector of the economy is examined in further detail in the following section.

Employment Patterns

One other factor that must be considered under the general heading of Latin American industry is the amount of employment provided by this sector. Despite the growth of labor-intensive industry in many of the countries, manufacturing has not been able to compete with agriculture and government as a source of new jobs. The average percentage of the labor force employed in industry or manufacturing is 14 per cent, half of which are engaged in handicraft making (Inter-American Development Bank, 1970, p. 13). In none of the countries does manufacturing employ more than 20 per cent of the work force. As noted in the previous chapter, all of the Latin American countries are characterized by rapidly growing populations which require a mushrooming number of jobs. Industry, in the form that it has taken to date, has not been providing the solution. Since the work force in industry is the only true working class in any of the countries, political parties anxious to build their programs around this group have not been successful. In general, the industrial sector has reinforced, rather than changed, existing social and political patterns in each of the countries of the area.

THE GOVERNMENTAL SECTOR

As in the rest of the world, government as producer, consumer, and investor is becoming of increasing importance in the economies of the Latin American countries. Decisions as to where and how the government will intervene are usually based on political preferences and premises. Intervention occurs at a variety of economic levels and in several different fashions depending on the country involved and who is carrying out the action.

Types of Intervention

Interventions in the industrial sector of the economies are the most common form of intervention in all of the nations. These actions are of two basic types. The first casts the government in the role of entrepreneur, establishing industries previously not found in a particular country, either because of a lack of capital in the private sector or because nongovernmental domestic and foreign capital sources have not regarded a particular venture as profitable. Enterprises which the various governments have established range from international jet airlines and steel mills to business such as a monopoly on cocoa leaves chewed by the Indians of Peru. In most countries the interventions have not followed a particular pattern, but seem to have occurred in response to demands by one or another interest group for a product or service not available locally.

Through the efforts of the United Nations Economic Commission for Latin America, particularly when it was headed by Raúl Prebisch, many of the twenty nations adopted national plans and established planning ministries with varying degrees of success. A major variable determining their success has been the amount of political support afforded the plans and their ministries.[7] Most of the countries have adopted the "backward linkage" theory of economic development, which follows the principle that large basic industries must be established before smaller plants will grow up around the big ones. One example of this theory in action is the steel mill established by the government of Mexico in Monterrey in 1916. The premise upon which the government worked was that a number of smaller industries would grow up around the steel mill and reshape the city. This has occurred, but the tremendous waste of resources (even in the 1960's the mill operated at 50 per cent of capacity) makes the backward-linkage theory questionable for countries already deprived of resources.

The second form of intervention is the expropriation of foreign-owned enterprises. Although many foreigners have the impression that this form of intervention has occurred in Latin America with great frequency, it is a highly unusual course of action and has been very limited in scope. At times expropriation has resulted in nationalization and the return of a business to private hands, but in most cases the government has retained ownership. Utilities in Brazil, the railroad network in Argentina, oil refineries in Peru and Bolivia, the banks in Costa Rica, oil refineries and mines in Mexico have all been expropriated in the past fifty years. When grouped together, these appear to be impressive evidence of a tendency on the part of the Latin American nations, but when it is considered that these actions have been taken by twenty countries (an all-inclusive list is not available) containing more than 230 million people and over a half century, expropriation can be regarded as the exception rather than the rule. It should be added here that the country most notably absent from the discussion is Cuba, which has endeavored to carry out total intervention and expropriation. To discuss whether or not the Cuban expropriations could have been avoided is superfluous. It does appear that a revolution similar to Cuba's is unlikely. This issue is discussed in the final chapter of this volume.

The government has intervened in the agricultural sector of the various Latin American countries, but to a much lesser degree than in the service and industrial sectors. What intervention has occurred has taken the form of agrarian reform, which has not been carried out extensively in any of the countries except Cuba and Mexico.

Demands for Intervention

Demands on the decision makers to intervene in their nation's economy have originated in both the international and domestic environments. Figure III-1 illustrates the origins and types of demands from each sector.

Most of the Latin American nations have provided participation opportunities to those citizens in the lower reaches of the prestige class, sometimes called the "middle sectors," and few efforts have been spared to coopt them into the prevailing value system. This group, which can hardly be termed a class, because of its concern for technology and its own well-being has managed to engineer many of the interventions in the economy. Especially as the size of the sector has increased with more educational opportunities, the ability to pressure decision makers for further intervention has become stronger. Not the least of the middle sector's interests has been the abundance of good white-collar jobs resulting from governmental interventions. Although this group has at times formulated alliances with the working class, it has been willing to forget the needs of the masses as a condition for its own social ascent. Classic cases of this use of lower-class support by middle-sector groups to gain political power and access to the decision-making apparatus, followed by conspicuous subordination of the demands of their allies, have occurred in Argentina, Uruguay, and especially Chile. In Chile the Radicals, with Socialist and Communist support, gained control of the governmental machinery in the early 1940's and were so successful in building up a large, "radicalized" bureaucracy that even now their domination of some parts of the public administration is obvious and well known.

UNDEREMPLOYMENT AND UNEMPLOYMENT

Because resources are scarce and the scarcity is correlated with limited technology, an underemployment syndrome exists in all of the Latin American countries. Underemployment persists despite the fact that most of the Latin American constitutional documents clearly

INTERNATIONAL SOURCES		DOMESTIC SOURCES	
United Nations Economic Commission for Latin America	(demands for central planning, regional integration, and government entrepreneurship)	Military	(demands for stability, coupled with technological progress)
Alliance for Progress and Agency for International Development	(demands for infrastructural investment and agrarian reform)	Landowners	(demands for status quo or agrarian reform with compensation)
		Industrialists	(demands for stability and protection from competition; planning is formally permissible)
Foreign Private Enterprise	(demands for status quo, special protection, and stability)	Middle Sectors	(demands for stability and government provision of certain goods and services)
		Working Class	(apathetic or discounted by decision makers)

AUTHORITATIVE DECISION MAKERS
(increasing government
entrepreneurship, but limited
expropriation and little formal
planning or agrarian reform)

FIGURE III–1. DEMANDS FOR GOVERNMENT INTERVENTION.

define work as a right of each citizen, rather than a privilege. The reason for labeling the situation a syndrome is that large pockets of unemployment coexist with a seemingly unending demand for trained personnel. While the working class, particularly agrarian labor, experiences a great deal of unemployment, members of the prestige classes commonly hold down two or more full-time jobs; one of these, significantly, is usually in the public bureaucracy.

The fact that so many members of the prestige classes depend at least in part for their income on jobs in the public administration has given these persons a great stake in the bureaucracy. Interestingly, salaries are the principal expenditures of the public administration in several of the countries. Data for 1963 on seven countries containing nearly 80 per cent of the population for the entire region show that between 50 and 65 per cent of governmental expenditures in each of the countries has been spent on personal salaries (Organization of American States, 1966, p. 196). It is safe to ask, then, whether the stated goals of the bureaucracy are as important as its function as a tension-management device of the prestige class. By providing members of this class with employment, the bureaucracies limit possible disruptive demands from this source. It may be that government intervention occurs in Latin America not as a response to the need for a particular good or service, but as the result of a demand for more white-collar jobs.

Another symptom of the employment situation has been a concentration of personnel in the service sectors of the various economies. As is common in economically underdeveloped societies, many persons are engaged in work which in societies like those of North America and Western Europe would be termed at best marginal and which in many cases is little more than disguised unemployment. The ready availability of household servants is one symptom of the abundance of personnel in the service sector. A barbershop with only two chairs but with a cashier, a shoeshine boy, and a manicurist is not unusual. Tiny grocery stores with as many employees as a modern supermarket, full-time balloon salesmen, and countless lottery-ticket vendors are all symptomatic of concentration in the service industries.

The problems of employment pose a particularly difficult challenge to economic-development planners. Modern industry is becoming increasingly automated, with fewer and fewer opportunities for employment, a situation which is forcing more and more North Americans and Western Europeans into the service sectors of their countries. If Latin American industry is ever to compete successfully in the world market, it will have to become as modern as the industries of the economically developed countries. Yet the pressure for jobs is so strong that in most of the countries obsolete plants requiring great amounts of labor are being built, insuring their inferior productive status in the future.

INFLATION

The lack of resources in all of the Latin American countries, the highly specialized economies, the preponderance of imports over exports, all place pressure on decision makers to print more money. Thus acute inflation has been the result in several of the twenty nations. Chile has been suffering most from inflation, although Brazil, Uruguay, and others have had similar problems.[8]

There are two schools of thought on this inflation problem and the methods for resolving it.[9] One school, the "structuralists," views some inflation as essential to the process of economic development and believes that the monetary problem is a symptom of the basic "structural" problems in the various economies and societies. The other school of thought, the "monetarists," including world bankers and the owners and managers of many foreign enterprises as well as others, believes that inflation can be curbed by using strict monetary-control methods. This school has held sway in most of the Latin American countries at one time or another. During these times they have adopted wage and price controls, exchange restrictions, and a series of measures designed to curb the money supply but which have not always been successful.

Inflation has meant that either many Latin Americans are unwilling to save (savings are for internal capital formation) or if the means are made available they convert their money into dollars and place them in another country. Many Latin American banks permit local residents to make dollar deposits and to maintain accounts in United States currency as long as a minimum amount is retained, an amount sufficiently large to exclude all but members of the prestige class from enjoying this antidevaluation privilege. The efforts of some governments to restrict this conversion practice have resulted in the development of such an extensive and well-developed currency black market that governments have been forced to largely ignore it. Whether they refuse to save money, export their funds, or keep their holdings in United States dollars, the Latin Americans engaged in these types of actions are having negative effects on the economic-development processes of their respective countries.

THE PREFERENCE FOR IMPORTS

Among the prestige classes of a number of Latin American societies, there is a method for acquiring status which is not conducive to economic development. This practice involves the purchase of foreign-made luxury commodities. Members of the prestige classes pride themselves on possessing well-stocked liquor cabinets; imported scotch, brandies, and liqueurs are served to friends and relatives despite their high cost. Television sets, refrigerators, furniture, automobiles, clothing, and other commodities manufactured abroad are much more highly valued than are locally made similar products.

The effects of these practices are not difficult to discern. Not only does local industry suffer, but the disdain for national products displayed by the few members of society with real buying power has effects on foreign-exchange holdings and on the sorts of export crops produced, and is revealed in the scramble for dollars so obvious in many of the countries. In a handful of the nations, nationalism has been coupled with a "buy national products" campaign. But in most of the nations political decision makers of the prestige class, principal consumers of imported products, have done little in the realm of education to stem this propensity to import.

SUMMARY

All of the Latin American nations are basically agrarian societies and they suffer from a scarcity of resources, unemployment, overconcentration of production in a few primary commodities, and inflation. These problems are similar to those faced by agrarian societies in other parts of the world. The difference is that in Latin America the structural causes of underdevelopment have been institutionalized, making change much more difficult to achieve. With per-capita income growing at a somewhat faster rate than population, the economic situation of the average citizen in many of the countries is actually deteriorating. If economic problems are to be solved at all, it seems safe to assume that they will have to be tackled through the auspices of the political decision-making process. But the structures of the political system, and as a result the political process itself, are closely dependent on the socioeconomic system for resources, and the role structure of the former is modeled on the latter. The result is quite often immobilization. New groups participating in the decision-making process, notably the "middle sectors," have assumed the same roles played by their upper-class mentors in the political system.

NOTES

1. See Higgins (1959) for one example of a discussion of this indicator.
2. All data in this paragraph are from Inter-American Development Bank (1970, pp. 27, 30).
3. See Johnston and Mellor (1961), esp. pp. 566–572.
4. Petras (1970, p. 260, and note 6 on that page).
5. For one interesting account of this period, see Seers et al. (1964).
6. An excellent discussion of the changes in evidence is found in Pearse (1966).
7. See Denton (1969) for one analysis of this problem.
8. For an interesting analysis of inflation in Chile, see Hirschman (1965).
9. For a discussion of the two schools of thought, see Hirschman (1961).

SUGGESTED READINGS

Anderson, Charles W. *Politics and Economic Change in Latin America.* Princeton, N.J.: Van Nostrand, 1967.

Baer, Werner. "The Inflation Controversy in Latin America: A Survey." *Latin American Research Review,* 2, No. 2 (Spring 1967), 3–25.

Campos, Roberto de Oliveira. *Reflections on Latin American Development.* Austin: University of Texas Press, 1967.

Dell, Sidney. *A Latin American Common Market?* London: Oxford University Press, 1966.

Diamond, Sigmund, ed. *Economic and Political Trends in Latin America.* New York: Columbia University Press, 1964.

Frank, André. *Latin America: Underdevelopment or Revolution.* New York: Monthly Review Press, 1969.

Gordon, Wendell C. *The Political Economy of Latin America.* New York: Columbia University Press, 1965.

Hirschman, Albert O. *Journeys Toward Progress.* Garden City, N.Y.: Doubleday, 1965.

Lagos, Gustavo. *International Stratification and Underdeveloped Countries.* Chapel Hill: University of North Carolina Press, 1963.

Lauterbach, Albert. *Enterprise in Latin America.* Ithaca: Cornell University Press, 1966.

United Nations Economic Commission for Latin America. *Development Problems in Latin America.* Austin: University of Texas Press, 1970.

Urquidi, Victor L. *Free Trade and Economic Integration in Latin America.* Los Angeles: University of California Press, 1962.

Véliz, Claudio, ed. 1965. *Obstacles to Change in Latin America.* London: Oxford University Press.

THE INTERNATIONAL CONTEXT

New York Governor Nelson Rockefeller's fact-finding tours of Latin America for the Nixon administration in 1969 were symptomatic of the interest in the countries of this hemisphere held by the United States chief executive and by the American people. It should be noted that while the President personally visited nations of Europe and Asia soon after taking office, he sent a non-policy-making emissary to the Latin American nations. The message was not lost on the residents of the great land masses to the south of the United States, many of whom believe that the North American "colossus" has always ignored them. While it may be possible for certain presidents of the United States or for the American people as a whole to ignore Latin America, it is not possible for the twenty nations and their peoples to ignore their giant northern neighbor. The nations share the predicament so aptly described by Canadian Prime Minister Pierre Trudeau in referring to the relationship of his own country to the United States. Trudeau reportedly said that living next to the United States was like "sleeping with an elephant. No matter how friendly and even-tempered the beast, one is affected by its every twitch and grunt."

In general a study of the international context of Latin American politics need include only two variables: the relationship of the countries to the United States, and the relationship of each country to the others. Although European nations were important components of the Latin American international environment during the nineteenth century, they are no longer—for reasons which will be discussed. Cuba poses a different problem, however, which is given special treatment at the end of this chapter.

POLITICAL RELATIONS WITH THE UNITED STATES

The Monroe Doctrine

In 1823, President James Monroe issued a unilateral declaration of United States foreign policy, which has come to be known as the Monroe doctrine. Largely ignored in Europe, Latin America, and the United States at the time it was promulgated, the doctrine nevertheless set the stage for later actions by the United States in this hemisphere. Essentially the doctrine contains three clauses:

1. The United States would permit no further colonization by the European powers in the New World.
2. The United States would permit no further extensions of monarchy in the New World.
3. Since the European powers would not be permitted to become involved in the New World, the United States promised not to involve itself in the affairs of the Old World.

The third clause has always been ignored by world policy makers, and analyses of the Monroe doctrine usually do not refer to it. During the nineteenth century the clause was irrelevant simply because the United States did not have the means to become involved in Europe, while in the twentieth century it has become so involved in the Old World that Latin Americans complain they receive only secondary attention. The Marshall Plan, NATO, the permanent stationing of United States military forces in the Old World, all point to the fact that at least one portion of the Monroe doctrine is not being enforced. Latin Americans, in complaining about their second-class status in the eyes of the United States, point out that the Marshall Plan (which was relatively successful) was formulated fifteen years before the Alliance for Progress (which has been relatively unsuccessful).

In fact the United States has ignored one or another of the clauses of the Monroe doctrine ever since it was formulated as official policy. During the nineteenth century many events occurred which evoked no response from the United States. For example, the British established a colony in Central America, named it the Mosquito Coast, and placed a king in the supreme political position there. Great Britain also attempted to capture the port city of Buenos Aires, with little or no reaction from Washington. A monarchy was established in Brazil which lasted almost half a century, while a much more short-lived kingdom was established by the Hapsburgs in Mexico. The Dominican Republic determined it could not survive independently and rejoined Spain. The list of violations of the doctrine, with no response from the United States, is indeed lengthy.

Worse yet, from the standpoint of the Latin Americans, while the United States has only sporadically enforced the provisions of the Monroe doctrine, it has felt quite free to intervene in the nations of the hemisphere and most particularly those of the Caribbean area. During the nineteenth century the United States acquired large tracts of Mexican land; Texas, New Mexico, Arizona, California, Nevada, Oregon, Utah, and Colorado were all taken by force from Mexico. Although the filibusterers did not receive formal support from the United States, Latin Americans have not forgotten the incursions of the American adventurer William Walker, who became dictator of Nicaragua for a short time.

The Roosevelt Corollary

By the time Theodore Roosevelt assumed office the "Roosevelt corollary" had been informally appended to the Monroe doctrine. The corollary, which was actually more like a "Roosevelt doctrine," sanctioned United States intervention in any of the Latin American nations if the government in Washington considered such an action necessary for the welfare of the United States. Intervention was virtually obligatory if it was believed in the American capital that failure to take action would result in the armed intervention of a European power. By the end of the nineteenth century, then, the United States had assumed the role of international rule enforcer in the hemisphere and intervened in the authoritative decision-making process of many Latin American nations with some frequency and considerable effect.

In 1898, the United States acquired as the spoils of the Spanish-American War Puerto Rico, the Philippines, and Cuba. The latter, which had experienced a violent decade of revolutionary activity just prior to 1898, was granted its independence in 1903, but only after the United States had supervised the writing of Cuba's constitution. The controversial Platt amendment, which authorized the United States to intervene whenever it was considered necessary to do so, was included in the constitution of the island nation. Between 1903 and 1923 United States troops occupied portions of Cuba no less than five times.

The acquisition of the Panama Canal Zone was another example of United States intervention during the period of the Roosevelt corollary to the Monroe doctrine. The isthmus of Panama had been a province of Colombia most of the time since Nueva Granada had declared its independence from Spain in the early decades of the nineteenth century. The United States had been bargaining with Colombia for rights to build a canal through the province of Panama for several years, but the legislature of Colombia proved to be a difficult bargaining partner. By 1903 a group of Panamanian elites, many of whom owned shares in the nearly defunct French Canal Company, became alarmed that the United States might look elsewhere for a canal site. Assured of American support, this group declared the Panamanian isthmus an independent country and shortly thereafter signed a canal treaty with the United States. When Colombian troops arrived to quell the rebellion, they found a United States warship blocking the access to the port of Colón, or Aspinwall as it was then known.

Other countries which experienced United States intervention during the first decades of this century included Haiti, the Dominican Republic, Nicaragua, and Mexico. The most famous of the incursions occurred when United States troops entered Mexican territory in an attempt to capture Francisco "Pancho" Villa. The Mexican people had considered Villa something of a bandit and a nuisance, but the United States intervention served to make "Pancho" a folk hero.

The Good-Neighbor Policy and After

The "good-neighbor policy" of President Franklin D. Roosevelt, announced in 1933, promised to end these interventions and to restore the Monroe doctrine, but the meddling has continued nevertheless. In 1954 the United States Central Intelligence Agency backed an invasion of Guatemala which resulted in changing the authoritative decision makers of that country. The Bay of Pigs invasion of Cuba in April of 1961, albeit unsuccessful, was another example of intervention, while in 1965 the administration of President Lyndon B. Johnson ordered United States troops into the Dominican Republic. Ostensibly the 1965 action was aimed at protecting the 6,000 United States citizens who resided in that country, but it eventually led to the restoration of a group of authoritative decision makers whose policies would be more agreeable to the United States.

That the long history of United States intervention in affairs of the Latin American nations has colored relations between the North American "colossus" and the individual countries is understandable. However, military interventions are only one variable in the relationships of the Latin American nations with the United States. Others will be discussed in subsequent sections.

THE ORGANIZATION OF AMERICAN STATES

The Organization of American States (OAS) is tangible evidence of the special relationship which exists between the nations of this hemisphere. Through it and its forerunner, the Pan American Union, the United States and the nations of the Latin American area have attempted to achieve certain foreign-policy goals. At times the foreign-policy goals have coincided and the OAS has been a rather spectacular success, but more often the goals of the United States and those of Latin America have conflicted. Because of its economic and military capabilities the United States has been able to maintain hegemony within the OAS. The fact that the headquarters of this regional organization are located in Washington, D.C., is the least significant evidence that the United States is the dominant member of the organization. Formally the OAS was regarded as the organizational incarnation of a multilateralized Monroe doctrine. Informally the relationship of the OAS to the Monroe doctrine is more difficult to discern.

The Pan American Union

The nineteenth century boasted only two meetings of the nations of the Western Hemisphere. The first took place in 1826 in Panama with Simón Bolívar as its host. The United States was not invited to participate in this meeting because the Latin American republics regarded it as an unimportant factor in their international environments. By the time the second meeting occurred, the participation of the United States was regarded as so important that the nations were unwilling to hold it without their North American neighbor. At the meeting, which took place in 1890, the Latin American nations made a strong plea for multilateralizing the Monroe doctrine by establishing a special political relationship with the United States. The mood of the United

States prior to the Spanish-American War was one of "manifest destiny," coupled with a distaste for any alliances. However, the Washington government did agree to the formation of the Pan American Union, which was to be restricted to the consideration of commercial and cultural relationships between the nations of the hemisphere. American business had begun to realize the potential of the Latin American area for investment purposes and viewed the Pan American Union as a method with which to deal with all twenty countries collectively rather than individually.

United States Overtures

The Pan American Union functioned in a rather obscure fashion over the following decades, largely because the United States was employing more direct methods of dealing with the various nations of the area. The announcement of the good-neighbor policy, which came only a few years before the United States became embroiled in World War II, represented an effort by the North American nation to establish the special political relationship so long desired by the twenty Latin American nations. However, the Great Depression was in full swing at the time of the formulation of the policy, 1933, and many of the nations were suddenly apprehensive of a close relationship with the United States. Many were striving to establish close ties with the nations of Europe in order to lessen their dependence on the United States.

Ironically, at the time the United States most desired and needed a special relationship with the Latin American nations, it was unable to establish one. After the war, when the relationship was solidified in the form of the OAS, the United States really did not need it. This is not to say that the nations of the Western Hemisphere did not meet prior to the founding of the OAS to discuss common problems. In 1939, at the First Inter-American Consultative Conference of Foreign Ministers, all of the nations of the hemisphere except Canada declared their neutrality. At the Third Inter-American Conference, held in Rio de Janeiro in 1942, the United States proposed that all nations in the hemisphere sever relations with the Axis powers, revealing the extent to which the United States had not mended its diplomatic fences so badly damaged prior to 1933. Although the proposal was passed, several of the nations did not comply with the proposal until much later, when they were more capable of assessing the drift of the war. Argentina did not declare war on the Axis powers until three weeks before Germany surrendered.

Latin American Overtures

After the war the nations of Europe were shattered economically, and the Latin American republics, realizing the strength of the United States, were anxious to comply with United States efforts to establish a special political relationship between the nations of the hemisphere —a formal alliance. No doubt, many Latin American leaders believed that just as the United States would aid its European allies and enemies to recover from the war, it would also provide massive economic assistance to its allies to the south. When it became apparent that no such aid was forthcoming, a great deal of bitterness surfaced. In 1945 a meeting took place in Mexico which was to have significant effects on both international and domestic decision making in the hemisphere. The Act of Chapultepec, which was ratified at the conference, paved the way for the establishment of the OAS and insured that Article 52 of the United Nations Charter would be written at the behest of the United States meeting later with its allies to establish the world organization. Article 52 states:

> Nothing in the present Charter precludes the existence of regional arrangements or agencies for dealing with such matters relating to the maintenance of international peace and security as are appropriate for regional action.

In effect, this sentence represents the confirmation by all nations of the world that the United States retains hegemony in this hemisphere. (The significance of this article and its interpretation by the United States was not lost on the Soviet Union, which multilateralized its special political relationship with the nations of Eastern Europe with the signing of the Treaty of Friendship, Cooperation and Mutual Assistance on May 14, 1955.) This hegemony has rarely been challenged, as it was during the 1962 Cuban missile crisis, and its effects on authoritative decision making in this hemisphere have been profound.

Ratification and Eclipse

In 1948 in Bogotá, Colombia, the charter of the Organization of American States was formally ratified. Also ratified was the Pact of Bogotá, which provides for the obligatory peaceful settlement of disputes between the signatory states. This pact grew out of the Treaty of Reciprocal Assistance of 1947, in which each of the nations agreed that an attack on one would constitute an attack on any of the others.

From the speeches made by the Latin American officials at Bogotá, during a meeting punctuated by the most violent urban disorder ever experienced in Latin America, the *Bogotazo*, it was clear that the United States was expected to render economic assistance as evidence of its good faith.

However, by that time the United States was looking elsewhere, and during the succeeding decade little attention was paid to either the OAS or any of the individual nations. The OAS functions in much the same fashion as had its forerunner, the Pan American Union. The supreme organ of the OAS, the Inter-American Conference, which was intended to deal with large political issues, has met very infrequently. Thus the organization has devoted its attention to commercial and cultural problems throughout most of the period of its existence. The advent of Fidel Castro changed this situation, for suddenly the United States realized that the very thing it was attempting to keep from happening elsewhere had occurred at its very borders.

The Act of Bogotá of September 1960, significantly enough ratified at a time when relations between Cuba and the United States had deteriorated to an all-time low, laid the groundwork for the Alliance for Progress and the long-awaited economic assistance desired by Latin Americans. The United States pledged $500 million for what was regarded as the beginning of a comprehensive development program.

THE ALLIANCE FOR PROGRESS

In March of 1961, one month before the Bay of Pigs invasion, President John F. Kennedy officially announced the Alliance for Progress. Although it was announced as a multilateral development program to be administered under the auspices of the Organization of American States, it was from its inception essentially a United States effort. It became, intentionally or not, still one more avenue through which the United States could intervene in the authoritative decision-making processes of the various nations by providing more of the scarce resources they so badly needed. Since the Nixon administration took office in January of 1969 the program has been declared defunct. However, it would have been academic to discuss the future of the Alliance for Progress even if it had not died at the inauguration of a Republican administration in Washington. It must be admitted in all fairness to the Nixon administration that the Alliance for Progress had been faltering since the death of John F. Kennedy. The reasons for its failure are numerous:

1. The United States did not provide the scarce resources which it had originally promised. The seemingly large amounts of resources claimed by the United States as having been granted through the Alliance for Progress actually included all aid, direct or indirect, flowing to Latin America, whether in the form of military aid or loans from the Inter-American Development Bank. The amounts allotted to the new program were not as large as they first appeared. And contrary to much propaganda, a large portion of all aid came in the form of low-interest loans rather than outright grants. The Latin American nations were obligated to repay these loans, and have been doing so.

2. Although the organizers of the Alliance for Progress were partly successful in selling the program to the public of Latin America as a self-help plan, it was usually presented in the United States as an anticommunist device, not as a Marshall Plan for the Western Hemisphere. As a result, military aid formed an increasingly large percentage of the funds.

3. The funds which were not military-oriented were often used to finance construction projects such as housing, schools, and other infrastructural projects which authoritative decision makers in Latin America would normally have had to provide through local means. The resources for the projects were often available locally, but suppliers of the prestige class no doubt preferred to be paid in hard United States currency. Because of their relationship to decision makers, they were assured that a good share of the resources would be brought in from abroad. Resources were not used in the main to import capital goods, which would have resulted in a long-run increase in the gross national product of the countries involved.

4. The Alliance for Progress had a profound psychological effect on Latin American decision makers. They worked under the impression that in a crisis someone would bail them out. As a result, the radical reallocation of resources or a more equitable distribution of the available land, schooling, consumer goods, hospital facilities—the principal goal of the alliance—was never achieved.

5. In general the Latin Americans refused or were unable to carry out structural reforms of their socioeconomic/political systems because the Alliance for Progress served to buttress the position of those in power and to preserve stability rather than to bring reform.

The demise of the Alliance for Progress does not represent the end of the Organization of American States. However, since the Castro scare has been eclipsed by other problems facing the United States in the world political arena, Washington appears to be no longer interested in a special relationship with Latin America on a political plane. As a result, the OAS is once again functioning as a commercial and cultural link between the nations of the hemisphere. When the United States needs the alliance for a particular purpose, it undoubtedly will once again come to political life.

ECONOMIC RELATIONS WITH THE UNITED STATES

As stated in Chapter I, Rosenau (1966) has hypothesized that the degree of penetration by the international system in the authoritative decision-making process of a country is related to the amount of resources it has. The fewer the resources, the more probable the intervention.

Foreign-Investment Patterns

The most overt interventions by the United States into the politics of the Latin American nations have been viewed from a historical perspective in this chapter, as has the organization through which the United States has funneled its diplomatic actions toward the twenty countries. However, less overt and yet extremely important are the relations of the United States to the nations of Latin America aside from the world of diplomacy. Despite the Alliance for Progress and other aid programs since World War II, the United States has extracted more resources from Latin America than it has provided. Table IV-1 provides some basic data on the activities of United States private enterprise in Latin America from 1950 to 1969. The amount of resources which these firms have managed to extract is formidable. To a great extent United States foreign policy, despite the existence of the Alliance for Progress, has been designed to permit this extraction by American enterprise to continue. The amount of reinvested earnings and government grants to these countries does not come close to making up the difference revealed in Table IV-1. Table IV-2 data show the distribution by country of cumulative United States investment in the area.

TABLE IV-1. United States Annual Investment and Income
from Investment, excluding Cuba (millions
of dollars).

Year	Annual Investment	Income	Balance[a]
1950	45	513	-468
1952	302	569	-267
1953	137	561	-424
1955	167	672	-505
1956	618	800	-182
1957	1,163	880	+283
1959	218	600	-382
1960	95	641	-546
1961	141	711	-570
1966	276	911	-635
1969	299	1,049	-750

a. The figures are presented as negative ones because, except for
1957, they represent an outflow of resources from 19 of the
countries.

Source: United States Department of Commerce: *Balance of Payments,
Statistical Supplement* (Washington, D.C.: Government Printing Of-
fice, 1961), pp. 176, 186; *U.S. Direct Investments Abroad, 1966--
Part I, Balance of Payments Data* (Washington, D.C.: Government
Printing Office, 1970), pp. 40, 94; *Survey of Current Business*, 42,
No. 8 (August 1962), pp. 22-23, and 51, No. 10 (October 1971), p. 34.

Foreign-Trade Patterns

The trade relations of the Latin American nations with the United
States are little different from their political relationship. A considerable percentage of Latin America's foreign trade is with the United
States, which is the largest customer of all of the nations as well as their
supplier, as the data in Tables IV-3 and IV-4 show. In 1967 the United
States purchased 33 per cent of all Latin American exports, a decline
of 10 per cent from 1958, while 42 per cent of all imports to the Latin
American nations came from the United States, down 6 per cent from
1958 (United Nations Economic Commission for Latin America, 1967,
p. 61).

Some analysts assert that it is primarily United States business interests which have been making foreign policy toward the twenty nations
of the hemisphere. Kolko (1969, p. 81) has stated: "The relationship
between the objectives of foreign economic policy and direct political
and military intervention, therefore, has been a continuous and inti-
mate one—indeed very identical."

Although the manner in which foreign policy is made in the United
States is beyond the scope of this volume, it must be stated that private

TABLE IV-2.   Distribution of Cumulative Direct Investment (millions of dollars).

Country	1950	1959	1961	1966	1968	1970 (preliminary)
Argentina	356	366	656	1,031	1,148	1,288
Brazil	644	828	1,008	1,246	1,484	1,843
Chile	540	729	748	844	964	748
Colombia	193	401	425	576	629	691
Cuba	642	956	-	-	-	-
Dominican Republic	106	87	107	a	a	a
Guatemala	106	132	127	a	a	a
Honduras	62	110	95	a	a	a
Mexico	415	758	826	1,244	1,459	1,774
Panama	58	327	498	793	922	1,233
Peru	145	428	436	518	692	691
Uruguay	55	45	49	a	a	a
Venezuela	993	2,690	3,012	2,678	2,620	2,696
Others	131	242	268	923	1,092	1,239
Total	4,445	8,098	8,255	9,854	11,010	12,203

a. Totals are included in "Others" for these years.

Source: For 1950, 1959, and 1961, United States Department of Commerce, *Survey of Current Business*, 42, No. 8 (Washington, D.C.: Government Printing Office, 1962), p. 22. For 1966, from *Survey*, 47, No. 9 (September 1967), p. 42. For 1968, from *Survey*, 50, No. 10 (October 1970), p. 28. For 1970, from *Survey*, 51, No. 10 (October 1971), p. 26.

investors have appeared to possess a considerable voice in policy making in Washington, particularly as the process affects Latin America. Since foreign peoples have little or no constituency in the United States and the general public pays little attention to United States–Latin American relations, it is probable that the small group that is interested—the representatives of business—is exerting an influence on policy making well beyond what its numbers alone would warrant.[1] The fact that Alliance for Progress money usually had to be spent in the United States is evidence of the influence of big business.

As mentioned in Chapter II, all of the countries are extremely specialized in terms of the export crops which they produce. This monoculturalism makes them particularly vulnerable to the sway of the international markets. The sale of exports abroad has not helped to alter the situation, for the resources which the Latin American nations exchange abroad for commodities are declining in value on the international market. Figure IV-1 provides a picture of this situation during recent years. The net terms of trade for the Latin American nations has deteriorated since World War II; they pay more for what they import and receive less for what they export.

SOCIOCULTURAL RELATIONS WITH THE UNITED STATES

Sociocultural relations are extremely difficult to measure, particularly in the international arena. The effects that sociocultural variables have on other kinds of interactions between nations are almost impossible to verify. Nevertheless, it is interesting to know the images and preconceptions one national group has about another, if for no other reason than the amusement they provide. The North American, when he thinks of Latin America, views it as a dirty, poor, revolutionary area peopled by lazy, shiftless aliens. This stereotype is disseminated through the mass media and predominates despite the new glamour acquired by such names as Acapulco, Rio, and Viña del Mar. The Latin American judges his North American neighbor on the basis of a stereotype gleaned from several sources. Hollywood has given him glimpses of a fabulously wealthy, immoral, and glamorously violent America. The tourist has not dispelled this image to any measurable degree. The Latin American intellectual, who in all probability has visited the United States, often adopts the Ariel-Caliban dichotomy of Rodó. On the one hand is the Latin American (Ariel), nonmethodical, emotional, philosophical, spiritual, nonmaterialistic, and moral. On the other hand is the North American (Caliban), methodical, machine-like, emotionless, materialistic, and immoral. These stereotypes can not only help the student to focus on the relations which exist between the United States and the Latin American nations, but they probably also play a part in the manner in which diplomacy is conducted between the countries. The principal variables have already been assessed. In the final analysis the United States desires stability in Latin America, both to facilitate the activities of American foreign enterprise and to avoid the possibility of another Castroite revolution in any of the countries. Latin American authoritative decision makers, in the main as anxious for stability in order to preserve their positions of status, are willing to cooperate, particularly if this cooperation assures a continuous flow of resources into their countries, resources which they can personally tap.

REGIONAL INTEGRATION

Until the early 1960's a person desiring to place a telephone call from Managua to San José had to be connected by the international operator in White Plains, New York. This communication problem was symp-

TABLE IV-3. Source of Imports, excluding Cuba (millions of U.S. dollars).

Country	Year	Total	United States Value	United States Per Cent of Total	Latin America	United Kingdom	Germany, Federal Republic	Italy	Other Western Europe	Communist Areas[b]
Argentina	1958	1,232	203	16	285	102	115	59	236	56
	1967	1,096	243	22	257	69	112	79	194	22
Bolivia	1958	80	37	47	13	5	10	3	9	c
	1967	151	62	41	19	7	18	2	18	2
Brazil	1958	1,353	483	36	247	44	141	29	195	29
	1967	1,670	572	34	230	58	168	52	261	80
Chile	1958	415	213	51	49	28	47	5	44	2
	1967	727	258	35	191	49	92	13	80	3
Colombia	1958	400	238	60	15	17	46	5	53	2
	1967	497	225	45	50	33	51	9	76	10
Costa Rica	1958	99	51	51	6	6	10	2	11	1
	1967	189	74	39	45	12	15	3	14	–
Dominican Republic	1958d	130	80	62	4	6	8	2	12	1
	1967d	175	96	55	5	7	10	4	20	–
Ecuador	1958d	90	46	51	3	7	12	2	14	c
	1967d,e	220	99	45	21	10	26	6	35	–
El Salvador	1958	108	53	49	15	5	10	2	16	c
	1967	224	70	31	68	14	16	5	24	c
Guatemala	1958	150	89	59	9	8	15	3	12	–
	1967	248	101	41	56	10	25	5	21	c
Haiti	1958f	40	25	62	c	2	2	1	5	c
	1967e	38	25	66	c	2	1	1	5	–

Country	Year									
Honduras	1958[d]	66	39	60	6	2	5	1	4	c
	1967	165	79	48	43	5	9	2	12	1
Mexico	1958	1,129	869	77	10	37	57	21	81	2
	1967	1,748	1,102	63	45	68	132	34	212	5
Nicaragua	1958	78	43	55	8	3	6	1	6	c
	1967	204	88	43	59	5	14	3	18	c
Panama	1958[d]	93	51	55	3	3	4	1	7	c
	1967[d]	227	91	40	54	7	8	3	16	c
Paraguay	1958[d]	33	9	27	8	2	4	–	3	–
	1967[d]	58	11	19	13	3	9	5	6	–
Peru	1958	335	158	47	26	27	36	9	51	1
	1967	813	299	37	103	36	100	31	113	3
Uruguay	1958	152	16	11	61	8	6	6	31	ε
	1967	172	24	14	47	14	17	5	23	6
Venezuela	1958[d]	1,428	819	57	16	102	121	94	162	2
	1967[d]	1,342	668	50	38	71	122	69	183	9
Latin America	1958	7,411	3,522	48	784	414	655	246	952	104
	1967	9,964	4,187	42	1,344	480	945	331	1,331	141

a. Includes Yugoslavia.
b. In Eastern Europe and Asia.
c. Less than $500,000.
d. f.o.b.
e. Derived from partner country data.
f. Year ending September.

Source: Adapted from Office of Program and Policy Coordination, Agency for International Development, *Latin America: Economic Growth Trends* (Washington, D.C.: Government Printing Office, December 1969), p. 27.

TABLE IV-4. Destination of Exports, excluding Cuba (millions of U.S. dollars).

Country	Year	Total	United States Value	United States Per Cent of Total	Latin America	United Kingdom	Germany, Federal Republic	Italy	Other Western Europe	Communist Areas[b]
Argentina	1958	994	128	13	131	237	95	64	225	64
	1967	1,465	124	8	285	139	79	229	470	70
Bolivia	1958[c]	65	21	33	8	33	2	d	1	–
	1967[c]	166	72	43	10	68	8	d	4	–
Brazil	1958	1,243	534	43	146	54	79	34	248	46
	1967	1,655	548	33	163	62	135	109	406	97
Chile	1958	389	157	40	36	55	64	11	58	d
	1967	913	168	18	83	124	71	74	279	2
Colombia	1958	461	319	69	6	8	44	2	40	2
	1967	510	222	44	30	21	68	4	114	16
Costa Rica	1958	92	46	50	6	1	25	2	4	–
	1967	143	68	48	32	d	11	2	19	d
Dominican Republic	1958	128	72	56	1	29	2	1	11	d
	1967	156	136	87	1	2	2	1	11	–
Ecuador	1958	133	77	58	13	1	18	4	17	d
	1967[e]	242	100	41	14	1	47	18	42	–
El Salvador	1958	116	46	40	8	1	38	2	7	–
	1967	207	55	27	79	d	46	1	7	d
Guatemala	1958	103	66	64	5	1	16	1	10	–
	1967	198	62	31	60	1	24	5	24	–
Haiti	1958[f]	42	21	49	d	d	1	7	13	–
	1967[g]	40	21	53	d	d	1	4	11	–

Honduras	1958	70	43	62	9	1	4	1	4	–
	1967	156	69	44	23	1	37	8	9	–
Mexico	1958	736	549	75	24	14	19	3	41	1
	1967	1,143	621	54	82	10	21	14	117	9
Nicaragua	1958	64	21	33	3	3	12	2	12	–
	1967	152	42	28	19	3	21	2	10	2
Panama	1958	33	31	93	1	d	–	d	d	–
	1967	84	65	77	2	1	2	–	1	–
Paraguay	1958	34	8	24	14	4	2	–	4	–
	1967	48	12	25	14	10	1	1	8	–
Peru	1958	291	111	38	43	26	18	7	55	1
	1967	774	328	42	40	17	85	20	149	19
Uruguay	1958	139	11	8	14	21	9	4	48	30
	1967	159	12	8	17	34	9	12	52	12
Venezuela	1958	2,319	976	42	189	144	54	17	143	–
	1967	2,886	977	34	212	186	43	38	247	d
Latin America	1958	7,452	3,237	43	657	633	502	162	941	144
	1967	11,097	3,702	33	1,166	680	711	542	1,980	227

a. Includes Yugoslavia.
b. In Eastern Europe and Asia.
c. c.i.f.
d. Less than $500,000.
e. Derived from partner country data.
f. Year ending September.
g. Principally exports of crude petroleum to Netherlands Antilles for refining.

Source: Adapted from Office of Program and Policy Coordination, Agency for International Development, *Latin America: Economic Growth Trends* (Washington, D.C.: Government Printing Office, December 1969), p. 26.

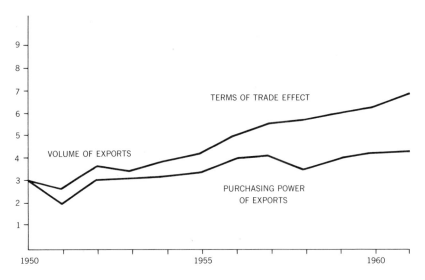

FIGURE IV-1. PURCHASING POWER OF EXPORTS AND
TOURISM (THOUSANDS OF MILLIONS OF 1950 DOLLARS). *Source:* United
Nations, *The Economic Development of Latin America in the Post War Period,*
New York: United Nations, 1964, p. 13.

tomatic of the relations between the Latin American countries in
general. Very little interaction of any type has occurred between the
twenty countries during most of their histories. During the 1950's
Raúl Prebisch, head of the United Nations Economic Commission for
Latin America (ECLA), began to call for a program of regional integration for Latin America. According to the proponents of integration,
the plan would succeed because:

1. The adverse effects suffered by the Latin American nations individually could be counteracted by the nations banding together to
adopt common customs barriers, to use their scarce resources more
judiciously, and perhaps to engage in joint marketing.

2. The adverse effects of the small money markets in many of the
countries could be offset by permitting industry locating in one of the
countries to sell in the entire integrated area at a lower per-unit
cost.

3. The duplication in industries in neighboring countries and the
resultant waste of scarce resources could be avoided.

4. Despite the fact that many of the countries evince essentially the
same industrial and economic structures, the competition would not
damage, but improve them.

Most of the literature dealing with regional integration in Latin America has concerned itself primarily with the Latin American Free Trade Area (LAFTA), which now includes all of the South American nations as well as Mexico—90 per cent of the population of Latin America. However, the more successful Central American Common Market (CACM), which includes Guatemala, El Salvador, Honduras, Nicaragua, and Costa Rica, has received little or no attention.[2]

The Latin American Free Trade Area

A principal distinction between LAFTA and the CACM is that the latter is a common market and the former is envisioned more limitedly as a free-trade area. Because a free-trade area does not involve coordinated industrial development or concentration of resources in areas where they are needed most, LAFTA has been only moderately successful.

The initial goal of LAFTA was to achieve free trade within the area by 1973. The failure to negotiate a common list in 1967 in accordance with the timetable of the Treaty of Montevideo, ratified in 1960, made negotiation of a new timetable necessary. The new deadline for achieving free trade within the area is 1980. Over the years member nations have joined together to eliminate tariffs on industrial products manufactured in the area; but in view of the limited number of these commodities, the over-all effects on trade and the development of resources have not been far-reaching. A primary difficulty for LAFTA is the economic diversity of the member states. Brazil, Argentina, and Mexico have relatively strong industrial and manufacturing sectors with large markets, while Paraguay and Ecuador are characterized by tiny markets and virtually no modern industrial or manufacturing sectors. A second significant factor has been the increasing realization by major sectors of the business community that the risks of competition, in comparison with their present protected security, are great enough to require strenuous opposition. To note rather extreme situations, all of the countries are afraid of the competition of Argentine wheat and beef, Uruguayan sheep products, Venezuelan oil and iron ore—making reduction of tariffs in those products next to impossible. But the fear extends to a wide variety of other products and businesses. Furthermore, even the large countries have been intent on protecting prestige industries such as steel, petroleum, and the airlines. Other problems—size of the region, inadequate infrastructure, inflation, low levels of original intraregional trade—should not be underestimated. Until the LAFTA members are willing to throw their customs doors open to the agricultural products of the area or until they permit the extension of the association into a true common market, there is doubt about its future and the 1980 deadline may well be postponed.

The Central American Common Market

The CACM is designed to permit the nations of the Central American area to form part of what eventually will be called the Latin American Common Market (LACM), a merger of all of the regional arrangements at some future date. The five nations of the isthmus formed their own association because it was believed that their weak resource base, even in relation to other Latin American nations, would put them individually at a disadvantage in the long-talked-about LAFTA. Actually the CACM predates LAFTA. In contrast to LAFTA the Central American organization includes provisions for free trade, common customs barriers, and an integrated industrial program. The success of the CACM can be assessed in part in terms of the rapid growth of Central American intraregional trade, a growth rate four times higher than for Latin American intraregional trade as a whole, in the period 1958–1965.

The "soccer war" of 1969 between El Salvador and Honduras may have had profound effects on the CACM. The senseless incident, in which more than 500 people were killed, brought relations between the two countries to a standstill. With no trade occurring between the two countries, and with Guatemala isolated from Nicaragua and Costa Rica because of the battleline, the entire integration movement may have been undermined. Honduras has taken this opportunity to withdraw almost completely from the CACM. The strategic location of Honduras gives this move considerable importance. According to one analyst (Nye, 1967), a prime factor in the original success of the CACM was the fact that authoritative decision makers have been willing to view the integration movement as something apart from the wiles and innuendos of diplomacy. The "soccer war" may have changed all this.

The Andean Group

Five LAFTA countries—Chile, Bolivia, Peru, Colombia, and Ecuador—dissatisfied with the progress made by the association by the mid-1960's initiated an effort to organize a regional grouping on the order of the CACM, except on a much broader scale. Especially important in providing impetus to the Andean Group (Grupo Andino) were the integration-minded Presidents Frei of Chile and Lleras of Colombia. The Declaration of Bogotá, a document of intent more than anything else, was signed by the five countries, plus Venezuela in early 1967. The latter, the most vulnerable of the countries to tariff reductions, has since broken with the group after heavy pressures from the other members to comply with the original goals.

Andean integration has three expressions: 1) an Agreement aimed at creating a common market; 2) a Corporation for stimulating production; and 3) agreement for industrial complementation, of which the most significant thus far has been petrochemicals (Sanders, 1968, p. 5).

In May 1969 the five remaining countries signed the final agreement, which calls for free trade in the zone by 1980, encouragement of integrated industries, and reduction of red tape on commodity trading.

For example, in July 1968 the five, excluding Ecuador, signed a complementation agreement calling for coordinated planning for 57 petrochemical products. Production of each product was assigned to one or more of the countries, with the other countries agreeing not to allow competing plants to be set up in their territory. In all cases, Ecuador and Bolivia have been given preferential treatment because of their economic weaknesses.

The Andean group has tremendous potential. The countries contain 50 million population with a total product of $19 billion, making the five comparable to Brazil as an economic unit. Furthermore, present intraregional imports are very low (3.6 per cent of their totals), suggesting that there exist considerable possibilities for expansion. None of the countries has more than 10 per cent of its imports coming from the other group members, including Venezuela. The problems loom large, however. Transportation and communication are enormous problems between countries as geographically separated as Chile and Colombia or Ecuador. The traditional enmities of Chile, Peru, and Bolivia in particular may arise in disruption and noncooperation. The wide differences in governments—from the dictatorship of Velasco Ibarra in Ecuador to the military regime in Peru to the Marxist socialism of Chile—would seem to harbor potential problems. The notorious institutional instability of Bolivia gives no cause for comfort. Two more immediate questions concern the role of Venezuela, whose entrance could both strengthen and weaken the group, and the attitude of the Allende government of Chile. Allende and a number of high leftist advisers have expressed grave doubts about the advantages for Chile.

CUBA'S RELATIONS WITH THE UNITED STATES AND
THE SOVIET UNION

Prior to 1959 Cuba shared many of the problems common to the nations of the Latin American area in their relations with the United States. The Cuba of the 1960's and early 1970's has managed to create a new international environment for itself, although Rosenau's hypothesis is no less relevant to the island nation than to its neighbors in the hemisphere. The new international environment faced by Cuba, dominated by the Soviet Union, does not mean that the United States is not capable of placing tremendous pressure on the country's authoritative decision makers. The Bay of Pigs invasion, the missile crisis of 1962, and the rather effective economic embargo—which places any nation trading with Cuba in the bad graces of the United States State Department—have apparently made an impact on the nation's economic and political systems. In short, the United States is still capable of making authoritative decisions affecting Cuba despite the fact that the two countries do not maintain diplomatic relations with each other.

Somewhat replacing the United States in the authoritative decision-making process internally in the island nation is the Soviet Union. This does not mean that Cuba has become a "satellite" of that nation, as it was quite definitely of the United States prior to 1959. But it does mean that certain decisions cannot be made in Cuba without prior consideration of the reaction in the Soviet Union. Cuba sells much of its sugar crop to, and imports most of its manufactured goods from, the Soviet Union. Although accurate statistics are currently unavailable, there is no doubt that the Soviet Union is subsidizing the present Cuban authoritative decision makers.

Cuban decision makers must consider the Soviet Union when making the following kinds of decisions:

1. What the island will produce for export; how much land will be used in producing the exportable commodities; and most significantly for a Marxist society, how much labor will be employed for this purpose.

2. What commodities will be imported—with the recognition that the Soviet Union usually attempts to barter, rather than buy and sell using "hard" currencies.

3. How almost all resources are allocated—which because of Cuba's heavy dependence on the international environment is influenced by the Soviet Union.

Cuban decision makers must consider the United States when making the following types of decisions:

1. How much of their resources they will commit to defending the island.
2. How much of their resources they will commit to the attempt to establish friendly decision makers in other Latin American nations.
3. How to proceed to trade with noncommunist countries.

Authoritative decision makers in Cuba must be careful in their dealings with their counterparts in the Soviet Union to avoid sanctions, but certainly no more careful than many of the other Latin American leaders in their dealings with the United States. In fact, in foreign-policy making Cuban decision makers have been permitted greater latitude by their international environment than have other Latin American decision makers by theirs.

During the 1960's the Soviet Union adopted a new foreign policy toward Latin America, one which does not encourage the fomentation of revolution in any of the countries (Dinerstein, 1967). Duncan (1970, p. 4) notes that "the Soviets no longer envisage the Cuban model being reproduced in Latin America. . . . Nor does Moscow foresee the victory of traditional Communist parties south of the Rio Grande." Partly as the result of its experiences with Cuba—the expenses incurred in subsidizing the nation at a time when Russian consumers were demanding a greater share of their own resources and the missile crisis of 1962—the Soviet Union now desires more industrialization and economic development for the nations of the Latin American area before it views them as ready for a move toward socialism. Economic development would create a nonagricultural working class, so necessary for revolution in Marxist doctrine.

As the expedition under "Che" Guevara to Bolivia in 1967 demonstrated, the government of Cuba, in direct opposition to the plans of the Soviet Union, has supplied resources for revolutionary efforts in at least one Latin American nation. The life-giving trade links between Cuba and its trading partners make it essential for the island nation to establish relations with countries closer to its own borders. It should be noted that diplomatic relations with Cuba were reestablished by the republic of Chile in 1970. The United States embargo has made it impossible for any of the Latin American nations, except Chile, to trade with Cuba. As a result, Castro has viewed as indispensable the establishment of friendly authoritative decision makers in nations which have supplies sorely needed by Cuba. With the failure of the

Guevara mission, perhaps Cuban decision makers will attempt a more conciliatory approach to the problem and to the United States. Whether or not the United States is prepared to soften its stand on Cuba is a problem outside the ken of this volume. However, other nations in the hemisphere can be expected to follow Chile's lead during the 1970's.

SUMMARY

The Latin American nations, without exception, are highly dependent on their international environments, largely consisting of the United States. The latter plays a formidable role in the authoritative decision-making process of all the nations including Cuba. And as this island nation demonstrates, until the very structure of a country's economy can be changed, causing a rapid growth in available resources, dependence on the international environment is inevitable.

NOTES

1. There are a number of excellent analyses of the processes of making American foreign policy. See, for example, Sapin (1966), Radway (1969), and Wagner (1970).
2. See Cochrane (1970) for one of the few works dealing with the CACM.

SUGGESTED READINGS

Adams, Richard N. *The Second Sowing.* Scranton: Chandler, 1967.
Alba, Victor. *Alliance Without Allies.* New York: Praeger, 1965.
Blanksten, George I. "Fidel Castro and Latin America." In Morton Kaplan, ed., *The Revolution in World Politics.* New York: Wiley, 1962. Pp. 113–136.
"Che Guevara's Bolivian Campaign Diary." *Evergreen Review,* 11, No. 57 (August 1968), 33–40.
Connell-Smith, Gordon. *The Inter-American System.* London: Oxford University Press, 1966.
Cornelius, William G. "The 'Latin American Bloc' in the United Nations." *Journal of Inter-American Studies,* 3, No. 3 (July 1961), 419–435.
Dinerstein, Herbert S. "Soviet Policy in Latin America." *American Political Science Review,* 61, No. 1 (March 1967), 80–90.
Dozer, Donald M. *Are We Good Neighbors?* Gainesville: University of Florida Press, 1960.

Dozer, Donald M., ed. *The Monroe Doctrine*. New York: Knopf, 1965.

Gil, Federico. *Latin American–United States Relations*. New York: Harcourt, Brace, Jovanovich, 1971.

Glavert, Earl T., and Lester D. Langley. *The United States and Latin America*. Reading, Mass.: Addison-Wesley, 1971.

Goldenberg, Boris. *The Cuban Revolution and Latin America*. New York: Praeger, 1965.

Johnson, Leland L. "U.S. Business Interests and the Rise of Castro." *World Politics*, 17, No. 3 (April 1965), 440–460.

Mecham, J. Lloyd. *A Survey of United States–Latin American Relations*. Boston: Houghton Mifflin, 1965.

Urquidi, Victor L. *Free Trade and Economic Integration in Latin America*. Los Angeles: University of California Press, 1962.

Whitaker, Arthur P. *The Western Hemisphere Idea*. Ithaca: Cornell University Press, 1954.

THE LEGAL-INSTITUTIONAL CONTEXT

The number of constitutions written since the Latin American countries achieved independence grows larger with each decade. According to one analyst, the number of these documents had reached 195 by the year 1965, or an average of 6.75 per country (Edelmann, 1965, pp. 371–391). In assessing this state of affairs, Mecham (1959) wrote that it was difficult to determine the exact role played by constitutions in the conduct of Latin American politics.

Perhaps the best indicator that Latin American constitutions do not reflect basic beliefs and values lies in the very frequency of change, in at least some of the countries. At the same time, the frequency of change may be only a symptom of deeper social divisions, of the inability to achieve consensus or reach compromises on basic values and goals. While there is little doubt that the constitutions of the Latin American countries do not, by and large, perform the same functions they do in the United States and Western Europe, it would be grossly incorrect to assert that they perform no function at all.

In view of the fact that the twenty Latin American nations are relatively new states, have strong intellectual and political ties to Europe (especially France, Spain, Portugal, and Italy), and have been dominated in practically all respects by the United States, it is not surprising that many of the ideas contained in their constitutional documents have been imported from those areas. The relative success of the United States document, especially since United States independence occurred only shortly before that of most of the Latin American countries, made it especially desirable as a model (in the same way that the writers of the constitution of this country borrowed from the British). This transplantation of form, ideas, and institutions from one society to another, sometimes almost unaltered, has been a principal factor contributing to the short lifespan of so many of the documents. The practices and patterns of one culture, when grafted onto another, usually do not yield the desired results.

THE FUNCTIONS OF CONSTITUTIONS

It might be asked whether it is necessary at all for the Latin American countries to pen constitutions—whether in fact this type of activity is primarily suited to wealthy and industrialized societies. This question leads to one of the reasons Latin American countries expend the effort to write a constitutional document.

International Status

Quite simply stated, the international system as represented by the United States, Western Europe, and the United Nations expects all nation states to adopt this type of document as one of the trappings of sovereignty. Thus, a primary function of the constitution is to secure international status both for its writers and for the country. Prestige among nations is prized because the elite decision makers—especially the nonnationalistic, imitative elites of Latin America—often have more in common with elites in other nations than with the masses in their own countries. In addition, international status is essential for obtaining foreign aid, negotiating trade agreements and quotas, and protecting the rights of citizens in other countries.

Articulation of Goals

If the Latin American constitution is regarded as an *ideal type* of sociopolitical, economic system, then the importance of this type of document cannot be overestimated. It may well be that Latin American leaders outline their nation's long-range goals instead of describing a contemporary political state of affairs, as has been true elsewhere (Wheare, 1966). It would appear that in Mexico, at least, this is exactly what the authors of the 1917 constitution had in mind. The revolutionary leaders of Mexico who penned this document included a large number of provisions, laws, and even idealistic statements which bore no resemblance to the existent state of political affairs. However, over the succeeding decades, the Partido Revolucionario Institucional (PRI) has gradually activated these clauses, shaping reality to the document rather than vice versa.

To cite only two examples of this process: (1) The 1917 constitution declares that the state is the sole proprietor of all subsoil mineral resources in the country. It was not until President Lázaro Cárdenas expropriated the oil refineries and other properties of British and United States firms in 1938 that the relevant portions of the constitution began to be enforced. As late as the 1950's, there were still several small, private oil operators working in the country. (2) The 1917 constitution under Article 123 states that a share in the profits is the right of all Mexican workers. It was not until 1962, under the administration of President Adolfo López Mateos, that this clause of the constitution was activated.

As analysts of the United States political scene have stressed, the great secrets of the constitution of 1789 are its brevity and its resemblance to the sociopolitical system which existed at the time, rather than representing an effort to change the system. Latin American constitutions are usually lengthy documents, their writers having attempted to incorporate as many details and to account for as many possibilities as they can. Unfortunately, this inclusiveness often makes the documents inflexible and dated almost before they are ratified. In this sense the documents resemble many individual state constitutions of the United States. While state constitutions have not been tossed aside with the frequency found in Latin America, it is not because they are any more relevant to contemporary political life. The discrepancy between document and reality has become so pronounced that a number of states in the United States—where constitutions are regarded with something close to reverence—have revised or are in process of revising their constitutions.

Effecting Change by Writing Laws

An extension of this general attitude toward constitutional documents is the tendency for Latin American decision makers to attempt to execute change by writing laws. It is not difficult to place a law on the books in most of the countries of the Latin American area; much more difficult is the enforcement of the same law. It may very well be that problem solvers, perceiving a demand for something which they cannot or will not grant, nevertheless decree a favorable decision in order to curb or diffuse the demands being placed on them. Constitutions are often written during crisis periods; but once the political processes have been normalized, the laws which are distasteful to decision makers can be ignored.

The history of Cuban politics provides another illustration of how Latin Americans view the function of their constitutional documents. The Cuban constitution of 1940 resembles the Mexican constitution with its compendium of long-run elite goals, rather than being a reflection of sociopolitical reality in the period before World War II. One theme that was continually repeated by Fidel Castro during the 1950's, in his speech "History Will Absolve Me" and elsewhere, was his intention of "returning" his country to the tenets outlined in the 1940 document. When, after assuming power, he began to fulfill his promises, many of the groups which had supported him began to fall away, regarding him as a traitor to the prestige class of his country.

Enumeration of Civil Rights

Besides asserting national goals, Latin American constitutions usually outline the form and authority of national institutions and describe the civil rights which are provided to the citizens. These rights usually can be and are suspended by the president of the country if he declares the nation to be in a state of siege. And it can be expected that when the military is actually in command, these rights are also suspended or at least curbed.

As outlined in the constitutions of Latin America, civil rights are often very extensive, including the right to hold a job and even to obtain political asylum in the embassy of a foreign country. In general, all of the constitutional documents written in Latin America provide for freedom of speech, press, and religion. *Habeas corpus*, a common right in the Anglo-American legal tradition, is not as pervasive or extensive in the twenty countries, although there is usually at least one high court which can make a ruling of this type.

CENTRALIZATION VERSUS DECENTRALIZATION

During the colonial period of Latin American history, decision-making authority was highly centralized in all of the twenty nations.

The representative of the European monarch usually was vested with supreme authority, although certain forms of local self-government, such as the *cabildo*, thrived. Geographical separation, poor transportation, rugged terrain, and other physical factors sometimes negated the practical impact of centralized decision-making power. Since attaining their independence, many of the nations have experimented with one form or another of decentralization, often as part of an effort to curb the tendency toward one-man rule, which is characteristic of the area as a whole. Regardless of the extent to which a federal or even a confederal type of governmental system was established, national decision makers have still retained the paramount responsibility and authority. Geographical decentralization has normally not been successful. The debate waged so furiously and often violently between supporters of a unitary system (usually urbanites who wanted national markets and modern societies) and supporters of a confederal system (usually coalitions of local *caudillos* and large landholders, anxious to maintain their abilities to govern as they wished in their individual fiefdoms) has now largely been settled in favor of a centralized government. This victory has not always meant a blow against the landholders, as they have maintained their independence as the price for compromise. The odd-man-out has been the local *caudillo*.

Exceptions to Centralization

In the two nations where decentralization is the most extensive, Argentina and Brazil, the reasons are largely related to their vast territorial size and to the fact that informal decentralization existed prior to the establishment of the formal trappings of federalism. The states into which Brazil has been divided by one or another of its constitutional documents have usually resembled informal regional arrangements which were established because of the nation's huge expanse of territory and the difficulties in communication which this represented. Residents of Buenos Aires vied for control of the formal decision-making apparatus with the great landowners of the *pampas* for so long and with such mutually unsatisfactory results that it was necessary for them to reach some form of working arrangement. The government in Buenos Aires has usually retained a tight control over the country, but the actual decision-making roles have remained in the hands of the *pampeños* more often than in the hands of the urban elite. At the same time, local legislatures in Argentina have retained, during periods of civilian rule at least, some measure of decision-making responsibility.

The imposition of decentralization on Mexico prior to the revolutionary period of its history almost brought about national disintegration. During the nineteenth century, Mexican states seceded and then were reunited to the federal government in what nationalists must have regarded as disheartening regularity. When a fifth column from the United States participated in one of the secessionist movements, involving the northern portion of the state of Coahuila known as Texas, the result was the irretrievable loss of that territory.

Most of the Latin American nations are subdivided in some fashion geographically. The subdivisions are variously titled states, provinces, departments, and cantons. In most cases, these subdivisions are merely convenient centers of administration for the central government or places where local citizens can participate in minor decisions related exclusively to their particular area. In several of the Central American nations, for example, the municipalities elect their aldermen, while the mayor is appointed by the president of the republic. Almost nowhere do the local councils have any significant autonomous functions, except to perhaps serve as patronage payoffs and training grounds for aspiring political figures.

THE CHIEF EXECUTIVE

Traditionally, the Latin American countries have favored the strong-executive form of government. The systems are so strongly overbalanced toward the executive that one observer has termed them "regimes of presidential dominance" (Lambert, 1967, esp. Chaps. 13, 16). The strength of the president varies from country to country, from time to time, and according to the individual who occupies the office. All of the nations have tried or have been forced to submit to a fairly broad variety of chief executives, ranging from the absolute monarchs of Mexico and Haiti in the nineteenth century to the collegiate system which prevailed in Uruguay for over a decade in this century. Predictably, the two extremes have been found unsatisfactory, and today the chief executive in all of the countries, although more powerful than any other single individual or branch of government, is subject to certain restrictions on the scope, duration, or authoritativeness of his decisions.

Chief of State/Commander in Chief

In all of the countries, except Cuba, the role of chief executive or principal administrator is performed by the same person who fulfills the role of chief of state. Cuba's president, formally the chief of state of that country, is not its chief executive, a role which Premier Fidel Castro reserves for himself. In many respects, however, Castro is the informal chief of state as well. The chief executive in any of the Latin American nations is reinforced in his decision-making role by possessing more formal status resources than any other individual in the country.

Although formally the roles of chief executive and chief of state are also combined with the role of commander in chief of the armed forces, informally this is not always the case. In nations where the military has been prone to intervene in the national political process, the merger of the two roles has occurred only when the chief of state/chief executive has been selected or imposed from the ranks of the armed forces. In 1971 in nine of the countries this was the actual situation.

Dependent on whether or not the president is the commander in chief of the armed forces is his ability to use the formal power of declaring his nation in a state of siege. If the military does not support him, it is unlikely that he can utilize this broad, formal power. The commander in chief/chief of state has resorted to this formal constitutional power with frequency, and as a result perhaps as many as one third of all Latin Americans have been formally deprived of their civil rights.

Chief Legislator

Although the role is not formally assigned to him, the president is often the chief legislator of his country. By monopolizing political communications and information and by preserving a formidable organizational strength, he is able to control the content of legislative considerations—assuming the legislature is even permitted to function. The president has a number of powerful weapons which he can use in his dealings with the national legislature, in addition to the charisma which accrues to him on the basis of being chief of state/commander in chief. For one, most presidents are in possession of a very broad decree power. By declaring their country in a state of siege, they acquire exclusive rule-making power and can actually close the legislative assembly and deprive congressmen of their normal political immunities.

Another important power is his control of the political spoils system —whether he is a military-supported chief executive or a civilian with some kind of political-party backing. In some of the countries, legislators cannot stand for reelection; in others, they are dependent on their party for continued support and election. The men or women who occupy legislative roles must cooperate with the president and his confidants either to stay in office or to obtain a patronage position once they are out of office.

Limitations on Presidential Power

The president is the principal and most important decision maker in all of the Latin American countries. Although various controls are placed on his power in most of the countries, he remains the most important single figure in the authoritative decision-making process. However, decision making and problem solving do not necessarily go together. Despite all of the president's power, his ability to make radical problem-solving decisions and to ensure their implementation is restricted. The principal force working against his ability to enforce decisions is the so-called executive branch of the government.

For many years, analysts have assumed that bureaucracy was merely an instrumentality available to the president—a machine which followed orders unquestioningly. It is rapidly becoming evident to political scientists researching countries which have scarce resources such as those of Latin America that the bureaucracy is anything but a tool at the disposal of the president (Riggs, 1964; Heady, 1966; LaPalombara, 1963). In fact, it may be the single most effective instrument working against presidential power in many of the countries. Unfortunately, so little empirical research has been conducted on this problem that it is virtually impossible to provide a detailed discussion, although an effort will be made in Chapter X. It can be stated briefly, however, that in the Latin American countries jobs in the public administration are filled in the main by members of the prestige class, a group which even in the lower reaches is interested in maintaining the status quo. The prestige class uses the bureaucracy to stabilize or institutionalize the system and thus to preserve its own position.

In view of the desperate problems facing many of the Latin American nations, it is not surprising that from time to time a man is elevated to the presidency who is interested in tackling some of these difficulties. However, his means for alleviating hunger, instituting agrarian reform, or combatting inflation are locked within the bureaucratic machine. Covered by civil service, protected by informal communications, shielded by kinship relations, and cloaked in secrecy, the bureaucracy in a typical Latin American nation is difficult to activate. Betancourt of Venezuela, Belaúnde of Peru, Frondizi of Argentina, Orlich of Costa Rica, Frei of Chile, and Goulart of Brazil—men of different characters and ideologies but similar commitment to reform

—have been confounded at least partly by the very bureaucratic machine which is supposed to help them. Administration's growing role in drafting and enforcing its own rules is characteristic of the modern administrative state, but is accepted in Latin America by the rapid growth of bureaucracy and the lack of strong, autonomous legislative or judicial controls.

When the new chief executive is of the military forces, he has even more problems, for it was a bureaucracy which placed him in office in the first place. He cannot afford to move against the military machine, and yet he may find the armed forces to be as much of a liability as an asset in his dealings with the civilian bureaucracies which he has acquired.

A theme repeated throughout this volume is that the *personalismo* which is so prevalent in Latin American nations insures that certain patterns of political behavior will invariably emerge. One of these is the seeming inability of Latin Americans to attach themselves emotionally to political aggregates such as parties; this lack is coupled with the need of a single person, or *patrón*, with which to identify. This characteristic tends to strengthen further the man who becomes the chief of state and to make any limitations on him difficult to implement.

In Mexico the solution has been to give the president almost unlimited power, and then through the Partido Revolucionario Institucional (PRI) to force him to relinquish it at the end of a six-year term. In Chile an arrangement of strikingly similar characteristics has developed, primarily over the past twenty years, except that party competition for the high post does exist. In various countries terms of office have been imposed on the chief executive; but usually these have been enforceable only through acquiescence or support of the military forces. Parties of national mobilization, such as the Mexican party, are a rarity. One problem is that once the military assumes the task of leadership selection, it is virtually impossible to wrest this authority from it. Even when the military is out of power, it remains as a veto group over selections.

Many of the other limitations imposed on Latin American chief executives by their constitutions are only valid when a civilian, duly elected, holds office. Typically, the chief executive cannot leave the borders of his country without the permission of the legislature, which usually places a time limitation on his absence. While a president is out of the country, a vice president is sworn into the presidency. Only a few countries, such as Brazil, elect a vice president who actually carries out formally assigned duties and receives a salary while in office.

THE LEGISLATURE

A great deal of space could be consumed in discussing the legislative structures of each of the Latin American countries. Statistics could be presented on how many representatives there are, whether the assembly is unicameral or bicameral, and how much seniority is required to assume a committee position. However, at the beginning of the 1970's, only four or five legislatures were actually participating in the decision-making processes of their countries, and these had quite limited functions. As a result, a lengthy structural analysis would be largely academic. Instead, a brief discussion is presented about the functions of the various legislatures when and if they convene.

Leadership Recruitment

Latin American legislatures serve as centers of political-leadership recruitment. It is in the chambers of these organizations that many decision makers are first given the opportunity fully to become acquainted with the authoritative allocation of values as it takes place in their particular society. It is also the place where they are able to acquire certain political skills, whether in oratory, campaign and communications management, or simply "wheeling and dealing."

Communication of Demands and Decisions

The operating legislature serves as a place where various elite factions can communicate their demands to one another and to the nonapathetic citizenry. It can also serve as a sounding board for the president, who in most cases can send a cabinet officer to the national legislature to make an address or to propose certain programs at any time. Although decisions may not be made by the legislature, the debates which take place serve to advise the people of a country about the decisions being made elsewhere.

Political Socialization

The legislature serves as an agent of political socialization. Speeches, campaigns, meetings, committees, all serve to keep the people aware of their national political processes. In a country where this awareness has resulted in too much social mobilization and where decision makers are being pressed with demands, perhaps even conflicting ones, this socialization process may have to be stopped and the legislature closed.

Decision Making

The ineffectiveness of legislative bodies, where they are allowed to function, to make the significant allocations of values and scarce resources has been discussed, and it is necessary only to note that while very limited this power has not been completely lost by all of the legislatures. The bodies of three major countries—Venezuela, Colombia, and especially Chile—play some role in the final decision-making process. In these countries, the amount of control the executive may exercise is definitely related to his political support in the legislature. President Frei of Chile, for example, could do virtually nothing in terms of real reform in that country until his party's victory in the congressional elections of 1965. The congress in Mexico has on occasion amended laws in substantial ways, and even more often wrought informal changes in legislation and its implementation.

Representation

The representation function of legislators should also be noted. While there has not developed anything near the same importance attached to representation of particular interests or areas as exists in the United States, legislators in those countries mentioned above in particular are clearly and in important ways voices of their constituencies. Radical party congressmen representing Chile's southern region behave in a markedly different fashion from those in the central area and especially different from those in the north. At the same time, the role of the legislative bodies should not be overemphasized. The Latin American systems clearly do not find their focus here.

THE JUDICIARY AND THE LEGAL SYSTEM

The principal distinctions between Anglo-American jurisprudence and Latin American law are that in the latter there is no common law, effective judicial review of political decisions, or the concept of *stare decisis*. As a result, judicial policy making, the capability of Latin American judges and lawyers to set or limit authorative decision-making processes, is not extensive.

Latin American legal systems or codes can often be found succinctly summarized in a very few thick volumes, in considerable contrast to the hundreds of volumes which are required to contain the legal code of the United States or Great Britain. A judge or lawyer in a country of this hemisphere, with the exception of the United States and Canada, quite often finds himself strictly limited in his prerogatives for action. Precedent does not bear on a decision in Latin America.

As Edelmann (1965, p. 450) has pointed out, by far the major influence on the legal codes of the Latin American nations has been Roman law. For a lengthy period of time, Roman law provided the basis and content of the law in both of the nations of the Iberian peninsula and also had considerable influence on French legal codes. Certain facets of common law have been imported from England and the United States, however. Common-law marriages, *habeas corpus*, and the broader writ of *amparo* were adopted or modified from Anglo-American codes. Other codes and practices have been imported at particular times into certain countries. In 1830, Bolivia adopted verbatim the civil code of France, to cite only one example (Edelmann, 1965, p. 452).

Most of the Latin American countries have incorporated three independent branches of government into their institutional system. However, the supreme court, like the legislature, is usually eclipsed by the presidency. Like judiciaries around the world, the Latin American supreme courts have not been permitted to implement or enforce their decisions with their own military or police force. Instead, they must depend on the executive branch, more specifically the president, for enforcement. As might be expected, if a president finds a judicial decision politically ill-advised, he will enforce it only halfheartedly or perhaps not at all.

Although at times a supreme-court justice takes a stand in opposition to the president, in general the Latin American supreme courts attempt to stay out of the political arena. Since it is within the political arena that most important decisions are made, the Latin American supreme courts deal with less important social problems. Moreover, the administration of justice, or more aptly the rule-adjudication function, is carried out within the narrow confines of a political context highly influenced by the socioeconomic environments.

Most of the countries do not provide their supreme-court justices with lifetime tenure. Sooner or later, these men must face the problem of seeking reappointment, returning to private practice, or attempting to secure another political position. This situation clearly must have an influence on the manner in which the supreme-court justices reach their decisions.

SUMMARY

In making a demand on the authoritative decision makers of his society, the individual Latin American or the group to which he belongs would certainly be wiser to articulate his interests to the president or to a member of the executive branch rather than to either the legislature or the supreme court. For it is in the executive branch of the government and within the institutions which help the president to control that branch—for example, the military, the political party —that the important decisions are made.

SUGGESTED READINGS

Christensen, Asher N. *The Evolution of Latin American Government.* New York: Holt, 1951.

Davis, Harold E., ed. *Government and Politics in Latin America.* New York: Ronald Press, 1958.

Edelmann, Alexander T. *Latin American Government and Politics.* Homewood, Ill.: Dorsey Press, 1965.

Gomez, Rosendo A. *Government and Politics in Latin America.* Rev. ed.; New York: Random House, 1963.

Mecham, J. Lloyd. "Latin American Constitutions: Nominal or Real?" *Journal of Politics,* 21, No. 2 (May 1959), 258–275.

Pierson, William W., and Federico G. Gil. *Governments of Latin America.* New York: McGraw-Hill, 1957.

POLITICAL ISSUES

For systems which, superficially, appear to be very unstable, there is a great deal of consensus supporting the political systems of all of the Latin American countries. The underlying consensus does not mean that there is no debate on issues, for Latin Americans show as great a propensity for rhetoric as do their North American neighbors. Moreover, very real differences are displayed on some issues within the elite groups that dominate the decision-making process. However, on the most fundamental issues, a generalized accord can be expected among prestige-class interests. There may be considerable haggling over specific policies, but in terms of broad goals and values there exists a strong base of consensus among those elites having control of or access to decision-making positions.

In order for a problem or situation to qualify as a political issue, there must be more than one side to the question. Consensus very often does not provide issues. It is necessary to have differing opinions, demands, and supports placed on authoritative decision makers as they distribute economic and social resources. The great majority of Latin Americans do not have a share in the resources of their nations. They do not have access to decision making and are systematically excluded from most aspects of the political process. Thus, to write about political disputes between the haves and the have-nots, as has been done with some frequency in the press, is to distort the situations. To have dispute would require that those Latin Americans who command very few resources have an active role in the system—be capable of making demands, applying pressures, and having a reasonable chance of seeing favorable outputs from the system. Such a characterization does not seem accurate for most of the countries.

LAND REFORM

Agriculture is the mainstay of both the socioeconomic and the political system of all the Latin American nations. At the same time *minifundio-latifundio* ownership patterns reinforce economies of low productivity, the need for large amounts of imported commodities, and low capital intensity within that sector of the economy.

International Pressures

Land reform was not a political issue in most of the countries until demands for changes in land-tenure patterns began to emerge from the international environments. The peasantry has been extremely apathetic to its own plight, and domestic leadership groups have not been inclined to support significant reform efforts. In countries without an open, competitive system for the selection of high officials, the oligarchies (civilian or military) are most unlikely to allow any opposition forces to agitate and organize in the countryside and even more unlikely to arouse peasant hopes for change themselves, as such a policy would amount to political suicide, given their prestige-class interests. Even in the competitive systems—such as Colombia, Uruguay, Costa Rica, and Guatemala—the competition that exists is usually between prestige-class groups which are in agreement on opposition to major changes in the countryside.

Since 1960, however, the situation has been altered somewhat. Demands have come from Alliance for Progress officials, United Nations experts, academics, and even some high-level United States officials. The difficulty (for reformers) is that the demands for reform which have originated in the international environment have not come from sources or institutions capable of exerting a strong influence on Latin American authoritative decision making, such as American private enterprise or the United States military. Thus, there has been no significant action in some countries and little land-tenure reform in others, resulting in the continuation of the status quo in the agricultural sector.

Only since the establishment of the Alliance for Progress has land reform, essentially an economic problem, been perceived by Latin American political decision makers as worthy of their consideration. Prior to the Punta del Este Charter of 1961, only three of the countries (Mexico, Bolivia, and Cuba) had embarked on a program of agrarian reform oriented toward the more equitable distribution of farmland. The lesson that in each of these countries land reform was closely tied to a nationalistic, anti-American, anti-private-entrepreneur social revolution was not lost on policy makers in Washington. The experience of Bolivia and especially Cuba, which was a major precipitating factor for the Alliance for Progress, weighed heavily in the United States decision to encourage reform as a means of thwarting further revolutionary efforts.

In order to reap the anticipated financial harvest from the Alliance, Latin American leaders called for more equitable landholding systems and for the general amelioration of the small farmer's situation. Most of the nations enacted laws to meet the demands of the Alliance for Progress charter, legislation which recognizes the social function of property ownership and establishes an agency to remedy or reorganize prevailing land-tenure systems.

Reform Alternatives

Figure VI-I provides some insight into the politics of land reform. There are, it is suggested, five basic positions which can be taken on this issue, though they are not the only reform possibilities. The positions along a continuum are designed to permit a simple, basic exami-

DEGREE OF REFORM

1   2   3   4   5

1 = Increased productivity
2 = Diversification
3 = Voluntary redistribution
4 = Involuntary redistribution
5 = Involuntary redistribution without remuneration

FIGURE VI-1. POSITIONS ON THE LAND-REFORM ISSUE.

nation of the principal questions and issues. Of special interest for this analysis is the question of which groups in the polity support which positions and how successfully each group has supported and promoted its stand.

For many years, members of the landowning elite, which held virtually all of the viable agricultural property, were unwilling to accept any of the proposed reforms. An increase in productivity, for example, usually requires more capitalization, and the old Latin American oligarchy was unwilling or incapable of raising the money required for such efforts. However, since World War II, the Point 4 program, and the Alliance for Progress, the position of the elite on this issue has changed. Increasingly in the twenty nations there is no room for a position to the left of Position 1 on the continuum. This is particularly true if there is money available for the purchase of tractors, seed, fertilizers, and other necessities through an internationally funded program.

Diversification of crops, if financed correctly and if the proper incentives are provided, can also be accepted by elite landowners. It is often more difficult to convince the small farmer not to produce his country's traditional export crop than the large landowner, who is more cognizant of world-market conditions. Colonization usually involves no threat to the large landowner's position and can also be accepted.

It is in the areas marked 3, 4, and 5 on the continuum that land reform becomes a hotly debated political issue. Although the land-reform laws which have been passed during the 1960's do not require compensation, most expropriated landlords have been paid in cash or bonds for the loss of their holdings. As Delgado (1962) points out, even in Bolivia and Mexico, where land-reform programs have had longer lives than in other countries, the practice of paying members of the prestige class for their lands has been the rule rather than the exception. These payments have usually been in long-term bonds or at underevaluated rates. Only Venezuela, with its oil riches, has been able to afford a short-term, full-value remuneration program. In that country many landowners have voluntarily given up their lands to the peasants in exchange for remuneration.

Those who hold Position 5 on the continuum of land reform have had little influence in the politics of their countries and little or no backing from groups or organizations in the international environment. They have also encountered problems in arousing enough domestic support from the landless to either elevate themselves into decision-making positions or permit them to pressure those in power.

Radicalization of an unpoliticized rural peasantry is a most difficult project. Without the strongest possible organizational efforts and other assists, leftist movements have historically been ignored or opposed by peasants.[1] As a result, in those countries where land-reform programs are now in progress, a compromise has been achieved between Positions 3 and 4, a compromise that almost always includes payment for property either before or during the distribution process. Because of the shortage of resources, the need for payment has meant that land redistribution has proceeded very slowly; expropriations are delayed or minimized until funds are available to finance them.

Prior to 1960 the Point 4 program, which reflected official United States policy on land reform in the twenty countries, advocated increased production and diversification, but evaded the subject of land redistribution. The Alliance for Progress went further, but was unwilling to permit the use of its funds, understandably, to purchase lands from Latin American elites for later redistribution. Alliance officials were emphatic in their support of voluntary redistribution with remuneration, but were wary of Positions 4 and 5 on the continuum.

Class Attitudes

The problem of remuneration for expropriated lands could become *the* Latin American political issue of the future if land-reform programs are continued. For expropriation with remuneration does not bring the full effects, socioeconomic and political, which were envisioned by the proponents of land reform. As Delgado (1962) points out, to reimburse a member of the elite for the loss of his lands is to replace one form of wealth and sociopolitical power with another. The position of the individual losing his lands remains unchanged in the sociopolitical system of his country. It would be as if in the United States persons with high incomes, paying 40 per cent in taxes, were later to be reimbursed. Under these circumstances, the egalitarian objectives are obviously forfeited. Since land reform has as its objective to make Latin American politics more participatory as well as to redistribute wealth, improve opportunities for upward social mobility, and upgrade the agricultural sector, reimbursement for expropriated lands may be working against all of these. As long as members of the prestige class maintain a tight grip on the authoritative decision-making process and gauge their own social and economic status at least partly on the possession of land, reform will not be widespread.

The lower levels of the prestige social class, the middle sectors, generally do not maintain a position on land reform or they actively support the more conservative alternatives. A typical pattern for a rising member of this class is to invest his first earnings surplus in land, as a means of establishing his prestige status and as a hedge against inflation. Members of this group are employed in the bureaucracies which have been established to bring land reform to the Latin American countries. To the extent that agrarian reform does not interfere with other bureaucratic goals and with their own status aspirations, it can be expected that the lower levels of the prestige class will work toward these goals in an incrementalist fashion. A more wide-ranging commitment is unlikely, given the sociopolitical environment.

Organized labor in most of the countries has never made close alliances with the peasantry and does not usually maintain a position on agricultural reform. As will be elaborated in Chapter VII, organized labor is a small but privileged stratum that has little interest in forming coalitions with the peasantry except possibly for simple reasons of political expediency—an arrangement that normally does not strike a lasting bargain.

Objectives

Land reform means different things to different people.

North Americans . . . tend to regard land reform as a type of amelioration of the socio-economic situation in the rural area, but with consideration of increased productivity foremost and social redress very much a secondary aspect (Schaedel, 1965, pp. 76–77).

Barraclough (1968–1969) argues that there are three implicit objectives of land reform: (1) greater social equality; (2) redistribution of political power; and (3) improvement in economic efficiency. In some contrast, Myrdal (1958, p. 87) argues that breakup of the old class structure is distinctly the primary reform function, with elevation of production a distant second.

The meaning attached to reform is quite important. As long as reform means only an increase in productivity, then a substantial sector of the landholding elite in Latin America would support it, especially when the reform program includes governmental aid and advice in capitalization, mechanization, planting, and fertilizing. Some would oppose even this kind of change if it affected social relations in the countryside. But if reform involves social equality and redistribution of political power, then opposition becomes strong and general. Ultimately, these goals imply substantial redistribution of property, and reform then becomes a revolutionary step. One of the most able observers of the agrarian situation, Antonio García (1967, pp. 132–138), does not seem to even consider the possibility of peaceful reform if it means real changes in social relations. Another long-time student of agrarian reform and presently head of the reform program in Chile, Jacques Chonchol (1970), has emphasized the drastic change required in social relations and government's role.[2]

In the Latin American context, these arguments seem to be well founded. The only serious reform efforts involving redistribution of land and changes in social relations in Latin America have occurred during or after major social conflicts and revolutions. The Chilean case may break this pattern, but even there reforms have not come without severe disruptions and some bloodshed in the countryside.

The Mexican Experience

The Mexican experience with land reform dates back to the 1920's and 1930's. However, land redistribution on a large scale took place only under the administrations of a few presidents, such as Lázaro Cárdenas (1934–1940) and Adolfo López Mateos (1958–1964). In the late 1960's, approximately 60,000 Mexican families a year were receiving their own lands (Inter-American Development Bank, 1970). Yet even in the early 1960's, 75 per cent of the available farmland was in the hands of 10 per cent of the farmers of Mexico.[3] It seems unlikely that recent efforts are broad enough in scale to change this pattern substantially, especially in view of the importance of prestige-class support for the present Mexican political balance. The very high rural birth rates have increased pressures for more distribution.

Mexican decision makers, however, have been able to pursue various methods of reform. Colonization, investment for purposes of stimulating productivity on large holdings, and outright redistribution have been tried, although redistribution is increasingly difficult in the more institutionalized, prestige-class-dominated decision-making process of the 1970's. The Mexicans have also experimented with a type of collectively owned but privately operated farm known as the *ejido*, with roots in the precolonial period. In the early period of *ejido* development, this type of farming operation simply led to the creation of more *minifundios*, and debate still rages over the social and economic value of the *ejido*.

The Bolivian Experience

Bolivian revolutionary decision makers did not intend to incorporate land reform into their program when they assumed power in 1952. But when peasants in valley areas remote from La Paz began to seize the lands they had been cultivating without the authorization of the fledgling government, officials of the National Revolutionary Movement (MNR) determined to legitimize the actions of the *campesinos*. The MNR proceeded to take the lead in meeting and expanding peasant demands to the point that the government effectively controlled the entire reform process. During the twelve years of MNR government, land redistribution continued at a rapid pace. However, since 1965 very little redistribution has been accomplished, and the official policy is that the government is interested in consolidating the position of peasants located prior to 1965 before distributing property to other landless families.

The Cuban Experience

The Cuban land reform has constituted the most extensive program of the three cases, but in the late 1960's data on the experience were scarce. Seers and his associates (1964) provide an interesting assessment of the early years of the Cuban land reform and of the role of the National Institute of Agrarian Reform (INRA), but the program initiated in the immediate post-1959 period has been drastically overhauled. It seems clear that the Cubans have completely reshaped landholding patterns, with at least some of the major holdings being farmed as collectives. This bold experiment, if successful, has important ramifications, especially as a precedent for the plantation areas of the Caribbean.

The Chilean Experience

The Chilean case seems much more relevant for the rest of Latin America, inasmuch as most observers do not foresee the imminent possibility of more Cuba-like revolutions in the hemisphere. Furthermore, the situation in Chile has included many of the same problems faced by the sister republics and has been relatively well documented.

The Chilean case is illustrative of our general points, yet is exceptional in that the debate on land reform has moved to a point not yet reached in countries without the recent experience of a social revolution. The public-policy debate now revolves around compromises between Positions 4 and 5, not between 2 and 3, or even 3 and 4, as remains the case in virtually all the other countries. The movement to the more extreme position on the continuum is largely a result of some unique domestic political factors.

In the early 1960's, under heavy pressure from its international environment, the Chilean government made the first hesitant steps toward passage of land-reform measures. This is not to say that authoritative decisions relevant to agriculture had not been made previously. In fact, the large landholders of the central-valley region, together with the small holders of the south, had long been successful in seeking and receiving government aid in marketing, exporting, irrigation, price supports, and production increases. They could also count on support from decision makers in conflicts with workers and tenants on their properties.

However, until the early 1960's there were few pressures for major changes in the countryside, especially of the redistributive nature. The conjunction of three factors, all felt, although in varying degrees, in practically every Latin American country, resulted in sharp changes in the decade of the 1960's:

1. The inability of the agricultural sector to produce enough even for domestic needs.

2. The increasing proletarianization and organization of rural workers by those supporting moderate-to-strong changes in the nature of social relations. (Three of the five major political groupings—the Christian Democrats, the Socialists, and the Communists—made very serious efforts to organize and attract support from the peasantry in the last two presidential races, 1964 and 1970.)

3. Pressure from international sources to meet the internal agricultural needs and especially to improve the conditions of the rural poor to neutralize their revolutionary potential.

The administration of President Alessandri (1958–1964), dominated by strongly conservative but mainly urban business interests, adopted the path to reform which was least objectionable to the elite. Essentially, the Chilean leadership chose to leave the tenure system intact but to mollify the critics, both domestic and external, by forcing landholders to make minimum improvements in their tenant workers' housing and labor conditions. Virtually no land was redistributed (some insignificant colonization efforts were initiated), little improvement of conditions was made, and the pattern of sociopolitical relations in the countryside remained unchanged.

What distinguishes Chile from the rest of the area, however, is the openness of the political competition and the strength of the urban and mining-based leftist parties. While other systems have been subjected to enough foreign and domestic pressure to move slightly farther than simple or symbolic gestures of aid to a still dependent rural mass, in Chile there exists strong domestic pressure from an institutionalized leftist movement. By the mid-1960's, as members of the leftist leadership became increasingly aware that support from the peasant could lead to their electoral success, strong efforts were made to organize the rural poor. This new perception, combined with the general economic malaise and ineffectiveness of the conservative Alessandri administration, resulted in a general leftward swing in the 1964 presidential election, which saw both major candidates advocating major reforms including reform of the land-tenure system.

The election of the moderate reformist Eduardo Frei for the period 1964–1970 saw the beginning of considerable movement in the countryside. The number of organized agricultural workers reached 125,-000 by 1970; 1200 *fundos* had been expropriated, embracing more than 3,000,000 hectares, with an estimated 28,000 peasants entering the program. While the program did not come close to the goals set by the Christian Democratic government, it constituted a substantial step ahead of previous efforts.

The relative lethargy which characterized the reform efforts and the aroused, yet often unfulfilled, hopes of the peasantry provided those favoring Position 5 on the land-reform continuum a golden opportunity, which was not wasted. The election of 1970 saw one candidate, Salvador Allende, vociferously advocating Position 5, another supporting a position very close to 5, and the conservative candidate pushing for reform somewhere near Position 3.

Interestingly, the stance of the large landowners in Chile has dramatically changed. They have moved from a policy of pure opposition against even the thought of fundamental change to a present policy of collaboration with a Marxist government. One cannot but be amused by the situation of the prestige-class president of the Chilean National Agriculture Society, whose ancestry includes presidents, senators, and others of the old oligarchy, flying off to Cuba to speak to the Castro government about agricultural exchange between the two countries.

It should be noted again that the pressures for reform are not as strong in the rest of Latin America as they are in the Chile of the 1970's. At the same time, a number of countries—Colombia, Peru, Venezuela, Guatemala, Brazil—have experienced enough pressure from one source or another to initiate very modest reforms. It is easy to overemphasize the scope of these efforts, simply because they are such marked changes from past policy. In all of these countries, the strength of the landowners and their prestige-class allies is such that reforms to date have been very limited, and are likely to remain so without the organization of the landless workers and *minifundistas* by political parties or by some other external force.

NATIONALISM

Nationalism is an issue of Latin American politics only to the extent that differing groups act, declaring their actions to be in the national interest. The actual importance of nationalism is the content of the nationalist sentiment and the uses to which it is put. All of the countries, with the exception of one or two of the Central American republics, display a high degree of nationalistic sentiment, which serves as a backdrop for political decision making.

Because of their tendency toward *personalismo*, Latin Americans are often unable to relate themselves to impersonal aggregates. Evidence of this problem is amply provided for Mexico by Almond and Verba (1963). The typical Latin American seems unable to develop a high degree of positive sentiment toward political parties, legislatures, agencies of the public administration, and other formal institutions. He can develop very strong loyalties for individuals within these institutions; but with the departure of the individual, the loyalty ends.

Silvert (1967a) describes three kinds of nationalist sentiment in Latin America: as ideology, as social value, and as patriotism. He asserts that only when nationalist sentiment is of the second type, can it be used by the decision makers of a country to mobilize the society for change —for example, toward reform of the land-ownership patterns of their country.

The Latin American is capable of developing strong positive sentiments toward abstract concepts, such as *la patria*, freedom, liberty, or reform. Latin Americans in general evince nationalism of an ideological or a patriotic variety. The difficulty facing authoritative decision makers in Latin America is to convert the nationalist sentiments or personal loyalties into social values.

Essentially, then, the question is whether or not Latin American nationalism can be converted into a device for mobilizing Latin Americans toward reform or change-oriented goals. Only in three countries of the area has this process even begun to take place, and in one, Mexico, the data demonstrate that loyalty to the polity has not permeated the population to any great extent (Almond and Verba, 1963). Nationalism as a social value is at least evident in the same three countries where agrarian reform began to take place well before the birth of the Alliance for Progress. Cuba, which has undoubtedly experienced the most far-reaching changes in its economy and society, was brought to that point because of Fidel Castro's ability to blend loyalty to himself and to the country with commitment to social change. *La patria o la muerte* ("Fatherland or death") is the motto with which Castro closes his speeches. In Bolivia, the third of the group, since 1964 nationalism has once again become synonymous with military interventionism.

Most common is the Latin American decision maker who attempts to tie personalism and ideological nationalism to his own charisma, with little more intention than to remain in power. An effort is made to blur the distinction among the individual and the government and the fatherland. Latin American military leaders are able to lead a coup, subvert a constitution, and overturn an elected government in the name of ideological and patriotic nationalism and because they believe it is necessary to protect the democratic principles upon which the country was established. What appears to be polynormativism to the outside observer is quite logical within the cultural context.[4]

The example of Fidel Castro within the context of nationalism is not likely to be followed by other Latin American decision makers, whether or not they claim to be desirous of achieving the goals now set forth on the island of Cuba. Payne (1968) has questioned the motives of Colombian decision makers in a manner which could be applicable to all of the nations of the hemisphere. Payne suggests that in Colombia, politicians seek decision-making roles not because they want to achieve certain sociopolitical and economic goals, but because they seek the status resources which the role will provide them. If Payne's propositions are correct and can be verified in terms of all of the Latin American countries, then the future of nationalism as a social value is a limited one. In view of the political culture of the various societies, it does not seem probable that leaders capable of blending personalism and ideological nationalism with social goals will emerge in great numbers. Two possible exceptions at the present time might be the incumbent Chilean and Peruvian regimes. In both administrations, the glorification of indigenous elements, appeals to national unity, efforts to integrate lower classes into the society, together with calls for significant changes in other sociopolitical relationships, give some credence to the argument that perhaps nationalism will be translated into support for reform.

COMMUNISM

Communism as an issue in Latin American politics can be viewed from a number of vantage points. First, as considered in Chapter IV, the issue can be the "threat" of the Soviet Union or China. Second, communism becomes an issue insofar as national Communist parties pose electoral threats, regardless of how close their ties with either Havana, Peking, or Moscow are (most have strong ties to Moscow). Third, communism is an important issue insofar as leftist-oriented guerrillas, urban or rural, adapt their ideological foundations from the "socialist" countries. While not all such groups are so oriented, the majority seem to have some ties in that direction. At the same time, in none of the countries does the present threat from this source to the regime in power seem significant.

While communism can certainly be labeled a major political issue in the United States, the authoritative decision makers of the twenty nations do not seem overly concerned by this phenomenon either as an ideology or as a political movement—to the dismay of North American officials concerned with Latin American policy. Typical of their thinking on the subject is the following statement by a Latin American political scientist:

> To judge by appearances, the Communist influence among intellectuals and students is considerable. But the truth is that the Communist movement has never been decisive in Latin America. The changes that have occurred, the movements that have appeared, the revolutions—including the Cuban—have all taken place without the participation of the Communists (Alba, 1969, p. 359).

At various times in response to United States pressures, direct or indirect, the Latin American nations have severed diplomatic relations with the Soviet Union and lately with Cuba and have declared various parties as illegal or unconstitutional, but basically there is little concern about the "threat" of communism.

Party Composition and Activities

In general, the Communist parties are small and composed of middle-sector or upper-class individuals. For many of these people, who have been members of the party since the depression years of the 1930's, the call for revolution has become a symbolic gesture—a plea which, above all else, has earned them a place in the social scheme of things. For others, it has been a method of gaining a comfortable spot in a university department or European embassy. The truth of the matter is that being a Communist provides status for some members of the prestige class. Although the Latin American Communist parties go out of their way to demonstrate their proletarian interests, there certainly are not many members of the proletariat in the parties. This is a simple reflection of the differences between the Latin American classes in methods for obtaining and achieving upward social mobility as well as attitudinal and occupational distinctions. Members of the lower classes must acquire economic resources to rise within their class, while the key to upward mobility for the prestige classes is the acquisition of status. Membership in the Communist party can bestow status, but since a decision-making rather than a gadfly role is necessary to become involved in the distribution of economic resources, and since the Communist party is highly unlikely to acquire a decision-making role in any of the countries, members of the lower classes are not interested in the movement.

The Communists in Latin America have worked actively to form labor unions among workers in agriculture as well as industry. However, these organizational efforts, most notable of which was the Confederation of Latin American Workers, have probably worked against the welfare of the laboring class in the long run, since Communist leadership in unions has given military and obligarchic groups an excuse to move against the movements and to crush them with the full support of the United States government and American-owned business. If a Soviet-line communist group can be differentiated from some other form of communist organization in a particular country, it is not unusual to find that the former shows little or no interest in the needs and plight of the peasantry. The dispute between the groups was nowhere more evident than in Bolivia after the fall of "Che" Guevara. One Bolivian communist supporter of Guevara, in referring to the Soviet-line party in his country, stated:

> The parties that claim to be in the vanguard of our people in the anti-imperialist struggle have the duty to be honest and to give an accounting of their actions to the people. . . . How can they explain the fact that they paid homage to the fallen guerrillas, but attacked them when they were preparing for battle (Paredo, 1970, p. 65)?

In 1961, a Mexican teachers' labor union with communist leadership went on strike because its members were being forced to complete one year of teaching duties in rural areas in order to become certified. Several clashes between the Chilean urban guerrilla movement, the

MIR, and the youth members of the Communist party in Chile have occurred, even after the Marxist socialist Allende had been elected, with the *miristas* charging that the party was so bourgeois that it could not truly represent the interests of the people. The old Soviet-line parties show a remarkable continuity of leadership, although none has displayed the longevity of such men as Ho Chi Minh and Mao Tse-tung. It is virtually unknown for leadership to change without death or voluntary resignation.

Insofar as an electoral threat is concerned, only Chile can be mentioned. In the other countries, Communist parties are either outlawed, sharply restricted, or so lacking in popular support that they provide little threat to opposition parties and groups. In Chile a long history of an active leftist movement, originating in the large mining sector of the work force, culminated in the election in 1970 of a Marxist, Salvador Allende, a long-time leader of the Socialist party (which at present leans farther to the left than the Soviet-line Communist group) and former national deputy and senator. Allende was elected in a three-way race with only 37 per cent of the ballots, and he was supported by substantial non-Marxist and certainly noncommunist parties and groups, with the regular Communist party being only one major group in the coalition. Allende rejects outright any "communist" label, saying that while his goals are those of Cuba's Castro, the means for reaching them will be strikingly different.

Radicalization of the Youth

The incongruities between ideals and reality, as well as other factors, create a radicalization of some groups among the youth and especially the students. Young members of the prestige classes, perhaps while at the university, have formed their own Marxist-oriented groups as a result of the conservative situation within the traditional communist and socialist parties. At times, they have aligned themselves with the preachments of Fidel Castro, and at other times have adopted their own nationalistic ideologies. These youth have organized and allied themselves with working-class youth—the mass of unorganized, unemployed, and underemployed urban young forming a tempting base—to challenge both left and right, but especially the left, in a number of countries. These include Chile, Argentina, Uruguay, Brazil, and perhaps Panama, Venezuela, and Bolivia. If these youth continue to resort to violence, then a further continuation of the policies of the 1960's can be expected, with the Latin American military forces helped by United States equipment and advice suppressing the youth.

EDUCATION

Analysts of the political-socialization process generally agree that there are three principal elements which contribute to the inculcation of political values into the members of a society: the family, the school, and the occupational environment.[5] Although much research remains to be carried out before generalizations can be made with considerable accuracy, some patterns are beginning to emerge in the literature.

It is becoming apparent that in the economically developed societies there are few discontinuities in this process; children in school are taught attitudes and norms of behavior similar to those they learn from their families. In societies with few resources, there may be sharp breaks in the socialization process as a person progresses from family to school to job. The result limits their effectiveness as students; this is true particularly of those in higher education in Latin America. It is for this reason, perhaps, that students become so active in politics, making demands often reformist in nature during their university careers. Since it is usually only children of elite families who manage to acquire enough education to facilitate admission to a university, the socialization disruptions apparently are restricted to them. The fact that these are the children of elites and that they have time to engage in politics as well as having the status to make their declarations heard means that education is one of the truly important issues of Latin American politics.

With the exception of Mexico and Costa Rica, in every nation of Latin America the military budget exceeds the resources allocated to education. To cut back on the military budget is virtually impossible, for decision makers who have made this mistake usually have not survived in office for long. Even an essentially noninterventionist force, such as the military of Chile, will take action if steps are taken to reduce its share of the resources. Twice in November of 1969, President Eduardo Frei found it necessary to declare a state of seige during confrontations of this sort. At the same time, to restrict the resources allocated to students can invite strikes and violence which in themselves may precipitate military intervention. Students strike and demonstrate over the raising of bus fares or even cafeteria prices and, in contrast to other members of the prestige classes, make alliances with working-class groups of all varieties. Students also protest the curtailment of civil liberties and other injustices which they perceive in their systems.

Education is a delicate political matter in Latin America. The continuous dispute between the students and the military over resources has made the two groups perpetual and deadly antagonists. Unless a decision maker happens to be a member of the military forces himself, he finds it necessary to placate both groups by providing the resources which they demand. Since it is generally at the university level that Latin American students are politically active, it is to this type of institution that educational resources are allocated, often at the expense of public primary and secondary schools. There are more than 150 universities in the Latin America of the 1970's. The paucity of resources allocated to high schools is probably functional to most Latin American political systems as a tension-management device. If free public secondary education were available to all students, tensions at the university level would probably become intolerable.

Before concluding that the university is only a place where prestige-class youth discover that poverty, disease, and other evils exist in their societies and that they have some capability to change the course of events, it should be noted that the university also serves as an effective device for inculcating elite values and making the personal contacts crucial to the facilitation of access to decision making in the future.

ECONOMIC DEVELOPMENT

As with other problem areas, there is a considerable amount of consensus on how resources are to be distributed in each of the Latin American countries as long as working-class groups are not permitted to participate in the authoritative decision-making process. In Argentina and Cuba in the 1940's, when labor was sufficiently well organized to make demands for resources, the military intervened and the labor groups were suppressed. A similar situation in Bolivia led to military intervention in 1964.

Incomes and wealth are highly concentrated in all of the countries (except Cuba), and concentration may be increasing (Lagos, 1965; Lauterbach, 1965). Even in countries where as much as 20 per cent of the labor force is organized, as in Mexico and possibly Chile, concentration of wealth is extreme, most capital is in private hands, and private business activities form the basis of economic activity.

Economic development, however, is always a Latin American political issue, particularly when methods for achieving more resources are being considered. Certain groups advocate a great deal of dependence on the international environment for achieving economic development. President José Figueres of Costa Rica is reported to have stated that his country would be economically transformed if only North Americans would be willing to pay a single penny more for a cup of coffee and remit that amount to his country. Other groups advocate increasing the amount of crops destined for export—an interesting policy given the pathetic terms of international trade in primary commodities. There are a few groups which advocate radical transformation in the structure of the socioeconomic environment in order to increase the number of resources available, and they are largely outside the decision-making arena. Certain splinter groups from the main communist party, a small group of students and professors, a few guerrillas, and an occasional priest or journalist constitute the normal source of support for this kind of action.

Thinking of the Figueres variety is becoming more obsolete, however, particularly with the failure of the Alliance for Progress. Increasingly, the trend is toward national solutions. Roberto Campos states:

> We must purify our own qualities rather than engage in the infantile sport of transfering to others—the monopolies, the United States, the angels, or the devil—the blame for our poverty. . . . No one will resolve the problems that we ourselves leave unresolved because of incompetence or cowardice (quoted in Sigmund, 1970, p. 137).

Even some of the least developed nations have evolved agencies or national plans to tackle their economic situation. For example, the government of Haiti now boasts a National Council for Development and Planning and a development program entitled *Le Demarrage*.

The Christian Democratic parties of Latin America talk in a more radical fashion about this issue. Two leading figures in the movement, Julio Silva Solar and Jacques Chonchol (1964), have advocated the development of the various countries in a noncapitalistic fashion. However, to this point their actions have not coincided very closely with their declarations—admittedly a common occurrence with politicians of all countries. Wherever the Christian Democratic parties have actually captured the authoritative decision-making roles of a particular society, capitalism has continued to flourish and the prestige classes have continued to prevail.

INTERNATIONAL POLITICS

Every country has a particular international issue which decision makers can utilize to mobilize people during political campaigns. Guatemalans rally to the cry of *Belize es nuestro* when politicians discuss British Honduras, while Venezuelans claim a portion of Guyana. Honduras claims Swan Island, a tiny piece of land in the Caribbean from which anti-Castro broadcasts were beamed into Cuba during the 1960's, while Panamanians demand an increased share of Panama Canal tolls.[6] Argentines claim the Falklands, dispute an island in the Platte River, and argue with Chileans over a chunk of the Antarctic, while the Bay of Pigs invasion has served Fidel Castro's need for heated rhetoric for years.

Undoubtedly, though, the greatest international political issue is the relationship of the countries with the United States. Anti-Americanism is a rallying point for most of the countries and in many cases forms the basis of nationalistic sentiments. As Victor Alba (1969, pp. 315–316), a Mexican political scientist, asserts:

There are, of course, historical and economic bases for many of the anti-American arguments, but these cannot explain the extent of anti-Americanism. . . . Perhaps it is to be found in the fact that the Latin American countries, owing to the oligarchic nature of their society . . . have not reached the stage of being nations. . . . The United States is blamed for everything. If there is a crisis, it is the fault of the United States, and if prosperity makes it impossible to find a parking space for one's car, that is the fault of the United States too.

If anything, anti-American sentiment is growing in Latin America. The governments of Chile, Peru, Ecuador, Argentina, Venezuela, and of course Cuba have all had serious international quarrels with the United States in the past few years. And in all the countries, even those with military regimes favorably disposed toward the United States, there exist significant pockets of hostility toward the colossus to the north. United States economic domination of the region and paranoia concerning the establishment of unfriendly regimes in the area make it an easy target for dissidents and nationalists of all varieties.

PUBLIC OPINION

Because data are very limited, it is extremely difficult to ascertain the role played by public opinion in the formation of political issues and in political processes themselves. The state of political-science research in the Latin American area somewhat resembles the countries it purports to study. It seems probable that the two-step flow of political communication and opinion formation discovered by analysts in the United States—for example, Campbell and associates (1966)—and other economically developed countries is probably more accentuated in the Latin American nations. A two-step flow of communications means that in every peer group there is an opinion leader, someone who devotes more time to following the political processes of his country. When it is necessary for an individual to take an action in the political system, he refers to this leader; and when a major decision is made by the authoritative policy makers, this opinion leader interprets the decision for his friends.

In the rural areas the *cacique* or perhaps the *patrón*, a member of the prestige class, serves as the opinion leader. Since, according to Oscar Lewis (1961), a great many Mexicans retain their rural life style even when living in urban areas, it may be that in other countries as well a form of *caciquismo* (personalistic political bossism) also exists in the cities.

Residents of the rural areas, still nearly half of all Latin Americans, probably are involved in politics and political issues only at election time. During election campaigns, caravans of politicians fan out from the capital cities, set up tents, provide beer or some other harder alcoholic beverage for one and all, and in general take the small towns, villages, and market centers by storm. Music plays from loudspeakers which intermittently carry speeches. Promises are made, hands are shaked, babies are kissed, and then the *políticos* return to the city—not to be seen or heard from again until the following election. Military governments deviate little from this pattern, although the occasion for a visit to the rural areas is probably not an election. Most residents of the rural areas are unlikely to note any differences between civilian and military authoritative decision makers. Resources are primarily allocated to the cities regardless of which form of essentially the same political system is presently adapted in the capital city.

Furthermore, if research in the economically developed countries has any relevance for an area such as Latin America, then we would expect to find a strong tendency toward communication of political information from decision makers to the masses, rather than the reverse. Research in the United States and Western Europe suggests strong correlations between lack of education and willingness to accept with little or no question what authoritative decision makers say or do. Thus, what political opinions the working-class populations have may be largely products of the words and actions of the decision makers themselves.

At present, however, it is possible only to speculate at the answers to questions of how public attitudes are formed and what the content of those attitudes is. Since so few of the countries are actually holding elections in the early 1970's, it is even more difficult to measure citizen response and attitudes with electoral data unavailable or unreliable.[7] Fitzgibbon (1957) wrote that he willed a study of Latin American political parties—which until then had been largely ignored by the discipline—to a whole generation of graduate students. The task of studying public-opinion formation in Latin American societies is so vast that it will certainly require more than a few dozen graduate students to carry it out.

SUMMARY

Essentially, the role of political decision makers is to retain the stability of their respective polities. They avoid whenever possible any moves that might mobilize the citizenry on serious and dysfunctional issues such as land reform, economic development, and the distribution of resources, where there would undoubtedly be major differences of opinion. Instead, the elites dispute among themselves, within their own small and closed groups, over the distribution of resources, while they guide the attention of those citizens capable of understanding to such issues as civil liberties, anti-Americanism, and a minor international dispute or two.

NOTES

1. Ayres (1970, pp. 79ff) documents this pattern for Chile, where there has been active, open competition (including a Socialist and a Communist party) for a number of years.

2. See the relevant section in Chapter III for a more complete analysis.

3. For an extensive discussion of this problem, see Vernon (1963).

4. For an interesting analysis of polynormativism, see Riggs (1964), Chap. 1.

5. An excellent analysis of this process is Langton (1969). One of the few analyses of this process in Latin America is Goldrich (1966).

6. Swan Island was turned over to Honduras in 1972.

7. The most thorough analysis of the electoral data of any country is Ayres (1970).

SUGGESTED READINGS

Alexander, Robert J. *Communism in Latin America.* New Brunswick, N.J.: Rutgers University Press, 1967.

Duff, Ernest A., and John F. McCamant. "Measuring Social and Political Requirements for System Stability in Latin America." *American Political Science Review,* 62, No. 4 (December 1968), 1125–1143.

Horowitz, Irving Louis, ed. *Masses in Latin America.* New York: Oxford University Press, 1970.

Horowitz, Irving Louis, Josué De Castro, and John Gerassi, eds. *Latin American Radicalism.* New York: Random House, 1969.

Johnson, John J. *Political Change in Latin America.* Rev. ed.; Stanford, Calif.: Stanford University Press, 1965.

Martz, John D. "Doctrine and Dilemmas of the Latin American 'New Left.' " *World Politics,* 22, No. 2 (January 1970), 171–198.

Martz, John D., ed. *The Dynamics of Change in Latin American Politics.* Englewood Cliffs, N.J.: Prentice-Hall, 1965.

Petras, James, and Maruice Zeitlin, eds. *Latin America: Reform or Revolution?* Greenwich, Conn.: Fawcett, 1968.

Silvert, Kalman H. *The Conflict Society.* New York: American Universities Field Staff, 1966.

Stycos, J. Mayone. "Politics and Population Control in Latin America." *World Politics,* 20, No. 1 (October 1967), 66–82.

Véliz, Claudio, ed. *Obstacles to Change in Latin America.* London: Oxford University Press, 1965.

Véliz, Claudio, ed. *The Politics of Conformity in Latin America.* New York: Oxford University Press, 1967.

Von Lazar, Arpad, and Robert R. Kaufman, eds. *Reform and Revolution: Readings in Latin American Politics.* Boston: Allyn and Bacon, 1967.

INTEREST ARTICULATION

It has only been in the past decade that the function of interest articulation and the groups which perform it have become subjects of political-science research in Latin America. This has been true for all except two groups: the military and the church. The military is so important that a separate chapter, Chapter VIII, will be devoted to it.

As in all systems, access to decision makers and to decision-making positions in Latin American countries is sharply limited. There is evidence of rather strong correlations between wealth/education/high occupational status and the propensity to participate in political activities.[1] In practical political terms, this means that because of the great concentration of resources—education, wealth, income, property—in the prestige class, a very small percentage of the population in any of the countries is able to participate effectively, particularly in the *effective* articulation of interests. Even in the countries where voting participation is relatively widespread, as in Uruguay, Costa Rica, and Chile, the laboring classes can be largely ignored because of their lack of meaningful resources, such as informal contacts or economic pressure, which could be translated into political power and their inability to consistently and persistently apply pressure on elites.

As expected, most interest articulation in Latin America originates in one social class, the prestige class, and the demands expressed and supports provided usually reflect the perceived interests of those making them. In general, interests articulated by members of the prestige class, whether individually or in groups, involve the allocation of status values. However, one group of prestige-class individuals, the students, makes demands not only for status but also for economic resources and political services, not only for itself but also for members of the working class. In the process, considerable status is acquired by the students.

INSTITUTIONALIZED BIAS

There are two main factors to bear in mind when examining the interest-articulation function in Latin America. First, because of the class origins of the interests expressed and the groups which formulate them, their interactions generally tend to restrict the authoritative allocation of resources to benefit their own class exclusively. Thus, unless the prestige class itself chooses to distribute resources to groups and activities outside its own sphere of self-interest, the distribution of political resources, or resources capable of conversion into political resources, is such that the working classes are likely to receive few of the benefits of government action. The abundance of resources in the United States and Western Europe allows decision makers to distribute social goods perhaps unevenly but still satisfying some minimum requirements of most of the population. In Latin America, in contrast, even without domination of the political machinery by the small elite classes, the lack of resources would deny the distribution of substantial political goods. But the present arrangements assure a very skewed distribution for the benefit of the privileged few.

The second factor is that because resources are so scarce in the twenty countries, one of two results occurs if a lower-class interest group does become capable of articulating demands or providing supports. One result is that the lower-class group either refuses to compromise or is incapable of compromising, so that its demands will be aggregated with those of other groups in the society. This situation makes for immobilism, such as has occurred in Argentina, Chile, and Uruguay. The alternate result is that the lower-class interest group aggregates its interests in a coalition with one or several groups of the prestige sector, leading almost invariably to its subordination to the prestige sector. While the classic instance is the 1938–1946 alliance of the Communists and Socialists with groups from the lower prestige sector in Chile, this type of alliance has occurred time and again with the same result—the abandonment of the weaker, lower-class interests when the prestige group believes that its demands have been met or its position is stable enough that it can safely ally with the other prestige-class groups and ignore the former allies.

Once a working-class interest group or coalition becomes strong enough to threaten seriously the fundamental interests of the prestige class, the entire spectrum of prestige-class interest groups will bury their differences and work to limit or halt the activities of the "usurpers," as they would be regarded. If a stalemate occurs, it is not unusual for the prestige-class groups or members of that class acting individually to ask the military to step in.[2] The first case study below exemplifies what can happen when a working-class group makes an alliance with a prestige-class organization; while the second case study is an example of a situation where a working-class group gains considerable strength but refuses to compromise in any way whatsoever with the elite.

CASE STUDY 1: THE LABOR MOVEMENT IN COSTA RICA

During the depression years of the 1930's, when economic conditions were particularly bad in Costa Rica, communist leaders decided that their best course of action lay in organizing a labor-union movement. Organizers were particularly successful in the banana-growing regions of the Atlantic coastal areas where, after a bitter strike, collective-bargaining contracts were eventually won for several thousand workers. Working from the organizational base provided by the banana workers, the organizers were able to extend their efforts to include labor from other sectors of the economy. By the 1940's, when the Popular Vanguard Movement was formally established, it had a formidable organizational base indeed. It rapidly began to make its interests known to authoritative decision makers and was able to achieve the distinction of having some of its demands met during the Calderón Guardia and Picado administrations in Costa Rica.

A young Roman Catholic priest, Benjamín Núñez, became concerned that a non-Christian ideology might be imposed upon the workers by the union leadership. Padre Núñez organized a new union, named Rerum Novarum after the papal encyclical of the same name.

During the 1940's the two unions competed with each other for membership with no loss in the strength of the movement as a whole. Union membership reached an all-time high during World War II.

The Popular Vanguard Movement was extremely influential during the administration of Rafael Calderón Guardia and managed to extract a very liberal labor code from this elitist president. In 1948, when Calderón Guardia attempted to perpetuate himself in office by annulling election returns, the Popular Vanguard lent its muscle to the effort.[3] Rerum Novarum joined the insurgent forces, headed by José "Pepe" Figueres, which after a bitter street-by-street battle through the capital city were able to oust Calderón Guardia and his forces.

The new constitution of 1949 specifically prohibits political organizations of a "subversive" variety. The Popular Vanguard Movement was prosecuted under the relevant clauses of the constitution, and was outlawed by a final decision of the supreme court in 1951. With the once powerful movement abolished, the membership was cast adrift.

Meanwhile, Rerum Novarum continued to collaborate with the National Liberation Movement, which was made up of a combination of young student elites and old-line oligarchic followers of Otilio Ulate Blanco. In 1952 the head of the National Liberation Movement, Figueres, became the elected president of Costa Rica and he named Padre Núñez as his minister of labor. Núñez thereupon merged his union with the newly formed National Liberation Party with the hope that the party would continue to aggregate the interests of the working-class group with those of its prestige-class but reformist-oriented members. During the four-year Figueres presidency, minimum-wage laws were passed and other benefits were extended by law to the workers. All of the collective-bargaining contracts won by Rerum Novarum were permitted to expire.

By the 1960's the Costa Rican labor picture was a stark contrast to what had prevailed in the 1940's. It was almost as if the entire labor movement had ceased to exist. Only one collective-bargaining contract was in force anywhere in the country, a contract which covered banana workers on plantations in the Golfito area. Minimum-wage laws were not enforced, and other security benefits were not proffered to the vast majority of the workers. Padre Núñez, still an official of the National Liberation Party, is a professor of sociology at the University of Costa Rica.

In summary, by allying themselves with the church and with an elitist party and by permitting their demands to be voiced by these groups, the working classes of Costa Rica ended up with very little to show for their efforts during the 1930's and 1940's through bitter strikes and revolution. Padre Núñez and "Pepe" Figueres have acquired enough of the status resources of the system—thanks in part to their labor-union supporters—that they have assured themselves of lifetime predominance in their country.

CASE STUDY 2: THE PERONISTA MOVEMENT IN ARGENTINA

In 1942 a group of young military officers, worried that their commanding officer at the time was contemplating a break in their country's close relationship with the Axis powers, staged a coup and set up a junta. Appointed to the post of minister of labor on the junta was a young colonel, trained in Italy, by the name of Juan Domingo Perón. Perón, who enjoyed a close relationship with Eva Duarte, a leader of the Argentine labor movement, actively began to court support from this working-class element. Working from his position as labor minister, he lent the full force of the government behind efforts by the working class to become organized. True to his fascist training, labor and management were invited rather forcefully to submit their disputes to his office for arbitration. His decisions consistently favored the laboring group.

By 1944 his fellow officers became alarmed about Perón's increasing popularity and removed him to an island in the Platte River. Labor unions immediately called for a general strike, and a demonstration in Buenos Aires may have numbered as many as 10,000 participants. The military officers undoubtedly could have suppressed the movement at that point, but they chose instead to capitulate and to bring Perón back. In 1945 Perón was elected to the presidency largely as a result of support from working-class groups.

During the entire period of his presidency, Perón actively worked to bring working-class groups into a position where they would be capable of making demands and lending support to the political system. In the 1970's it is estimated that labor organizations, dissolved by the military dictatorships which have succeeded Perón, list approximately 2.5 million members on their rolls, all of them *peronistas* (*Statistical Abstract of Latin America,* 1967, p. 96). As long as Perón was also capable of meeting the demands of the military and the church, he was able to remain in office—despite the fact that he had totally alienated both the industrial sector and the landowners.

In 1955 the military became disaffected and removed Perón from office. Then, in concert with all other interest-articulating groups, the military made an effort to eliminate the *peronistas* as an organization. However, the dictator's followers have retained a fanatical zeal, and each time the military forces have relinquished their hold on the authoritative decision-making process of Argentina, once to Arturo Frondizi and the second time to Arturo Illía, the *peronistas* have pressed their demands for more wages, better working conditions, and more resources from the system in general.

There seems little doubt that there was no way for either Frondizi or Illía to aggregate the demands and supports they were getting from the *peronistas* with the demands from all of the other groups in the country who regarded the followers of Perón as a threat to their status positions. Eventually one group or another in Argentina was able to convince a not unwilling military to step in and restore authoritative decision making. By 1971 the Argentinian people were well into what General Juan Onganía and later strongman General Alejandro Lanusse termed a ten-year military rule. Regardless of the military leader in power, there is little chance of his permitting the *peronistas* an opportunity to articulate interests.

Meanwhile, Perón lives in luxury in Spain, a guest of Generalissimo Franco, and *peronista* leaders continue to hold strategic conferences with him there. By becoming a cohesive force demanding a share of the political resources of Argentina, the *peronistas*, a working-class group, have brought the entire authoritative decision-making process to a standstill several times. And yet as the Costa Rican example, as well as others, amply demonstrates, if the *peronistas* cooperate or compromise, the result could be assimilation.

THE ROLE OF THE UNIVERSITY STUDENT

Table II-5 provided data showing the size of the university-student group in Latin America. In view of their numbers, students have been capable of exercising a disproportionate voice in the politics of the various countries. Lambert (1967) maintains that student participation in politics is as accurate an indicator of the scarcity of resources in a society as are such data as per-capita income and literacy. According to Lambert, in no economically developed nation has the student movement gained wide authority nor do students as a group play more than a marginal political role. Conversely, virtually every poorly endowed country has an active and influential student movement. In Latin America, students are prime movers in making nationalistic demands and are generally one of the few status-oriented prestige-class groups, if not the only group, which advocates a more egalitarian distribution of political resources. Particularly when allied with the organized labor groups, students are forceful participants in the political process throughout most of Latin America. For reasons elaborated below, their demands are almost always reformist if not radical in nature—a factor of some importance in reviewing their role.

Reasons for Student Influence

Students in Latin America are politically important for a variety of reasons. They have an advantage over some groups demanding a share of the resources because of their prestige-class status. The students have not yet been tied to their particular political system by prestige white-collar employment; yet they usually have enough free time for political participation. Moreover, they meet regularly as a recognizable group. The military forces, the traditional enemy of the students, realize the importance of the regular meetings on campus in strengthening the bargaining power of the students. As a result, it was not unusual for the military junta under the leadership of General Omar Torrijos, which took power in Panama in 1968, to close down the National University for six months as an immediate precaution.

Still another reason for the important position of the students is their relationship with lower-class interest groups. There has developed in most countries an informal relationship between student groups and the interest-articulating groups of the working class. The working-class groups ally themselves with the students because they desperately need leadership of ability and status to operate in a bargaining arena which is dominated by the prestige class. The working class needs literate leadership, but alliances with other elite groups has led to situations like the one in Costa Rica, where the working-class leadership gained status but the membership in general was deprived of its ability to articulate interests in the long run. The students have remained reasonably loyal to the working-class alliances, if not as individuals at least as groups. Student groups in Chile precipitated the overthrow of Chile's only twentieth-century dictator (a military figure as well), have regularly clashed with the police and the armed forces, harbor in their ranks significant elements of the left-wing urban terrorists (MIR), and have regularly supported reformist and revolutionary candidates and issues in alliance with the working classes and even the peasantry in the past few years. Students and a few *peronista* unions have been practically the only consistent and open opponents of the

military regimes in Argentina. Similar patterns are present in practically all of the countries of the region.

Another reason for the importance of students in the process of
politics in Latin America is that the various political parties in the
countries attempt to organize support on campuses and in fact
often wage campaign battles in the university area. Student elections are viewed as deadly serious events both on and off campus.
The rewards for the winning students involve larger shares of the
scarce status commodity so valuable to members of the prestige
class. At the University of San Marcos in Peru, student elections
have led to deaths from violence from time to time because of the
intense desire of the students to acquire that all-important resource,
status.

The Nature of the University System

One factor contributing to student activism in Latin America lies in
the nature of the university system. The lack of full-time professors
and the absenteeism and general aloofness of the part-time faculty,
who teach primarily to obtain a share of the status resources of their
country, have caused students to cry out for reform. As one analyst
notes:

> This usually means there is no time for research, no time for student
> counseling or tutorials, and none to devote to the running of the depart-
> ment or to the life of the university. . . . teaching is just a chore to be
> performed in a desultory fashion, or, if business is pressing, perhaps
> neglected altogether (Gale, 1969, p. 86).

The outdated organization of the universities of Latin America,
where each student forms part of a "faculty" and takes no courses
outside of it for credit, leads to a great waste of resources. For example,
at the University of Mexico, if an engineering student decides that he
needs to take an English course in order to be able to read certain texts,
he cannot go to the English department and take a course along with
students from other faculties. Instead, he must find a group of students
in the engineering faculty who, like himself, desire an English course.
A teacher is then hired and brought to the faculty to teach the group.
This system often means that different faculties of the same university
are providing instruction in the same subjects, with a consequent
duplication of teaching staff, equipment, and teaching and research
laboratories.

Status Resources and Prestige-Class Origins

The importance of the student in politics in Latin America is not merely an opinion held by students themselves or by foreign observers. Bonilla and Silva Michelena (1967) obtained a sample of opinion from a broad spectrum of the population of Venezuela, where groups were requested to rate themselves in status in comparison to the student groups. Students were selected as one of the two most highly reformist-oriented groups in the country. The opinions were based on attitudes toward a series of factors, including loyalty to the nation, the idea of citizen responsibility, and secularism. Table VII-1 shows how the groups were rated. The most important inference from the table

TABLE VII-1.   Types of Patriotism by Socioeconomic Status in Venezuela.

Types of Patriotism	Socioeconomic Status		
	High	Middle	Low
Reformist	High government officials University professors Staff in government	Student leaders Secondary-school teachers Primary-school teachers Labor leaders	None
Patriotic I	Oil-industry executives Industrial executives of central and western regions	Priests Municipal-council members Small-industry operators	None
Patriotic II	Agricultural entrepreneurs Industrial executives of eastern region Owners of cattle ranches	Government employees White-collar workers in commerce Oil-industry workers and employees	Industrial workers of western region
Apathetic	None	Small-business owners	Industrial workers of central and eastern regions Farmers in land-reform settlements Wage workers in agriculture Rancho dwellers Traditional subsistence farmers

Source: Adapted from *A Strategy for Research on Social Policy*, vol. 1 of *The Politics of Change in Venezuela*, p. 68, by Frank Bonilla and José A. Silva Michelena by permission of the M.I.T. Press, Cambridge, Massachusetts. Copyright © 1967 by The Massachusetts Institute of Technology.

is that Venezuelan students, by voicing reformist demands and supports, acquire a tremendous amount of the scarce status resources.

It must be emphasized that the Latin American university does not serve as an important vehicle of vertical social mobility for members of the working class, nor does student activism have anything to do with this function. According to Silvert (1967b), students from working-class families in Latin America rarely attend the most prestigious faculties or complete the full course of study. Student leadership reflects this situation. The prestige-class origins of Fidel Castro, for example, are not unusual for a radical student leader. An empirical study (Bonilla, 1960) of the leadership of the Chilean federation of students reveals that almost without exception the leadership of this movement for the past fifty years has been derived from the prestige class, and the federation has been a constant source of reformist and radical political activity. It should be noted, however, that the sons and daughters of the uppermost groups in the Latin American social systems are often educated abroad.

Student Tactics and Demands

The university students use strikes, demonstrations, protests, the press, sit-ins, blockades, and other methods which have become familiar to the North American student only in recent years. Student protests can involve a busfare increase, more participation in academic affairs, a larger share of the national budget for the university, or plainly nonacademic and nonstudent issues, such as land reform, a show of strength against the military, or as in the case of Panama in 1964 a demand that the United States fly the Panamanian flag in the American-controlled Canal Zone. Increasingly, the demands are for university or social reform.

As the United States press has revealed, the Latin American student tends to be anti-United States. The reaction in the United States is to view this tendency as part of an international conspiracy. However, it is usually a sentiment related to the students' traditional hatred of the military. Realizing the importance of United States military aid for keeping the military forces in their countries strong, the students transfer some of their frustration into an anti-"yanqui" hatred. It might be noted that with the military tightly in control of thirteen of the countries in the early 1970's, student activism has been considerably hampered.

Another factor important in explaining anti-United States feeling is the increasing awareness of Latin American intellectuals of the extent and significance of foreign control over their countries' economies. The transference of this information to the already nationalistic student reinforces a hostility which originates from other sources, such as his living next door to a wealthy and aggressive neighbor.

THE ROLE OF ELITE INTEREST GROUPS

In most countries of Latin America, the prestige class is cohesive on the few issues which are regarded of utmost imporance. For example, if the elite believed that resources which had been traditionally allocated to it were to be taken away because of demands from other groups, a concerted and unified effort would be made to stop such a dispersion. However, when issues involve the allocation of status, welfare, or other types of resources within the elite class, a plurality of interests does appear. Only rarely and in few countries do these groups experience the need to seek support from the working class in their efforts to compete with their peers. When lower-class support is sought, as in the case of Costa Rica discussed earlier, the prestige-class group or individuals usually manage to avoid making commitments to their lower-class supporters.

Interrelationships between Prestige-Class Groups

Virtually every country in Latin America boasts a landowners' association, an industrial syndicate, a chamber of commerce, and a Rotary Club. Very often the membership of each at least partly coincides with all of the others. Rather than giving birth to a new group of entrepreneurs or an urban bourgeoisie, industrialization has tended to reinforce the command of the landowners or old-line prestige class over the available resources of their society. The overlap between large landholders and major industrialists is marked in most countries. Industrialists in Latin America are no longer the pariahs they once were when the intellectuals of the area opposed the introduction of industry and modern technology to their countries. Industrialists now command a sizable share of the status resources of their societies, not to speak of the economic goods and services.

In some Latin American countries the relationship among the elite interest groups is an official one. In one of the very few studies of this type of association, Kling (1961) analyzed an overarching type of interest-articulating organization in Mexico. The Instituto de Investigaciones Económicas y Sociales, supported by a wide array of prestige-class interest-articulating groups, had as its sole purpose the dissemination of extreme right-wing propaganda throughout the country. The financial supporters of the institute do not particularly favor the ideas which the group espouses, but wish to have the propaganda widely and loudly aired so that advocates of the free-enterprise system and capitalism in general will appear as moderates within the Mexican political arena. A similar group, The Asociación Nacional de Fomento Económico (ANFE), operates in Costa Rica; while the Consejo Nacional de la Empresa Privada (CONEP) serves this purpose in Panama. CONEP officials talk of an international network of interest-articulating organizations in support of free enterprise in order to permit businessmen from nineteen of the countries to make unified demands on Washington and Wall Street decision makers.

It should be noted that these interest groups represent those having virtually all the resources of the Latin American states. Decision makers resist their demands only at great risk. What makes the weight of these industrial and commercial associations even more significant is their concentration even within the prestige class.

Furthermore, one must note the importance of the informal relations among the upper reaches of the elite. In practically every Latin American state, there is a handful of superior private schools to which the sons and daughters of elite families are sent, and there are a few private clubs to which elite families (or at least the adult males) belong. The concentration of the landholding, commercial, mining, and industrial potentates in the capital city facilitates the continuance of this pattern, reemphasizing the closeness of ties. Among the easiest ways to note its presence is to examine marital patterns in the elite class. Intermarriage among elite families is the rule; in fact, an important means of mobility is for a young man of the lower prestige class to meet, usually in the university, and marry the daughter of a higher-status figure. Note the example of Eduardo Frei, former president of Chile, and his successor as Christian Democratic leader, Radomiro Tomic, both descendants of middle-status immigrants but both marrying into the highest reaches of Chilean aristocracy.

THE ROLE OF THE CHURCH

Diminishing Influence

Once an extremely important political interest group in Latin America, the Roman Catholic church has gradually lost its ability to make demands for resources or to provide supports for particularly amenable authoritative decision makers. To a great extent, this is the result of a diminution in spiritual influence by the religious organization. Whereas at one time all Latin Americans were automatically considered to be Roman Catholics, the church itself has come to the realization that at most 10 per cent of the population of the twenty nations practice their faith (Houtart and Pin, 1965). Pope Paul VI made a trip to Bogotá in 1968 specifically to demonstrate the concern on the part of the Vatican about this situation.

There are other reasons for the diminishing influence of the church. For one thing, the organization has experienced a great deal of difficulty in obtaining recruits for the clergy. This in itself is reflective of the diminishing status that is to be obtained by taking a position in the religious organization. Not only does a priest receive very little status from the prestige class of modern times but even members of the working class refuse to defer to the clergy. The latter situation is no doubt at least partly a result of the fact that the priesthood is no longer regarded as a vehicle of upward social mobility for a member of the lower class. With the increased educational requirements of a religious career, it is nearly indispensable to enter the prestige class first, before embarking into the priesthood. According to the two French priests Houtart and Pin (1965), the priest-parishioner ratio in Latin America is approximately 1 for each 4,000 of the population. Foreign clergy are brought in, but they are often viewed with disfavor by the hierarchy and in turn are less willing to submit to pressures from the church bureaucracy.

Division in the Clergy

Another reason for the waning influence of the church as political interest-articulating group is a split which has occurred within the organization over what the mission of the institution should be and how it should be carried out. Certain elements in the church believe that its mission should be exclusively a spiritual one—to preach and teach—and that the organization should not have a social role.

Ivan Vallier (1967), a well-known analyst of the situation of the church in Latin America, has described the split as a four-way break rather than a simple division in the ranks. Figure VII-1 shows essentially how Vallier perceives the split. The "external" elites view the ability of the church to build its influence as relating to its involvement with secular groups and events, while the "internal" elites view the influence of the church as originating with its organization and rituals.

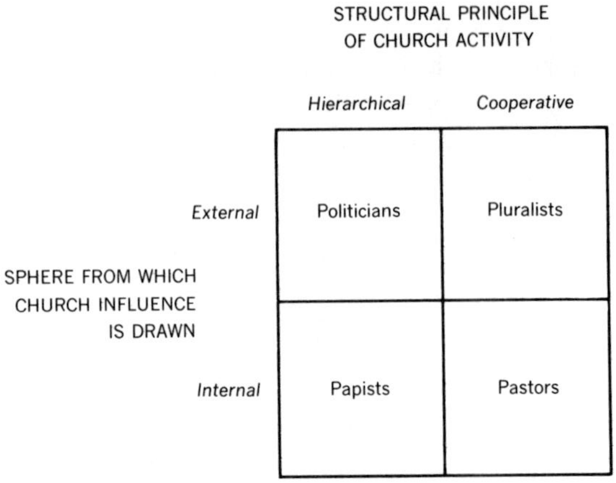

STRUCTURAL PRINCIPLE
OF CHURCH ACTIVITY

	Hierarchical	Cooperative
External	Politicians	Pluralists
Internal	Papists	Pastors

SPHERE FROM WHICH
CHURCH INFLUENCE
IS DRAWN

FIGURE VII-1. A TYPOLOGY OF CATHOLIC ELITES. *Source:* Ivan Vallier, "Religious Elites," in Seymour Martin Lipset and Aldo Solari, eds., *Elites in Latin America*, New York: Oxford University Press, 1967, p. 206. Reproduced by permission of Oxford University Press.

The other dimension of the typology is related to the organizing principle of religious-social relationships; when these relationships occur within the church, then the structural principle is termed "hierarchical," and when built outside the church, then it is termed "cooperative." According to Vallier, where such items as concordats or other constitutional clauses formalize the influence of the church, it is the "politician" cleric who tends to prevail. There are very few countries where a "pastoral" hierarchy prevails and this means that in most of the nations the clergy is either "papist" or "pluralist." Whatever the case may be, unless unity is restored to the church hierarchy, its influence as a political interest-articulating group can do little else but diminish.

Political Influence

Just as the spiritual influence of the church varies from country to country, so does its ability to command resources from the system. In all of the countries except Cuba, the church still retains a great deal of the status resources it once monopolized. It can place its demands and supports in such a fashion as to put bounds on systemic outputs relating to matters of the family and morals.

The church also has a tremendous impact on the educational process in all of the countries except Cuba. As noted earlier, in order to gain admission to a Latin American university it is almost essential to go to a private high school. Approximately 95 per cent of all private high schools in the twenty countries are in the hands of one religious order or another. The church is also anxious to have an influence in the public-education process, and religious instruction in the state-owned schools is the rule rather than the exception. In some countries, such as Colombia, this influence extends to the selection of textbooks.

In only a very few of the countries, including Peru, Colombia, and the Dominican Republic, does the church still receive a direct government subsidy. These subsidies are provided usually under the provisions of a concordat ratified with the Vatican.

THE ROLE OF LABOR UNIONS

Labor's Political Debility

Mexican analyst Alba (1962) has listed seven reasons for the weakness of the Latin American labor movement:

1. The lack of education among the working class.
2. The peasant origins of the workers and the fact that many workers retain ties to their villages, where they return for protracted periods of time.
3. The persistence of the isolated, peasant mentality in the city worker.
4. The fact that the industrial plant of the twenty countries is weak and only now is going through the transition from cottage-type artisanry to assembly-line, machine-model, organized industry.
5. The fact that women scarcely take part in industry.
6. The great number of children employed in industrial operations.
7. The general lack of interest in social problems among the workers.

Approximately 20 per cent of all labor-union members in Latin America belong to the *peronista* organizations in Argentina. In fact, this is the only country where labor is sufficiently strong to make its demands and supports continuously felt in the system. In some other countries, such as Mexico and Chile, organized labor is able to exert some influence, especially when in coalition with other groups, but is not powerful enough to receive a hearing for its demands effectively and consistently. The Latin American labor-union movement in general is a political movement just as virtually any organization or cause or process in the countries finds that it must articulate interests to authoritative decision makers if it is to survive. However, the political orientation of labor is particularly strong because the leaders of the movement have come to realize that dealing with decision makers in the political arena will enable them to gain a greater share of the resources than dealing or bargaining with individual employers. By entering the political arena, labor leaders acquire status resources personally.

In the past few decades, many Latin American labor unions have actually been founded by political parties. The party elites seek labor support and in return make various promises to the members of the working class—promises usually involving an increase in the economic resources allocated to the working class. The results often have been an official but unenforced labor code and minimum-wage law and a great deal of prolabor symbolic outputs from authoritative decision makers, while at the same time the decision makers keep the working-class groups under tight control. This has been the situation not only in Costa Rica but also in Mexico under the Partido Revolucionario Institucional (PRI), in Chile under conservatives and even the reformist Christian Democrats, and in Venezuela under the Acción Democrática (AD) government.

In countries where communists have organized the working class, a military takeover has usually meant the banning not only of communism (often to placate forces in the international environment), but also of the labor unions themselves. Whatever the communist motives in organizing labor, they have not done the Latin American working classes any favors by their efforts and, in fact, have often invited repression of the workers because of their involvement.

Empirical studies of the attitudes of labor-union members in Latin American are extremely scarce. In a survey made by Alex Inkeles in Chile, when labor-union members were asked, "In your opinion, which of the following should be the major task of a labor union?" the solid majority responded that it was to "improve the economic position of workers" (quoted in Landsberger, 1967). Leaders, who are more likely to have prestige-class orientations, were more concerned with status and other noneconomic issues than were the rank and file, who regarded economic gains as being the primary duty of the union while only 54 per cent of the leaders responded similarly. The Chilean situation is probably not atypical of the Latin American area as a whole.

At the beginning of the 1970's, only about 10 per cent of all Latin American workers were organized into unions, and the figure was this high only because of Chile's and Argentina's relatively high rates of unionization (20 per cent or better). In many countries, competing unions tend to limit the effectiveness of the groups in making their demands. Until the problems noted by Alba are resolved and until more members are recruited into the unions, the ability of the movement to demand a share of the resources of the various societies will be limited. Leadership is scarce and although the students as a group have shown themselves to be loyal allies, they have not been so loyal as individuals.

THE ROLE OF THE PEASANTS

Latin American peasants, individually or collectively, are undoubtedly the least articulate and influential group in any of the twenty nations. Even urban slum dwellers are likely to be more active and effective than the peasantry. This fact is particularly interesting since the peasantry forms the largest single group in practically all the countries.

The Potential Influence of the Peasantry

The vineyards of Chile, the plantation agriculture of Central America, Brazil, Colombia, and other countries, and the cattle-raising *estancias* of Argentina require some extended contact between workers. Even if they do not work together, the housing pattern throws agricultural workers more closely together in Latin America than in most areas of the world. Thus, the possibilities for organization and group activity are present, but are largely unexplored to this point. However, if and when land reform becomes a reality, it can be expected that the peasants will gain an increased voice.

The experiences of Venezuela, Chile, Mexico, and Bolivia seem to bear out this expectation. In these countries, the raising of possibilities for land ownership among peasants has led to sharp, almost overnight changes in peasant behavior. In the 1952 and 1958 presidential elections, the peasant in Chile, when he carried out the unusual act of voting, was supporting to some considerable extent the more conservative, status-quo candidate. By the 1970 election, however, after five years of tentative work toward land reform and peasant unionization, with both the Christian and the Marxist left openly encouraging peasants to place demands on the system, they were doing exactly that. Besides supporting the two candidates who promised complete redistribution of the land, they were taking over properties, striking, and in general making life difficult for the *terratenientes*. The pattern has been repeated in even more violent fashion in some parts of Bolivia.

Peasant Attitudes

Anthropologists have engaged in isolated analyses of peasant attitudes, but few attempts have been made to examine their political attitudes at the national level. Bonilla and Silva Michelena (1967) did so in Venezuela and have provided some fascinating data in the first volume of their series on that country. The non-land-owning peasant who was the least political of the group interviewed yet was typical of the majority of Latin American peasants stated that his personal economic situation had shown no improvement in the preceding five years and that his personal life was not very happy. More than 60 per cent of the non-land-owning peasants interviewed in Venezuela made these assertions (Bonilla and Silva Michelena, 1967, p. 129). Ironically, the peasant who received a parcel of land from the government under the national agrarian-reform program did not differ in his responses to questions about how happy he was.

Perhaps the most important result of receiving land is the change of attitude which becomes apparent toward group political activity and toward the articulation of interests to authoritative decision makers. Bonilla and Silva Michelena noted that political activity among the peasants increased between 20 and 50 per cent after receiving land. Undoubtedly, one of the most significant aspects of the Bolivian revolution of 1952 was the role played by the peasants in the National Revolutionary Movement after seizing the lands of their former *patrónes*. In general, however, Latin American peasants remain an apathetic lot. They are interested neither in organized political activity nor in revolution. It would appear that as long as social relations remain stable and urban influences are minimal, the peasantry is the least active participant of any major interest group in Latin America. One of the great disappointments faced by "Che" Guevara in Bolivia was the fact that the peasants were so apathetic to his efforts. At times he had to plead with them not to report him to the authorities while they refused to provide him with food, shelter, or supplies.

THE MEANS OF ARTICULATING INTERESTS

As discussed earlier, the articulation of interests in Latin America is usually an informal process, rather than the formal practice of delivering testimony to a legislative committee or even providing information or demands to presidential or congressional aides and assistants. This point deserves some elaboration. The highly developed class-consciousness of prestige-class members in particular emphasizes the tendency, present in practically all nations, of decision makers to restrict their contacts to members of their own social circles. The smallness of most of the Latin American countries and the extreme concentration of economic resources especially, but other kinds of resources as well, mean that the political decision makers of the prestige class often know personally or "know someone who knows personally" almost the entire socioeconomic elite. This pattern is accented by the concentration of the elites in capital cities and even in specific sections of the capitals, the practice of sending their children to the relatively small number of expensive private schools, and the extensive use of private clubs and associations as meeting grounds. The pattern is further reinforced by the long-standing tradition of *personalismo* and distrust of "outsiders," that is, those not known through kinship or close friendship ties. In short, prestige-class interests can be and regularly are articulated through informal rather than regularized, formal, open channels.

It should be remembered that interests must be not only developed and organized but also communicated to leaders. The communication between leaders and prestige-class interests is obviously no great problem. In sharp contrast, communication between working-class groups and leaders may well be a one-way process—leaders to masses—for several reasons. The working classes are very poorly educated, and education is an important attribute in the development of political demands and their forceful presentation. They have little time to devote to political activity. They have little financial support to offer leaders or prospective leaders. They are poorly organized, if organized at all. They lack personal contacts and the means for making these contacts. And their leadership, almost always of at least lower prestige-class background, is easily coopted into forfeiting lower-class goals for personal acquisition of status, prestige, and possibly economic reward.

Thus, as long as working classes can be kept uneducated and unorganized, an occasional symbolic reward is usually sufficient to maintain existing sociopolitical relations with no threat of system instability. Even when the lower class has access to the ballot, the lack of other political tools and advantages effectively restricts most opportunities for the attainment of a greater share of resources.

SUMMARY

Interest groups and interest articulation in Latin America are largely restricted to the members of the various sectors of the prestige class of the twenty countries. Alliances between working-class groups and prestige-class groups have invariably and, given the concentration of resources, almost inevitably been to the disadvantage of the former. A succeeding chapter will consider the general failure of the political parties to aggregate the interests of the two groups. The scarcity of resources, both economic and sociopolitical, which characterizes all of the Latin American countries has left no room for compromise and bargaining.

NOTES

1. Inkeles (1969) and Ayres (1970), to note only two recent and relevant studies.
2. Chile offers a possible exception to this pattern, insofar as working-class groups have succeeded in gaining access to decision-making positions by the election of the Socialist Allende with the backing of major lower-class interests, but this situation remains in too great a state of flux to speculate upon at this time.
3. For one account of these events, see Denton (1971).

SUGGESTED READINGS

Alba, Victor. *Politics and the Labor Movement in Latin America.* Stanford, Calif.: Stanford University Press, 1968.

Blanksten, George I. "Political Groups in Latin America." *American Political Science Review,* 53, No. 1 (March 1959), 106–127.

Bonilla, Frank, and José A. Silva Michelena. *A Strategy for Research on Social Policy.* Vol. 1 of *The Politics of Change in Venezuela.* Cambridge: M.I.T. Press, 1967.

Denton, Charles F. "Interest Groups in Panama and the Central American Common Market." *Inter-American Economic Affairs,* 21, No. 1 (Summer 1967), 49–60.

Goldrich, Daniel. *Sons of the Establishment.* Chicago: Rand McNally, 1966.

Houtart, François, and Émile Pin. *The Church and the Latin American Revolution.* New York: Sheed and Ward, 1965.

Illich, Ivan. "The Futility of Schooling in Latin America." *Saturday Review* (April 20, 1968), pp. 57–59, 74–75.

Kling, Merle. *A Mexican Interest Group in Action.* Englewood Cliffs, N.J.: Prentice-Hall, 1961.

Lambert, Jacques. *Latin America: Social Structures and Political Institutions.* Berkeley: University of California Press, 1967.

Lipset, Seymour Martin, and Aldo Solari, eds. *Elites in Latin America.* New York: Oxford University Press, 1967.

Mecham, J. Lloyd. *Church and State in Latin America.* Chapel Hill: University of North Carolina Press, 1966.

Peterson, John H. "Recent Research on Latin American University Students." *Latin American Research Review,* 5, No. 1 (Spring 1970), 37–58.

Pike, Frederick B. *The Conflict between Church and State in Latin America.* New York: Knopf, 1964.

THE MILITARY FORCES

The military forces in most of the Latin American countries play such an important role, both in the political system and in the general affairs of the society, that a separate chapter devoted to an analysis of this phenomenon is well warranted. The list varies from year to year, but Table VIII-1 provides some insight into the state of military affairs in a typical year, by demonstrating how much hegemony the forces actually maintain in the area. In 1971, thirteen of the twenty nations were ruled either directly or indirectly by their armies. The military in Colombia and Venezuela lurk in the background and usually are granted all of their demands for resources in the hope that they will not intervene again. The military forces of Chile in October of 1969 demonstrated that they are not a passive organization by any means by demanding, and receiving, more money for pay and equipment with no action taken against those who threatened the uprising.

PAST AND PRESENT FUNCTIONS

When North Americans think of the military forces in the Latin American

TABLE VIII-1. Type of Rule, 1971.

Type of Rule	Country
Military, direct	Argentina, Bolivia, Brazil, Ecuador, Haiti, Honduras, Nicaragua, Panama, Paraguay, Peru
Military, indirect	Dominican Republic, El Salvador, Guatemala
Civilian, with potentially interventionist military	Colombia, Venezuela
Principal interest group	Chile
Civilian, with subordinate military	Costa Rica, Cuba, Mexico, Uruguay

countries, they usually envision a semifeudal situation, with regional chieftains galloping through the countryside at the head of bands of ill-trained, poorly equipped peasants. These *caudillos*, such as Pancho Villa and General Santa Ana (named because of their familiarity to Americans), fought for a bewildering variety of causes, ranging from land reform to simple pillage, and they have gradually disappeared during this century. They have been replaced by professionally oriented generals, admirals, and colonels who command well-trained and disciplined troops. Military equipment, while not up to superpower standards, usually includes modern artillery, some jet aircraft, a few naval vessels, and enough trucks, jeeps, and tanks to move the troops around. Officers often have received some training abroad, usually from the United States military, which maintains missions in many of the countries and which operates special schools for this purpose, particularly at Fort Davis on the Atlantic side of the Panama Canal Zone and at Fort Bragg in the United States.

The *caudillos* did have something in common with their twentieth-century counterparts: the modern military leaders are no more oriented toward defense against attacks from abroad than were the men on horseback in the nineteenth century. Perhaps as an inheritance from the occupation troops stationed by the authorities in Spain, Portugal, or France during the centuries of colonial rule, Latin American military forces have traditionally been garrison forces. Their prime function has been to maintain internal order rather than to defend from without. From a functional perspective, the military forces have been the principal organization or structure performing the system-maintenance function in the societies. Clearly, the support or at minimum acquiescence of the military establishment is necessary for the effective operation of virtually all the Latin American political systems. It has often appeared to analysts that while performing this function, the forces have created more disorder than order, but those who have viewed the military as a creator of modified anarchy have usually assessed the societies under study from a very limited perspective.

The military functions in other politically relevant ways in Latin American societies. It is a powerful articulator of interests, usually rivaling in influence any group in the society. Furthermore, since the military has so often substituted its own rule for civilian leadership, it has the additional function of leadership recruitment in a number of Latin American systems. So little research has been done in this area that the analysis of this function will be quite limited and tentative. Finally, military men as authoritative decision makers must be examined, since they clearly function in that role in a number of the systems. Again, a lack of serious study precludes generalizations about military behavior in this area, but some tentative suggestions will be made.

COMMAND OF RESOURCES

The prominence of the Latin American military forces can be assessed from indicators other than the presence of military leaders in official decision-making positions. Since politics is defined in this analysis as the series of interactions involving the authoritative allocation of scarce resources, more important are the amounts of these values a particular military force can command whether in direct control of the authoritative decision-making process or simply operating in the background. As can be noted from Table VIII-2, the average percentage of the government budget expended by the military in Latin America is about 11 per cent.

Although the percentages are not high when compared to the United States, these are countries with very scarce resources and with little or no external defense problem. Furthermore, Latin American military forces are numerically quite small. Table VIII-2 provides the expenditure per military member in each country, giving a more accurate portrait of the situation. Powell (1965) suggests that those countries perennially governed by the military are characterized by a greater proportion of military expenditures going into weaponry and

TABLE VIII-2.   Military Expenditure as Percentage of Government Budget
and Gross National Product, excluding Cuba and Haiti.

Country	Government Budget 1961	Government Budget 1969	Gross National Product 1961	Gross National Product 1969	Expenditure per Member of Military, 1960[a] (thousands of dollars)
Argentina	13.2	11.4	2.8	2.2	2.46
Bolivia	16.2	8.8	2.6	1.7	0.34
Brazil	7.5	16.2	1.6	2.5	1.01
Chile	11.4	7.3	2.7	2.0	1.47
Colombia	12.4	10.5	1.5	1.3	1.82
Costa Rica	-	-	-	-	-
Dominican Republic	23.0	13.0	4.7	2.4	1.08
Ecuador	11.2	7.8	2.3	2.1	0.84
El Salvador	7.2	20.3	1.1	3.0	0.85
Guatemala	9.6	9.6	0.9	1.0	0.87
Honduras	11.6	14.3	1.5	2.2	0.71
Mexico	5.6	5.4	0.7	0.7	1.89
Nicaragua	15.8	11.8	1.6	1.5	0.73
Panama	0.5	0.7	0.1	0.1	-
Paraguay	14.4	11.2	1.4	1.9	1.00
Peru	15.3	19.5	2.2	3.4	N.A.
Uruguay	8.6	12.9	1.7	1.9	N.A.
Venezuela	6.9	7.6	2.1	2.0	3.51
Average	9.4	10.8	1.8	1.8	

a. Figures for 1960 are used in the absence of comparable reliable data.
Some figures for individual countries may have changed, but probably
not enough to significantly distort the total picture.

Source: Office of Development Programs, Bureau for Latin America, Agency
for International Development, Summary Economic and Social Indicators 18
Latin American Countries: 1960-1970 (Washington, D.C.: Government Printing
Office, April 1971), pp. 41, 42. "Expenditure per Member of Military"
computed from data on size of armed forces supplied in John Duncan Powell,
"Military Assistance and Militarism in Latin America," Western Political
Quarterly, 18, No. 2, Part I (June 1965), pp. 382-392, at p. 385. Reprinted
by permission of Western Political Quarterly and John Duncan Powell.

training best suited for maintaining internal security, while those
characterized by occasional intervention spend more of their defense
funds for high-cost items such as jet aircraft and aircraft carriers. The
nations never experiencing interventions are characterized by very
low levels of defense spending. There is certainly an underestimation
of defense spending, caused by the unavailability of accurate figures on
United States military assistance, which obscures even further the size
of the allocation to the military. The United States aid funneled
through the Department of Defense is also selective and, during the
past two decades, has gone to countries that have been dominated by
the military.

The military commands several other kinds of resources which are
more difficult to measure, but which help to explain its prominent

position. The level of technological advancement, as the result of modern training and a new professionalism, combined with tight-knit organizational hierarchies, has made the military forces the most institutionalized interests in their nations. While large landowners and the church have diminished in importance in the competition for resources in Latin America and at times have been joined by groups which have been able to compete with them, with only two or three exceptions the position of the military has been enhanced during the period since World War II.

SOCIAL ORIGINS

While the *caudillo* was often a member of his country's oligarchy, a landowner desiring more land or the control of his nation's government, the leaders of the modern Latin American forces are often of a new breed. Members of the traditional elite class are no longer attracted to military careers. Members of the prestige classes are still attracted to the naval and air forces in those countries which boast significant nonarmy services, and vestiges of social elitism are still to be encountered in institutions such as the Peruvian or Chilean naval academies. But the land armies have usually been the predominant force, and it is within these forces that the greatest changes in leadership recruitment have occurred.

Individual leaders such as Anastasio Somoza of Nicaragua, Rafael Leonidas Trujillo of the Dominican Republic, and Fulgencio Batista of Cuba—all from the Caribbean region and all men who rose from the obscurity of working-class or bottom-level prestige-class backgrounds to rule their nations—were not very different in social origins from the current crop of military officers. The social origins of military officers in the period since World War II are still another part of the explanation for the frequent political interventionism in the area.[1]

In many respects, the group which has at times been called the "Latin American middle class" resembles the upper class, and for this reason the two groups are placed into one category, termed "prestige class" in this analysis. The similarities between the groups in terms of occupational, kinship, and attitudinal criteria have already been assessed. But it is significant to note that military officers have been drawn mainly from the lower reaches of the prestige class and as a result are probably even more mistrustful of social change than is the oligarchy.[2]

Political Attitudes

At the same time, the military may be mistrustful of the elite, especially in countries where the potential for explosive lower-class protest against social injustices is substantial. Increasingly, the professionalized military is willing to blame the traditional elites for creating and perpetuating systems that are potentially very unstable and threatening, even to the military, and for political inaction in the face of challenges. The Peruvian case is one of the most obvious examples of this kind of distrust.

The military officers, often possessing fewer resources than the oligarchy, now view their careers as a definite way of improving their personal situations. Any rapid social change, such as occurred in 1952 in Bolivia or much earlier in Mexico, could threaten their own positions in the social sphere. When the Bolivian National Revolutionary Movement assumed power in 1952, it did in fact abolish the armed forces of the country. A new force was established, however, and it intervened with a coup d'état twelve years after the revolution. The events in Costa Rica culminating in the seizure of the government by the National Liberation Movement in 1948 also led to the abolition of the armed forces. The national guard, which replaced the military, is one of Costa Rica's weakest political organizations.

Members of the officer corps of the Latin American military forces, newly emergent into prominent prestige-class roles, regard any major social changes, whether to the right or to the left, as undesirable unless the results of the change can be predicted to a reasonable degree. Because of this attitude, the military often trusts only itself to bring change of any kind to a particular society. The military government of Peru is a good example of this situation in the early 1970's. This characterization does not mean that military officers are cynical in their attitudes and Machiavellian in their behavior. Frequently, the officers are quite idealistic, have decided that stability is the most desirable attribute for their country, and have concluded that their intervention is the only means of preserving the constitution and Western sociopolitical values. It is quite probable that when General Lanusse of Argentina led a move to depose General Roberto Marcelo Levingston, in the name of returning his country to representative democracy as soon as possible, he sincerely believed what he stated.

PROFESSIONALISM

During the many decades in which *caudillismo* flourished in Latin America, very few of the generals or chieftains or other soldiers considered the military as a lifetime career opportunity. This was true not only of the leaders of the forces, but also of the men who followed them. Regardless of rank, a soldier viewed his time in the military as a sojourn, after which he would return to civilian life as a farmer, tradesman, or peasant. The soldier-civilian often joined the armed forces with political ends in mind, as a way of making his demands for services or resources more forcefully to decision makers.

The professional soldier of the twentieth century in Latin America, despite the existence of conscription in some of the countries, places a different set of values on the organization with which he serves. As a result of training, often by international sources (by European missions prior to World War II and by the United States since then), a career ladder, and an esprit de corps of a more institutionalized variety, the modern soldier has adopted military goals and norms rather than external political ones. The temporary soldier displayed a great deal of enthusiasm as he followed his *caudillo*, but discipline and loyalty were not the strong points of nineteenth-century Latin American military forces.

The fact that the military has become professionalized and that the soldier-bureaucrat has replaced the soldier-civilian has not reduced the tendency for interventionism. The more advanced training of the modern soldier has made him more conscious of modern technology and its benefits in terms of both armaments and society as a whole. It has made him impatient with the tactics and turbulence of civilian politics and its seemingly never-ending inefficiencies, lack of discipline, and disorganization.

The rise in professionalization of the military forces has been the cause of still another political phenomenon. The *caudillo* usually was loath to share the responsibilities of making authoritative decisions with anyone; his was essentially a one-man, highly personalistic type of government. Today when the military assumes full authoritative decision-making responsibilities, it places a *junta* or group of officers at the forefront, a group which rules the country through a nominal chairman who becomes the chief of state. The bureaucratic training of the professional soldier has made him less prone to accept the personalism which still runs rampant through the civilian society. Military men are more accustomed to group decision-making and problem-solving techniques than are the civilians of their countries. The members of the *juntas* of the 1970's often appear drab and colorless in comparison to the flamboyant personalities of the civilian politicians and the *caudillos* who dominated so many of the countries throughout most of their histories.

There is one great difference between the military bureaucrats and

their civilian counterparts in various agencies of the public administration. While the civilian occupying a decison-making role often retains loyalties to a professional association and holds other positions
outside the bureaucracy where he is principally employed, the soldier
is usually exclusively employed by the armed forces and is dependent
for his social and economic status solely on his position within the
military organization. Trained in military academies at home or
abroad and often of a social-class background which would not provide
him with the status he has achieved in the armed forces, he cannot do
otherwise than remain loyal. Trained to obedience through one or two
decades in the lower ranks, by the time he has emerged into a decision-
making role he has been thoroughly indoctrinated in the military way
of doing things.

Part of the professional ethic instilled into members of the military
forces is a considerable amount of patriotic nationalism. Their pride
in their particular country often is disequilibrated by the nation's
inability to develop the technological skills already acquired and in
operation within the military forces themselves. Interestingly enough,
however, the officers generally do not seem to find it incongruous that
they are dependent on the United States or other foreign sources for
their arms and equipment. There is no contradiction, apparently, in
the minds of the military leaders between their patriotic pride and
their foreign dependence.

INTERSERVICE RIVALRY

One of the few factors working against military preeminence in the
authoritative decision-making processes of the Latin American nations
is the existence in some countries of interservice rivalries. The overthrow of Juan Domingo Perón in 1955 was at least partly the result of
one of these divisions. Although the army preliminarily remained
loyal to the Argentine dictator, when the air force began to make
bombing forays on the Pink House and the navy threatened to shell
the capital city, Perón capitulated. Such open divisions are unusual,
however, and the last occasion where one force openly warred on
another, resulting in the victory of something other than an army,
occurred in Chile in the last century, when the navy of that country
emerged victorious.

Usually the armed forces have remained well coordinated, or at least
differences are resolved without public dispute, largely because of the
massive strength of the land forces vis-à-vis the sea and air forces. This

does not mean that naval or air-force officers do not attain important decision-making positions, as revealed by the recent accessions of Admiral Wolfgang Larrazábal of Venezuela and air-force General René Barrientos of Bolivia. As the more elitist-oriented naval and air-force academies of certain countries open their doors to cadets whose origins are in the lower reaches of the prestige class and sometimes lower—something which the armies in the main have already done—the chances for serious divisions over major goals will become even more remote.

More probable are intraservice rivalries, in which groups of younger officers or noncommissioned officers or even cliques of higher-ranking military men conspire against each other. The Dominican Republic has been particularly susceptible, and, as a result, General Trujillo made it a habit of transfering his officers from division to division and from geographical location to geographical location with extraordinary frequency in order to make plotting against his rule more difficult. The losses in terms of efficiency were more than made up in Trujillo's plans by the security which this practice ensured him. The 1965 civil war in the Dominican Republic, during which a group of young officers under Colonel Caamaño Deño attempted to restore their country's constitutionally elected president in the face of opposition from some of Trujillo's old henchmen, is evidence that intraservice rivalry is an ever-present reality in that island nation.

As professionalism becomes even more imbued in the officer ranks of the military forces and as leaders are drawn from working-class backgrounds with increasing frequency, this sort of rivalry will also become less probable. Failure in this kind of a dispute for decision-making authority entails an almost automatic loss of status and role position. Colonel Caamaño Deño, who failed, has disappeared after being assigned to his country's embassy in London. Since promotions are becoming more automatic and since all military officers eventually obtain an opportunity to do some decision making of importance, the risks will be too high for most of the status seekers in uniform to break out of the pattern and attempt a coup.

REASONS FOR INTERVENTIONISM

Table VIII-3 demonstrates the frequency of successful coups in Latin America since 1930. Attention has already been given to several internal characteristics of the military that account for this heavy

TABLE VIII-3.   Number of Successful
Military Coups.

Country	1930-1971	Since 1950
Argentina	9	6
Bolivia	11	5
Brazil	5	3
Chile	2	-
Colombia	2	2
Costa Rica	1	-
Cuba	4	2
Dominican Republic	4	3
Ecuador	9	3
El Salvador	6	2
Guatemala	6	3
Haiti	5	4
Honduras	2	2
Mexico	-	-
Nicaragua	1	-
Panama	4	2
Paraguay	7	1
Peru	5	1
Uruguay	-	-
Venezuela	4	2
Total	87	41

involvement of the military in the political decision-making processes of the Latin American nations. These include their command of national resources, the cohesiveness of their organizations, their superior technology and discipline, and the social origins of their personnel; all have been assessed in terms of their effects on the behavior of the military organizations.[3]

Socioeconomic Reasons

While there is some disagreement among students of the military concerning the reasons for continual intervention, on one point there is near consensus. An adequate explanation of intervention must include an examination of the general state of the society. The stratification system, the concentration of resources, the ethnic composition, the levels of economic development, and similar social and economic background variables are key factors in determining the role of the military in politics. Disagreement surfaces when efforts are made to identify and specify more clearly which variables are most important. Fossum (1967) argues that intervention is positively correlated with

size and poverty, that it has occurred in periods of economic deterioration. Putnam (1967, p. 97) finds that economic development seems to
encourage, not inhibit, intervention.

Political Reasons

While noting that socioeconomic characteristics are important in
explaining military intervention, Putnam's (1967, p. 106) qualification
should be heeded:

> Over the last fifty years in Latin America the political sphere has become
> more autonomous; that is, factors other than socio-economic develop-
> ment have become relatively more important determinants of military
> intervention.

The fact that political considerations are increasingly paramount is
verified by Putnam's data on socioeconomic factors and especially by
Fossum's finding that coups are often concentrated around election
periods. The reason for the military's interest in the election results
would appear to be evident. As noted above, the military has certain
important political interests, in particular its own continuation as a
vital social force and permanent institution. Its basic needs—salaries,
equipment, personnel, and even its goals—are provided by the authoritative decision makers.

Not surprisingly, then, the military makes very strong efforts either
to control the decision-making process or to articulate its interests to
civilian authorities. The fringe benefits which military officers in
many of the countries enjoy are legendary. Beautiful officers' clubs
abound in the nations' capital cities; one club in Caracas compares
favorably with elite country clubs anywhere in the world in lavishness
and services. Interest-free loans, duty-free imports, pension plans, opportunities for further education and for travel abroad, and immunity
from many civilian laws and their nations' court systems make the
military career particularly attractive to men on the bottom rungs of
the prestige social class, men who could not live in this style if they
were engaged in any other occupation. These fringe benefits and other
facets of the military life have become still another reason for intervention in politics. Any civilian leader attempting to withdraw resources
from the military is gambling with his position and with the positions
held by other elected officials in his government.

A Tradition of Interventionism

Another important consideration in understanding the conspicuous role of the military and the functions performed by that establishment in the national political process is the tradition of interventionism which is common to almost all of the countries. The military has intervened before and, as a result, there is no traditional aversion to doing so again. When General Ovando seized the reins of government in Bolivia in the fall of 1969, it was the 185th time that the rulers of that country had been changed since it was founded by Simón Bolívar in the early part of the nineteenth century. On the other hand, the military in Chile, while an important interest group, has a history of nonintervention. Although there was strong encouragement from prestige-class interests during the early 1950's and again in the early 1970's, the military refused to intervene, even to prevent a Marxist regime from coming to power. To say that tradition causes political or military action is of course fallacious. But in countries where the military has intervened, it would seem more probable that it would do so again; the course of action is one which naturally will be considered by military decision makers.

The military leaders often view themselves as the ultimate guardians or defenders of their nation's constitution and heritage. National honor, patriotism, the fatherland, all are honored by the military. When members of the armed forces view the actions of certain politicians as unconstitutional, as they did many of Joao Goulart's policies in Brazil, they may believe it their sacred duty to remove the elected government from power even if it is unconstitutional to do so. The population at large also often holds the belief that the armed forces are the most patriotic element of their polity.

Civilian Demands

There is one more reason for the military interventionism so prevalent in Latin America. At various times, civilian interest-articulating groups or political parties, perhaps at a disadvantage in making demands for status and economic resources at least in comparison with other civilian groups, call on the military to side with them and to assume authoritative decision-making power on their behalf. Alternatively, the interest-articulating groups attempt to provoke the military into intervening, hoping to gain some long-run if not short-term advantage. Although the interest-articulating groups which engage in this type of tactic are usually oligarchical in social origin, there have been other groups which have attempted similar actions.

The classic case occurred in the early 1950's, when it seemed that the Colombian nation as a whole clamored for the military under Gustavo Rojas Pinilla to assume authoritative decision making power As a result of *La Violencia* which swept the country after 1948, claiming more than 200,000 lives, the entire country desired little else but order. Political leaders were to learn to their chagrin that the military is more difficult to remove from power than it is to place in the authoritative decision-making roles of a society. Thus in the 1970's, almost two decades later, many decisions cannot be made without first considering the reaction of the military forces. Interestingly enough, when Rojas Pinilla attempted to convince the Colombian military forces to intervene in his behalf after he lost the presidential election of 1970, he was unsuccessful. The liberal-conservative coalition has managed to keep the national armed forces placated since Rojas' days.

UNITED STATES MILITARY AID

There are several features of the Latin American military forces which appear almost ludicrous to unfamiliar observers. Regardless of the country and irrespective of how unsavory a particular general, field marshal, or admiral, after a coup d'état these men invariably find it necessary in their first speeches to declare that they are fervent anticommunists and are devoted to the principles of democracy. It is clear that these speeches are not designed for domestic political consumption, simply because few Latin Americans are worried about the threat of communism or enthralled with the principles of "military democracy." After a coup, members of the prestige class scramble into exile or attempt to establish new lines of political communication to replace those just severed. It is to the world, principally to the United States and the Pentagon, that these declarations are pointed. Through the years, Latin American leaders have learned that these are the things United States officials want to hear from them. Thus the sooner the proper symbolic pronouncements are made, the more rapidly will come diplomatic recognition of the new regime and the resumption of military aid.

Despite their inordinate command of domestic resources, Latin American military forces are dependent on international sources for equipment and certain types of supplies. Military aid creates many peculiar problems and also has its bizarre aspects. For forces with no international defense problem, some of the military organizations of the area have an inordinate amount of heavy equipment. General Trujillo of the Dominican Republic built up his navy until it became a task force of thirty-nine vessels at the height of his dictatorship. The force, including cruisers, minesweepers, and gunboats, was the second-largest in the Caribbean, the first being that of the United States. The Dominican navy has never seen action, despite the frequent invasions the country has endured over the years, mainly from the United States. The Brazilian navy owns a single aircraft carrier, upon which a Brazilian aircraft did not land for many years because of interservice rivalries. The navy wanted planes of its own, while the air force obdurately refused to land its planes on the craft. Peru reportedly possesses two submarines, but has never trained crews to man them. The Pacific coastal nation has recently acquired supersonic jet aircraft which, according to the Peruvian air force, are to be used in antiguerrilla warfare.

The large, unneeded pieces of expensive, used war equipment sold to the Latin American countries through the military-aid program is only part of the problem. In 1968 approximately 50 per cent of all funds appropriated for Latin America under the Alliance for Progress assumed the form of military aid. It is interesting to note that data on United States military aid to Latin America are particularly difficult to find. The *Statistical Abstract of Latin America* (1967, p. 193), which lists a category of "financing military sales" as a form of United States aid to the area, footnotes the category as follows: "Data for this category do not include total military sales and/or aid by the United States. Accurate statistics in this category have a way of hiding." The volume then lists a figure of $151 million for the period 1940–1966. Table VIII-4 provides a country-by-country picture of United States military aid over the eighteen-year period 1950–1968. The aid assumes many forms, including officer training, small equipment, uniforms, and military advisers. In the same eighteen-year period, despite the figures from the *Statistical Abstract of Latin America*, it is estimated the United States sold at a discount used equipment worth more than $1 billion. The discount is probably included in the aid figures produced by the Alliance for Progress for the period.

Since 1964 and the demonstrations of that year in the Panama Canal Zone, about one third of the salaries of the Panamanian national guard has been paid by the United States in an effort to strengthen the force and avoid further disorders in the area. Military training by the United States for Bolivian troops probably contributed to the capture and execution of Ernesto "Che" Guevara in the desolate jungles of that nation where he was attempting to foment an uprising.

TABLE VIII-4. United States Military Aid, excluding
Costa Rica, El Salvador, Haiti, Mexico,
and Panama (millions of dollars).

Country	1950-1967	1968
Argentina	23.5	10.9
Bolivia	15.8	3.5
Brazil	194.1	12.6
Chile	79.2	7.5
Colombia	67.5	12.2
Cuba	10.6	-
Dominican Republic	16.0	2.3
Ecuador	34.2	2.8
Guatemala	10.8	2.3
Honduras	5.4	1.0
Nicaragua	8.9	1.3
Paraguay	5.2	1.8
Peru	73.2	8.7
Uruguay	35.8	2.0
Venezuela	6.3	1.3
Total	586.5	70.2

Note: Figures represent military equipment and supplies
and expenditures for services. Includes equipment
and supplies procured for the military-assistance
program or from procurement or stocks of military
departments and services such as training, military
construction, repair and rehabilitation of excess
stocks, supplies, operations, and other charges.
Source: The Statistical Abstract of Latin America, 1968,
Kenneth Ruddle and Mukhtar Hamour (eds.), Publ. by the
Latin American Center, University of California at Los
Angeles (1970), p. 253. Reproduced by permission.

The case of the pickup trucks which were provided to Panama
through the Alliance for Progress ostensibly to build up the nation's
tourist industry is illustrative of the manner in which military aid is
camouflaged into other accounts in the United States budget. The
Alliance granted to Panama low-interest funds to purchase a fleet of
pickups which were supposedly going to cruise the nation's main
tourist arteries and to render assistance if required, following the
successful example of Mexico with their bilingual mechanics and mo-
torists' aides.

Panama did not receive a bargain on the trucks even though it used
Alliance funds which were loaned at subsidized interest rates. For one
thing, the trucks had to be purchased from American manufacturers.
And for another, they had to be shipped on vessels of the United States
merchant marine.

Upon reaching Panama, the vehicles were converted into paddy
wagons which are used by the national guard to control the country
which it now officially runs. The citizen of Panama is treated to the

sight of a military dictatorship which uses United States pickup trucks
—cruising urban streets, carrying heavily armed national guardsmen
—which bear on the outside of the doors the decal of the Alliance for
Progress symbol: two hands clasped in a handshake as a sign of cooperation. The educated Panamanian knows that the trucks are being used
for a distasteful purpose and at the expense of Panama's economic
development. The United States taxpayer believes that the million
dollars which went to Panama through the Alliance for Progress was
used to build the tiny nation's tourist industry.

Defenders of military aid have justified the program with several
arguments:

1. If the United States does not supply arms, the Latin American
armed forces will turn elsewhere for their weaponry and the United
States will have made enemies of "friends."

2. The Latin American armed forces are the area's best defense
against communism. Many of the military dictators have been
openly friendly with the tiny Communist parties of their countries,
for example, Trujillo of the Dominican Republic and Batista of
Cuba. As discussed in a preceding chapter, however, communism
hardly represents a credible threat to the stability of any of the
countries.

3. Military assistance is part of an over-all hemisphere defense plan.
However, since none of the Latin American armed forces is capable
of withstanding either a conventional or a nuclear attack, the equipment supplied under the program is being used for internal-security
purposes.

4. The armed forces of Latin America are promoting stability,
which fosters economic, social, and political development. The
number of coups in recent years belies this argument. Incidents
like the "soccer war" in July of 1969 between Honduras and El
Salvador, during which each nation bombed the airfields of the
other and five hundred people were killed, hardly vindicates this
argument. It is more probable that the military forces in Argentina, Brazil, Bolivia, Peru, Panama, and elsewhere have placed their
societies in straitjackets from which they may not be permitted to
emerge for many years. With the United States actively supporting
the military forces of Latin America and with these forces intervening in politics, it is little wonder that traditional enemies of the
military in nineteen of the countries, such as students, certain labor-union groups, and parties with predominantly working-class
appeal, have developed an anti-American attitude.

SUMMARY

Despite the seeming institutional instability caused by constant military intervention in the political arena, only one or two of the coups have resulted in significant social change. In fact, most of the military interventions have occurred to prevent the possibility of significant change (Needler, 1968, Chaps. 3, 4; Nun, 1965). It is difficult to predict what the future may hold, but it seems safe to assume that there will be little reduction in the influence currently enjoyed by the Latin American armed forces in the authoritative decision-making processes of their societies.

NOTES

1. While there are few reliable and recent areawide studies of the composition of the military, especially of higher-ranking figures, in terms of social background, some individual-country analyses exist. Among the best and certainly one of the most interesting is Einaudi (1970).
2. The classic article discussing this issue is Nun (1965).
3. For an excellent survey of the literature dealing with the military and politics in Latin American, see McAlister (1966) and Putnam (1967). Suggested Readings at the end of this chapter contain what we feel are the most important titles dealing with the subject. We might note Johnson (1964) in particular.

SUGGESTED READINGS

Fossum, Egil. "Factors Influencing the Occurrence of Military Coups d'Etat in Latin America." *Journal of Peace Research*, 4, No. 3 (1967), 228–251.
Johnson, John J. *The Military and Society in Latin America*. Stanford, Calif.: Stanford University Press, 1964.
Lieuwen, Edwin. *Arms and Politics in Latin America*. New York: Praeger, 1965.
Lieuwen, Edwin. *Generals vs. Presidents*. London: Pall Mall Press, 1964.
McAlister, Lyle N. "Recent Research and Writings on the Role of the Military in Latin America." *Latin American Research Review*, 2, No. 1 (Fall 1966), 5–36.
Needler, Martin C. "The Latin American Military: Predatory Reactionaries or Modernizing Patriots?" *Journal of Inter-American Studies*, 11, No. 2 (April 1969), 237–244.
Nun, José. "A Latin American Phenomenon: The Middle Class Military Coup." In Institute of International Studies, *Trends in Social Science Research in Latin American Studies: A Conference Report*. Berkeley: University of California Press, 1965. Pp. 55–99.

Powell, John Duncan. "Military Assistance and Militarism in Latin America."
    Western Political Quarterly, 18, No. 2 (June 1965), 382–392.
Putnam, Robert D. "Toward Explaining Intervention in Latin American
    Politics." *World Politics*, 20, No. 1 (October 1967), 83–110.
Wyckoff, Theodore. "The Role of the Military in Latin American Politics."
    Western Political Quarterly, 13, No. 3 (September 1960).

POLITICAL PARTIES

There are literally hundreds of political parties throughout Latin America, although the role of this type of institution has rarely been more minimal than in the early 1970's. An attempt to describe and compare each party would be as futile as would an attempt to examine all of the parties in the countries of Western Europe. In line with the functional approach of this volume, an attempt is made first to classify the most important Latin American political parties according to various criteria and then to generalize about the types of political functions which the parties perform. It should be pointed out here that in the majority of the countries the parties perform virtually no function at all.

Political scientist George Blanksten (1959) has provided a conceptual schema for classifying the political parties and other types of voluntary and involuntary associations in the twenty countries. Although there are a great number of methodological drawbacks involved in the use of this type of schema, the analyst wishing to compare the political-party structures of all of the nations of the area has little choice but to employ one. Hopefully, as the parties are discussed in terms of the functions which

they perform, some of the misconceptions arising from the classifica-
tory schema will be corrected.

ONE-PARTY SYSTEMS NONCOMPETITIVE

Blanksten's first major category of Latin American political parties
is the one-party system noncompetitive, a category which he divides
into two subparts. The first is a system where the dominant party
makes a concerted and official attempt to obscure the distinction between it and the government of the country. In this type of system,
the party is the main locus of authoritative decision-making roles and
overlaps with the institutional role structure. No competing parties
are permitted in this type of system. The only example of this type of
system in the Latin American area of the early 1970's is the one headed
by Fidel Castro in Cuba.

In the second type of one-party system in Latin America, the dominant organization always wins elections when they are held, but other
parties are permitted to exist and to campaign against the dominant
political organization. The only example of this type of system existing
in the early 1970's is the Mexican Partido Revolucionario Institucional
(PRI). That there are factions within the PRI makes the political process itself more competitive than it would appear with a superficial
analysis. But no faction has yet to break away successfully at the polls
and to compete for the votes of party loyalists.

Other examples of this kind of party system are really not comparable with the PRI, which is a party of national mobilization. The Partido Dominicano (PD) of dictator Rafael Trujillo also perpetuated a
one-party system where some competition was permitted. But the PD
and the PRI are so vastly different in a functional sense that to place
them in the same category in a schema is to distort reality.

COMPETITIVE PARTIES

Blanksten's second major category of political parties in Latin
America is that of competitive parties. Before an examination of the
various subparts in this category, a significant characteristic of Latin
American political parties should be noted: Even when they do compete, they may not be committed to the ideal of competition. The
existence of an official party, which the government in power supports
in an election, lending the party its resources, prestige, and military

muscle, is not unusual. The reasons for the existence of *oficialismo* are discussed below.

When there is a competitive party system in the Latin American area, it usually takes the form of three or more parties, rather than a two-party system. Although a great many factors contribute to this situation, one of the most important is the widespread use of some form of proportional representation in the electoral system. As Duverger (1961) has pointed out, proportional representation serves to lead to the multiplication of political-party organizations, while single-member districts have the opposite effects.

Pragmatic Parties

Blanksten's first subcategory of competitive parties is the pragmatic organization, the party which places no major ideological or philosophical demands on its membership. Instead, its sole reason for existence is to obtain or win authoritative decision-making roles (not necessarily elected offices) for its leaders or appointed candidates. Since these organizations do not evince an ideology of any significance, something which might possibly serve to bind the membership together, they must be successful at gaining positions capable of dispensing patronage on a fairly regular basis and in reasonably large amounts.

Pragmatic parties are divided by Blanksten into three principal categories, the first of which is the broad-based pragmatic organization. This type of organization is actually most common to the Anglo-American nations and the countries of Western Europe, but is found occasionally in countries which are less developed economically. In order for this type of party to survive, there is a need for a fairly broad consensus within the society as to social and economic goals and the political means for obtaining them.

Not surprisingly, there are and have been few Latin American political parties of this broad-based pragmatic variety because the countries' socioeconomic and political systems are not conducive to them. The two major parties of Uruguay, despite their many factions or sub-*lemas*, might be categorized as broad-based pragmatic political organizations since their differences are not ideological. A consensus built around a well-developed welfare state and the sharing of administrative responsibilities, despite the fact that the Blancos have dominated for four decades, has insured the survival of this system.

In the past the so-called radical parties of Argentina and Chile (they are not radical in the meaning of the word which has emerged on

United States campuses) could have been categorized as broad-based pragmatic organizations despite splits which at times seemed to occur along ideological lines. Unfortunately for the radicals, the consensus they attempted to create in Argentina was not broad enough to include a rapidly growing working class, different in many ways from that of other Latin American countries because of heavy European immigration. The appeal of Perón and the confrontations which occurred between working and prestige classes led to a polarization and an eventual military dictatorship. Similarly, the radical party in Chile has had difficulty in broadening its base to include politically emerging urban and lower-class groups.

Other observers would argue that the Christian Democratic parties of Chile and Venezuela and Acción Democrática (also of Venezuela) could be classified as broad-based and pragmatic, and to some extent they do seem to be moving toward a position that would allow them to make cross-class appeals. However, their strong ideological overtones argue for their placement elsewhere.

The second category of pragmatic party outlined by Blanksten is the narrow-based personalistic organization. This is the type of party which was predominant in Latin America throughout the nineteenth century and for much of the twentieth. With political parties disbanded or underground in so many nations as the result of military interventionism, it is difficult to ascertain what form of interest-articulating and voluntary organizations will emerge after the armed forces relinquish or are forced to give up some of their power. It seems safe to predict, however, that immediately after a military dictatorship it is the narrow-based personalistic party which will first begin to compete for values in the newly civilianized political arena, a party which will exist to promote the political fortunes of the colonel or general who has become the *oficialista* civilian candidate for elected office.

During the 1960's, personalist, narrow-based parties predominated in Panama until the military coup of 1968 led by General Omar Torrijos, and achieved varying degrees of ascendancy in Peru, El Salvador, Costa Rica, Guatemala, Bolivia, and the Dominican Republic. This does not mean that it is only in the small countries that this type of party has recently played an important role, but rather that several of the large nations have been ruled by the military for most of the past decade. Saying this should not obscure the rise of nonmilitary *caudillos* that even now can at times effectively compete. The Rojas Pinilla movement, led by the one-time military dictator of Colombia in 1969 and 1970, the Ibañez movement in Chile of the early 1950's, and various other movements lend credence to those who argue that the anti-"politics" feelings are not always converted into support for military intervention but can instead be funneled into support for *caudillos* who promise to "sweep the rascals out."

Personalist parties at times find it necessary to band together to achieve a broader base of support, which leads to a discussion of Blanksten's third type of pragmatic party—the narrow-based ad-hoc organization. The coalition which put José María Velasco Ibarra into the presidency of Ecuador in 1968 is one example of the narrow-based ad-hoc party. Significantly, with the subsequent cooperation of the military forces and Velasco Ibarra, the party has no longer been required. The Party of National Unification, which placed José Joaquín Trejos Fernández into the presidency of Costa Rica in 1966, is still another ad-hoc affiliation.

Ideological Parties

Blanksten's second subcategory of competitive political parties is the ideological party. The ideological parties cover a broad spectrum from communist to militant right-wing associations. At one point in the early 1960's, it appeared that the ideological organizations would emerge as the predominant form of political party in the area. However, their emergence led to a polarization of groups in many of the countries that was characterized by seemingly irreconcilable differences. The political paralysis which ensued led to intervention by the military forces in several countries. In the case of the one or two ideological parties which did survive the decade, the compromises to pragmatism which they made overshadowed their ideological stance, and it may very well be that in the 1970's these organizations should be labeled pragmatic rather than ideological.

The best-known group of ideological parties in the Latin American area is the so-called League of Social Democratic Parties, which includes Acción Popular Revolucionaria Americana (APRA) of Peru, Acción Democrática (AD) of Venezuela, Partido Liberación Nacional (PLN) of Costa Rica, Partido Revolucionario Dominicano (PRD) of the Dominican Republic, Movimiento Revolucionario Nacional (MNR) of Bolivia, and the Febreristas of Paraguay. Although APRA founder Raúl Haya de la Torre would have preferred to see his organization or the league become a genuine international movement and at times this group has been represented as such, actually it is an extremely loose coalition of nationalist parties. Few cooperative ventures have been successful. For approximately fifteen years the league did support a leadership-training school in a rural area of Costa Rica, the Inter-American School for Democratic Education. However, this school, which trained hundreds of party youth, was disbanded in 1969.

All of the league members favor some form of state interventionism and believe that active steps must be taken to lessen the dependence of their countries on the international market, most specifically the United States. They advocate land reform, with the exception of Bolivia's MNR, of an incrementalist variety, the elimination of illiteracy, industrialization, housing-construction programs, and the nationalization through expropriation of vital foreign enterprises if necessary. All of the parties also actively support civil liberties for their countries, including freedom of speech, the press, assembly, and so forth. All support the United States position on the Fidel Castro government in Cuba. As of 1970, only the PLN of Costa Rica, probably the least ideological of all of the parties, controlled both the presidency and the legislature of its country while keeping the military in a totally subservient position. Reforms which have been carried out by the PLN can be termed moderate at most, members of the urban prestige class being the principal beneficiaries.

APRA of Peru, the oldest of these Latin American Social Democratic parties and certainly several decades ago the most fervently ideological of the group, has never managed to achieve its goal of obtaining the principal authoritative decision-making posts of the country. There is some doubt in the early 1970's about whether it ever will have the opportunity to do so. Through a mystifying set of concessions to pragmatism at improper moments in time, the modification of ideology by long-time party leader Haya de la Torre, which includes the support of "imperialismo" and the strength of the Peruvian military forces, APRA has been experiencing a deterioration in popular support for many years. Since its victory at the polls in 1962, overturned by still another military coup, desertions from the party have snowballed.

The short-lived administration of Juan Bosch and the PRD, who fell victims after only seven months in office to latent Trujilloism in the Dominican armed forces, coupled with either an intentional or unintentional block by the United States of PRD return to power in 1965, has insured that this party and the ideological promise that it presented to the citizens of that country will probably remain unfulfilled. The fact that Costa Rica, during the administration of PLN President Francisco Orlich, sent a handful of policemen to the Dominican Republic to participate in the United States–OAS intervention there, has earned the enmity of not only the PRD, but also many of the other Social Democratic parties for the Costa Ricans.

The Social Democratic parties, led by well-meaning members of the prestige classes of several of the Latin American countries, have fallen victim to or become co-opted by their very social structures and economic systems. Although promising reforms and new benefits for the working classes, their goals once in office shifted to the provision of resources to the prestige classes through jobs in the bureaucracy and status through political participation. The shortage of economic resources in each of the countries has insured that after the demands of the prestige classes are met by these ideological parties, little has been left for distribution and allocation to the working classes. Their support of incrementalistic problem-solving styles and their efforts to avoid sudden disruptions of their economies and social systems have insured that little or no change has occurred during their tenure in the decision-making roles of their countries.

The other principal group of ideological parties in Latin America, a group which has as slight a relationship one to the other among its members as do the Social Democratic parties, is the Christian Democratic, which in the period 1968–1970 held sway in authoritative decision making in both Chile and Venezuela. Whether or not these particular parties remain in power in the future, it is safe to state that Christian Democracy is on the ascendancy throughout Latin America. The majority of the Latin American nations now boast a party of this type, the ideology of which is based on a religious-political philosophy derived from several papal encyclicals, including the *Rerum Novarum* of Pope Leo XIII and *Quadragesimo Anno* of Pope Pius XI, and the writings of Jacques Maritain whose *Humanisme Integral* has been widely distributed throughout the Latin American area. Pope John XXIII's *Pacem in Terris* is rapidly achieving the prominence of the earlier writings. The Christian Democratic parties advocate more or less the same programs as do the Social Democrats, except that their programs, couched in Christian theology, are often less moderate than those of the latter. From a preliminary assessment of the Frei administration in Chile, at least, it would appear that the Christian Democrats have been no more successful than the Social Democrats in achieving their declared goals and for similar reasons. Run by members of the prestige classes, by the time each of the parties meets the demands of its more vociferous and capable supporters, there is little energy, status, or economic resources available for members of the working classes.

Latin American Communist parties, another form of ideological party, were considered in an earlier chapter under the general discussion of communism as a political issue. In the main, even these organizations have been dominated by more pragmatic members of the prestige classes in the countries in which they operate. The same can be said for the Socialist parties where they are found. These latter are often further to the left on the political spectrum than the Communists.

PARTY FUNCTIONS

Neumann (1956, p. 396) defines a modern political party as

> the articulate organization of society's active political agents, those who are concerned with the control of governmental power and who compete for popular support with another group or groups holding divergent views. As such a party is the great intermediary which links social forces and ideologies to official government institutions and relates them to political action with the larger community.

If Neumann's definition is regarded as universally applicable, then most of the Latin American political parties are not modern at all. Some of the most articulate political agents in Latin American countries never join a political party; instead, they work through some other type of organization, such as the military forces or agencies of the public administration. Since the latter have had considerably more success in gaining and holding authoritative decision-making responsibilities, the fact that prestige-class members have not delegated as much attention to political parties is not surprising.

Still another reason that Neumann's definition is not applicable has already been introduced: several of the major Latin American party systems are noncompetitive. It might be added here that many of the parties which do compete do so unwillingly. *Oficialismo*, in which the party in control of a government during an election receives the support of the authoritative decision makers, the chief of state in particular, is quite common. The violence which marred the Guatemalan elections of March 1970 was an example of *oficialismo* in action. The Revolutionary party of incumbent President Mario Méndez Montenegro received the full support of the government as his proposed successor competed with two other candidates, principally Colonel Juan Osorio, who eventually emerged as the victor. During the campaign, Colonel Osorio asserted that he would take his protest of *oficialismo* to the streets if it was necessary. Revolutionary party members, of course, denied that the government was playing favorites.

The final portion of Neumann's definition concerns a function of Western political parties which is often referred to in the literature of political science as "interest aggregation." Most Latin American political parties are incapable of acting as intermediaries between diverse groups. As Scott (1967, p. 128) states:

> They are elitist in the sense that political initiative resides in a restricted leadership group, frequently consisting of the elite who control the functional groupings which are brought into the political movement en masse with minimal consultation of the rank and file. . . . They will not undermine their own authority with the rank and file and abandon the groups they represent in order to turn the party into a more neutral and broadly based aggregating mechanism.

The differences between socioeconomic classes in Latin America, the very great gap between prestige and working classes, is reflected in the political parties of the area. Most of them primarily articulate the status demands of their leadership and mobilize the lower class only in the most formal sense. Only two or three Latin American political parties, led by members of the prestige classes, have done more than formally articulate in a symbolic fashion demands for more resources for the working classes.

The only characteristic which the parties in Latin America have in common with the Neumann definition is that the associations are indeed usually concerned with controlling the political apparatus of the country in which they operate—capturing the centers of authoritative decision making. In many of the countries, where the military has assumed control, the parties have experienced abject failure in recent years.

National Mobilization and Stabilization

There are two functions of political parties in underdeveloped countries such as those of the Latin American area which Neumann did not consider. One is the function of national mobilization, where the political party mobilizes new groups of the population into the political arena as part of an effort to change the country. The other is stabilization, perhaps the opposite of mobilization.

Three Latin American political parties can be termed as parties of national mobilization, although one of these has been removed from power by the military forces. The three parties are the PRI of Mexico, the MNR of Bolivia, in power from 1952 to 1964, and the Communist party of Cuba. None of these parties actually permits or permitted members of the working class to assume decision-making responsibilities, but the prestige class made great efforts to gain the support of the working class by articulating its usually latent demands for economic resources. The result was a great deal of social change, irreversible in most cases, in all three of the countries. The leftist coalition that now governs Chile is moving in this direction, but seems far from being a movement of national mobilization at this time.

Another function of political parties in the economically under-developed areas is that of bringing stability to their respective polities. By institutionalizing and compromising, co-opting and controlling, political parties manage tensions in a system. In the Latin American systems, where political parties have been permitted to play active roles in the authoritative decision-making process, it would appear that they have had the opposite effect. By mobilizing elements into the political arena and teaching them to expect certain resources from their polity, the successful parties have created a situation where instability might result if successive demands were not met. However, as noted, only three of the Latin American countries have recently boasted a party of mass mobilization.

The *peronista* party of Argentina was also an organization of national mobilization. When it was later removed from office, in conjunction with its founder Juan Perón, the country became impossible to govern. The groups which had articulated and channeled their demands for political resources through the *peronistas* refused to work through any other political associations or to return to a state of apathy or alienation so common to other Latin American nations. The result has been that since 1955 the Argentine military has intervened several times, and despite claims by former President Levingston in 1970 that a return to democracy was imminent, it appears that the armed forces under General Lanusse plan to retain control over the authoritative decision-making process for an indefinite period of time in order to restore stability.

In the countries which have been more stable, it would seem that a situation such as that of Argentina has not occurred because their political-party systems have contributed to the general tone of politics and have been symptomatic of generally stable social systems. Latin American political parties are not creating a generalized consensus in any of the countries, nor are they achieving stability through the interest-aggregation process. Rather, they seem to be creating or at least reinforcing stability by acting as outlets for tensions and opposition, giving symbolic service to grievances, while maintaining the original balance of social relationships and arrangement of social rewards and privileges.

Leadership Recruitment

One of the functions which Latin American political parties perform in common with similar associations in economically developed countries is leadership recruitment. Even if a party is out of office for a long time, the experiences of members at meetings and negotiations, at giving speeches and writing articles, provide them with political skills which may serve them well later in a job within the public administration or in a less sheltered decision-making position. Even in the societies which are predominantly characterized by narrow-based personalist parties, this leadership function is an important one. Considering that the prestige classes are small and leadership skills in great demand, this function and its importance should not be underestimated.

Political Socialization

All of the Latin American political parties perform the function of political socialization to a certain degree. Running advertisements in the mass media, writing pamphlets, and giving speeches, party leaders are bound to have at least some influence on how people will view their political system. Parties have a great deal to do with what the people learn about political participation, about the personalities of their leaders, and about the nature of the government. Since so many Latin Americans have little contact with the formal educational process, in which political socialization is a principal function, the parties in their campaigns and other activities are regularly the only source of political socialization with which people become familiar, giving obvious importance to the content of party propaganda.

SUMMARY

It could very well be that political parties will play a principal role in the authoritative decision-making processes of all of the Latin American countries in the future, although they may not be parties which adhere to the standard Western model. Meanwhile, the parties which do exist usually are personalistic, characterized in general by a very small permanent organization and a stratified membership. Party militants are usually of the prestige classes, while the rank and file are not permitted a great deal of participation. Leadership does not fluctuate very much in either the few large broad-based parties or the narrow-based personalist parties.

SUGGESTED READINGS

Ames, Barry. "Bases of Support for Mexico's Dominant Party." *American Political Science Review*, 64, No 1 (March 1970), 153–167.

Anderson, Charles W. "Politics and Development Policy in Central America." *Midwest Journal of Political Science*, 5, No. 4 (November 1961), 332–350.

Blanksten, George I. "Political Groups in Latin America." *American Political Science Review*, 53, No. 1 (March 1959), 106–127.

Fitzgibbon, Russell H. "The Party Potpourri in Latin America." *Western Political Quarterly*, 10, No. 1 (March 1957), 3–22.

Kantor, Harry. *The Ideology and Program of the Peruvian APRISTA Movement.* Washington, D.C.: Saville Books, 1966.

Martz, John D. *Acción Democrática.* Princeton, N.J.: Princeton University Press, 1966.

Martz, John D. "Dilemmas in the Study of Latin American Political Parties." *Journal of Politics*, 26, No. 3 (August 1964), 509–531.

Padgett, L. Vincent. "Mexico's One Party System: A Re-evaluation." *American Political Science Review*, 51, No. 4 (December 1957), 995–1008.

Snow, Peter G. "The Class Basis of Argentine Political Parties." *American Political Science Review*, 63, No. 1 (March 1969), 163–167.

Williams, Edward J. *Latin American Christian Democratic Parties.* Knoxville: University of Tennessee Press, 1967.

BUREAUCRACY AND
DECISION MAKING

A major theme of this volume has been how and to whom scarce resources are allocated. In Chapter XI explicit consideration is given the question of to whom resources are made available, that is, who receives the political outputs. This chapter will focus on those actors whose primary functions relate to what was called rule application in the model in Chapter I. While rules are applied by other institutions and actors in some systems, the primary institution performing this function in all the systems is the public bureaucracy. However, this is not the only important function of the bureaucracy. In fact, public bureaucracy is the most clearly multifunctional structure in the Latin American countries. Most of this chapter will be concerned with outlining the most important of these roles, an understanding of which is essential if we are to see beneath the formalities of political decision making to the more basic patterns and forces that contribute to the final policy outputs.

Public administration as a focus of study in comparative politics is a relatively recent arrival (see Heady, 1966). Political scientists are beginning to devote research efforts to the bureaucratic phenomenon, and it can be expected that in a few years a considerable amount of data related to the subject will be made available (see Charlesworth, 1968).

As has been noted throughout this volume, Latin America is often relegated to last place by those in the social sciences most concerned with empirical research, and as a result data about organizational behavior in the twenty nations of the area are very scarce.[1] This chapter provides a preliminary assessment of bureaucratic behavior in the area and suggests some generalizations. It may be a long time before these generalizations are verified since research in this area requires access to and understanding of the most covert, easily obscured, politically sensitive arenas of decision making and political action.

The focus in this chapter is on the higher-level administrator. While the "line" worker's role is not insignificant and will not be ignored, clearly the key decision making and action takes place at the higher levels of the public bureaucracies and most of this discussion centers on this "administrative class" that occupies the higher-level posts.

THE COLONIAL ERA

The need to govern Spain's far-flung empire led to the establishment of an elaborate administrative structure in certain of the Latin American states. That these structures and practices have had an effect on current administrative practice is difficult to corroborate. But it is not inaccurate to assert that for a considerable portion of the nineteenth century, certain administrative structures in Spanish America were little more than nationalized versions of the colonial bureaucratic institutions.

Phelan (1960) has asserted the following about the Spanish imperial bureaucracy:

> Looking at the Spanish administration as a whole, one can see no single guiding goal or objective save that tendency common to all bureaucracies —the tendency toward self-perpetuation. Nor are there several goals commensurate with each other. . . . The standards to which individual agents were subject often clashed with one another, and no clearcut priority among these standards was available for the agents.

Phelan devotes most of his article to showing that because of these conflicting goals and the communication problems presented by geographic distance between Spain and its colonies, the appointed officials informally were actively involved in making Spanish colonial policy. There were checks on crown officials, such as the church and the *audiencias* (similar to municipal assemblies), but policy making by bureaucrats was common, nevertheless.

The efficiency of the Spanish bureaucratic system is best gauged by the enormous treasures extracted from America and returned to the Iberian peninsula, by the cities and fortifications erected throughout the New World, but above all by the extraordinary length of time that Spain was able to retain possession of her colonies while suffering tremendous naval defeats and losses in power in conflicts with European rivals. In contrast, the British colonial administration of the period, the one responsible for administering the colonies which now are part of the United States and Canada, can be labeled a shambles.

Neither the French nor the Portuguese colonial bureaucracy approximated the Spanish in effectiveness, although it can be assumed that officials of those institutions were as active in formulating policy as were the officials of Spain.

THE POSTCOLONIAL PERIOD

In the immediate postcolonial period, Latin American bureaucracies closely approximated the institutions which had been established by one imperial power or another. In Brazil the imperial bureaucracy officially survived most of the nineteenth century. During the twentieth century, various vestiges of what were considered good bureaucratic form in the economically developed nations at the time were transplanted to the Latin American nations. Civil-service rules, files, exams, appropriate spans of management control, incentive systems, and so forth have been introduced to achieve one goal or another. In the Brazilian case, Graham (1968, p. 4) notes that leaders in the public-administration field

> have attempted to create a "modern" public personnel system which will replace favoritism and patronage with rational recruitment practices and they have devoted considerable time and effort toward putting into practice ideas and techniques borrowed from the economy and efficiency movement in the United States.

He concludes that this effort has largely failed. The Brazilian pattern is a common one, and the results appear to be equally similar.

The period since World War II has witnessed a strong increase in the demands from certain sectors of the prestige classes, especially the new elites of industrialists and entrepreneurs of different sorts and the ever-increasing numbers of highly educated young people, as well as from some segments of the working classes, particularly the organized members of the industrial-labor sector. With the assistance and encouragement of experts from a wide variety of Western nations, these varied groups have pressured governments for the same kinds of goods and services available in the more economically developed countries. Scott (1965) argues that the strain on the public bureaucracies resulting from this change in their environments has been even greater than one might expect because of the lack of informal, mutually integrative, and self-enforcing political mechanisms, such as political parties and interest associations, that might help absorb the shocks of increased demands.

Among the various demands made on the public bureaucracies are the following:

1. Preserving system stability.
2. Bringing controlled socioeconomic change to the system.
3. Providing prestige white-collar jobs.
4. Establishing universal achievement criteria for personal advancement.
5. Producing an ever-widening array of economic goods and services.
6. Encouraging and attracting foreign capital into their countries.
7. Providing an ever-widening array of social goods and services— schools, hospitals, sewage-treatment plants, water-purification systems.
8. Raising the resources to pay for these services.
9. Assuming the role of chief national planner and problem solver.
10. Remaining apolitical.

As can be seen, the expectations placed on the public administrative structures are as dichotomous in the 1970's as they were in the 1770's if Phelan's assessment of colonial bureaucracy is accepted.

CHARACTERISTICS AND ROLES

On the basis of his study of several Southeast Asian countries, Riggs (1964) has developed several models of bureaucratic behavior. His "sala" model appears to be as applicable to the nations of Latin America as to those of Asia. Riggs notes several characteristics of the sala model, such as polynormativism, price indeterminacy, and selective enforcement of rules, that seem particularly pertinent to Latin America. Polynormativism is defined as value conflict within individuals which leads to support of new value orientations (reflected in behavior such as support for merit systems) on a verbal level while in practice exhibiting the traditional patterns (such as dependence on personal, friendship, or kinship ties to obtain employment) that the new values should have replaced. Price indeterminacy in this context means that salary and service levels vary according to the status of the beneficiary. Selective enforcement of rules is the use of one set of standards to govern relations with some groups or individuals and other standards for different individuals or groups, that is, those with the status or connections to gain exemptions from the normal patterns.

In his study of Brazil, Graham (1968, p. 6) argues that the

attempt to reform the Brazilian federal civil service through the use of American-style public personnel policies has led to the creation of an administrative system, characterized by a high degree of formalism, in which there is considerable discrepancy between norms and reality.

The difficulty lies in trying to apply norms in governing administrative behavior which conflict with the functional demands of the political and social systems.[2] Vernon (1963, p. 153), while focusing on different problems and issues, says much the same thing in his study of Mexican economic development.[3]

Further illustrating more specific instances of these "sala" characteristics and their meaning, Roberto de Oliveira Campos (1967, p. 286) Latin American official and theorist, notes:

The main drawback to improvement of public administration in Latin America is perhaps the tradition of State paternalism. . . . It affects the recruitment of employees, which is more often than not conducted by the system of affiliation or allegiance to political clientele rather than by systems designed to measure concrete achievement. . . . it explains the generally faulty nature of the control procedures over government operations and government enterprises.

Actually, there are some inherent contradictions in what Campos has to say, since at least theoretically the operation of a spoils system should lead to more effective political control.

Campos' statements are supported by Gomez' (1969) analysis of

Peruvian bureaucracy. Gomez notes, for example, that the recruitment of civil servants in Peru follows no particular pattern and that there is almost no uniformity in that country's administrative structure and behavior. Parrish and Tapia-Videla (1970, p. 467), in a report on administration in Chile, note that "there has been a proliferation of agencies and programs following no semblance of a rational plan, and a lessening of the flexibility to adapt to new problems." According to Scott (1965, p. 302), "Throughout the region, governments tend to create the formal structures of more highly developed and productive societies, but to ignore their content."

Fusion of Traditional and Modern Values

Speaking directly to the question of bureaucratic attitudes and values along much the same lines that Riggs has proposed, Scott (1965, pp. 303–307) notes that while all the Latin American bureaucracies are characterized by a fusion of traditional and more "modern" values (meaning more like those found in bureaucracies of the United States and Western Europe), there are clearly gradations from country to country in the degree to which the newer values have come to predominate and where there exists a reasonably successful intermingling of traditional and "modern." He maintains that the bureaucracies in Category I have experienced little attitudinal adjustment; that those in Category II have experienced change in some value patterns, but have related dysfunctionally with traditional values; that those in Category III have experienced considerable change in values and attitudes, and the fusion of modern and traditional is being modestly but successfully resolved. Note that only four states fall into the final group, and some sources would dispute the inclusion of Brazil, if not the others.

Category I	Category II	Category III
Guatemala	El Salvador	Uruguay
Honduras	Dominican Republic	Costa Rica
Haiti	Panama	Mexico
Paraguay	Bolivia	Brazil
Peru	Venezuela	
Ecuador	Colombia	
Nicaragua	Chile	
	Argentina	

The traditional bureaucratic system—the one that served quite well in a stratified, ordered, stable system—places value on authority, hierarchy, and formality. That is, those characteristics and behavior patterns that enable the bureaucracy to control effectively certain segments of the population and their demands, the law-and-order function, are emphasized. Strong elements of this system persist in all of the countries, in the face of the monumental rhetoric of change, modernization, and reform within the bureaucratic systems. If Scott (1965, p. 307) is correct in saying that the bureaucrats in Mexico have hindered change and that in the mid-1960's had a semiauthoritarian and dominating relationship with the working class, even after the bloody and thorough revolution in that country, it is probably safe to argue that such behavior and attitudes are prevalent in other Latin American countries, with the possible exception of Cuba.

Rule Making and Implementation

The increasing volume of demands placed on the political systems of the Latin American countries has enormous consequences in terms of the functions of the bureaucracies. The lack of effective intermediate organizations and the concentration of decision-making powers in the executive branches have meant the transference of these demands to the public bureaucratic agencies, vastly increasing the role of these institutions as rule makers and implementers. The lack of effective parties, aggregative interest associations, and similar groups and organizations results in the public bureaucracy also becoming an important force in the setting of goals and priorities, a key input function, and in providing support for the political system, becoming in many cases the most important source of input demands and supports. Given the increasing input demands from bureaucracies in countries of Western Europe and the United States, it should not be surprising that these structures have significant input roles in Latin America, where there are few other educated, organized, cohesive, and socially important institutions.

Prestige-Class Origins

Two additional factors that help explain bureaucratic influence and importance are the technical skill and experience in particular duties and the reflection by the Latin American bureaucrat of the dominant values of the prestige class that still prevails in practically all of these countries. In this context, it should be noted that bureaucratic positions, particularly in the higher levels being considered most directly here, require relatively advanced levels of education. These levels of education are beyond the reach of practically all of the sons and daughters of the working class. Thus, the Latin American civil servant is very likely to come from the middle and lower ranges of the prestige classes. (Usually, those in the upper reaches of the prestige class have the resources to pursue other, more lucrative, and higher-status activities.) Furthermore, the socialization experiences (school, church, family, and peer groups) are likely to be much the same for these higher-level civil servants, resulting in shared values and aspirations.

The educational barrier is so striking in most of these countries that the question of whether recruitment is by ascriptive or achievement standards is almost moot. Thus, Scott finds in Mexico, Peru, and various Central American countries the existence of "bureaucratic families," families in which the father, son, brother, uncle, and cousin all fill government positions. But Scott (1965, pp. 294–295) goes on to say that in countries such as Chile, Argentina, Brazil, and Mexico, where achievement standards are prevalent, the results in recruitment may be much the same; that is, individuals with the same values, behavior patterns, and aspirations will be filling the posts, just as if ascriptive standards had been used. Grimes and Simmons (1969) verify this finding in their study of Mexico.

Common socialization experiences, educational backgrounds, urban (usually capital city) origins, and other characteristics give the bureaucrats a moderate-to-strong sense of group identity or consciousness. Professional interaction is reinforced by personal and family associations to heighten the identity. Furthermore, as the pressures on government for increased services and greater efficiency have increased, the consciousness of the administrative class as a group of importance has also been raised.

In sum, the importance of the bureaucracies as centers of decision making is difficult to overemphasize. Possessing high levels of education, technical skill, organization, and politicization; being in key positions for translating inputs into policy; having direct contacts with other important prestige-class interests; and reflecting a high degree of group consciousness—the bureaucracies have enormous impact on the making of decisions.

Reasons for Ineffectiveness

This is not to suggest that the Latin American bureaucracies are especially effective or efficient. On the contrary, one of the overriding characteristics of the public bureaucracies in Latin American countries is their inability to carry out their most basic function—the implementation of demands made on them by conflicting social forces. A number of factors are responsible for this failure, but among the most important are lack of financial resources, lack of agreement among decision makers on priorities, incompatibility of the demands made on the public bureaucracy, and the desire among bureaucrats themselves for status and security. This last issue deserves some consideration.

The desire for status and security must be examined in the context of the Latin American society, with its limited resources and high class- and group-consciousness. The bureaucrat, dependent to some degree on the balance of political power in a threatening environment where that balance is often unsteady, must be constantly aware of the uncertainty of his position. The threatening nature of his environment results in a tendency to choose very selectively the kinds of demands that will be given attention. In fact, as long as the demands made on the bureaucracies do not necessitate action stimulating or creating significant changes in social relations, the security of bureaucrats is usually not threatened. In several of the countries, however, some pressures are arising from non-prestige-class sectors and even from some sources within the higher-status groups that would require basic social changes or shifts in the structure, composition, and behavior of the bureaucracy. It is difficult to believe that the public bureaucrat will consciously work to engineer change that would reduce the social and economic distance between the working class and the class of his relatives, peers, and himself, would threaten his job, or would alter the way he is accustomed to doing his job.

This inability to meet the demands placed on them results in a number of regularly noted characteristics of bureaucratic behavior, present to some extent in practically all bureaucratic organizations, public or private, but accentuated in Latin America. Most evident among these include the tendency to protect one's position by resort to rigidifying regulations, "red tape," and simple inaction. In a summary report by the United Nations Economic Commission for Latin America (1970) concerning the issue of planning and economic development, the authors state that

> the plans often encounter resistance from the traditional government administration, reluctant to institute changes and jealously guarding its policy making power against any possible transfer of power which may imply reorganization of the administrative structure to facilitate the establishment of the policy making machinery which planning requires.

Latent Functions

Latin American bureaucracies perform functions that very often are latent, subtle, and perhaps even unintended. Daland (1967, p. 210) has detailed a number of these more subtle roles of the public bureaucracy of Brazil, but they seem equally applicable to the other Latin American countries:

1. The provision of a channel for upward mobility for the educated middle class, a group which because of behavioral and attitudinal characteristics has been in this volume included in the prestige class.
2. The provision of a permanent income for that portion of the middle class which provides support for the regime.
3. The provision of opportunities for private entrepreneurship based on the powers attaching to certain offices.

The issue of job and income provision through the public bureaucracy has been raised previously, but the repeated appearance of the argument in the literature emphasizes its importance. What is not usually mentioned, at least not very clearly, is the real contribution of providing jobs and income. In effect, the expanding bureaucratic machinery makes work not only for substantial numbers of the economically active population but for those elements of the population that could, if alienated from the system, create considerable system instability. And not only are jobs provided for the prestige class but they are jobs that tie these elements to the existing system in the strongest possible ways, making their futures dependent on the continued smooth operations of the existing political relationships. It would be difficult to devise a more effective co-optation arrangement. Continued rapid expansion of the bureaucracies in the Latin American countries may be necessary, regardless of the need or lack of need for expanded government goods and services, in order to maintain system stability, to co-opt the increasing number of educated people seeking reasonably secure, relatively prestigious white-collar jobs. Thus, Scott (1965, pp. 302–303) justly concludes that the Latin American tendency to multiply agencies may be at least partly explained as a job-producing exercise. He argues that the formality and red tape are often nothing more than means to exercise the control needed to maintain stability.[4]

The third function mentioned above is simply a reference to the importance of the ties between the politically important economic groups in the private sectors—in some countries the landholders, in others the new industrialists, in most countries both groups—and the bureaucratic offices, especially the higher posts. While this function has not been given much attention to this point, Daland (1967, esp. Chap. 5) goes so far as to say that the industrial community acts as a veto group on most major bureaucratic actions in the Brazilian system, Vernon (1963) notes the prevalence of the ties in Mexico, Petras (1970, Chaps. 1, 2, 8) makes the same claim for Chile, and Scott (1965) charges that this kind of mutual accommodation is a general and widespread phenomenon in the Latin American area. As Vernon (1963, p. 153) notes:

> Extensive ties between public officials and private interests are part and parcel of Mexican life. Venality and corruption draw bitter public reaction from time to time, but the reaction is only transitory. And the "conflict of interest" problem in its more subtle forms is not a real issue and does not even draw an initial reaction.

In effect, there is, using Riggs' terminology, selective enforcement of the rules and probably institutionalized corruption in at least some of the systems. Those people who are able to exert the influence and make the inside contacts are exempted from the normal operating procedures that are used to control the "outsider."

CLASSIFICATION OF ADMINISTRATIVE STRUCTURES

Heady (1966) has developed a classification schema with which to compare preliminarily the public administration structures of the economically underdeveloped areas. His typology is based on using ecological considerations in comparing organizations. He delineates six types:

1. *Traditional-Autocratic System.* In this type of system, political elites owe their power position to a long-established social system which usually emphasizes inherited monarchic or aristocratic status. Administrative machinery is the principal vehicle for action, but its ability to operate is hampered by its own traditional characteristics and by the difficulties it faces in penetrating the community.

2. *Bureaucratic Elite System—Civilian and Military.* This is a system where the preponderance of political power is in the hands of career government officials—military or civilian or a combination. Traditional elites have been removed.

3. *Polyarchal-Competitive System.* In this system the most important

variable is genuine political competition. Heady's discussion of this system resembles the proliferation of "pluralist" type studies available about the United States polity.[5] In this type of system, the public administrators will be weak because of a lack of political support.

4. *Dominant-Party Semicompetitive System.* The dominant mass party is common in the developing nations, and Mexico's Partido Revolucionario Institucional is a striking example. A militant, centralized elite, through the party and the administrative structure, provides a continuity of program and goals not otherwise found in developing nations.

5. *Dominant-Party Mobilization System.* In this type of system, the dominant party permits no competition and actual or perceived coercion is stronger. Bureaucratic response to political decision makers would be more predictable than in Type 4.

6. *Communist Totalitarian System.* In this type of system, there is an insistent emphasis on responsiveness by the administrative apparatus to the party. The party maintains close supervision and control and often parallels the administrative apparatus with a political apparatus.

There are a number of problems inherent to the Heady classification schema. Undoubtedly, the greatest is that some of the categories do not encompass any of the Latin American systems accurately. Also some of the categories seem irrelevant to the Latin American scene. For example, there is some doubt that a totalitarian system could exist in any economically underdeveloped country. In order to establish totalitarianism, there must first be a fairly advanced degree of technology, coupled with a particular type of awareness by the citizenry. It could almost be asserted that totalitarianism cannot exist where there is a high degree of illiteracy. In underdeveloped countries which have been labeled totalitarian, it is only the elites, "the people who count," who have been subjected to the full pressures of the system.

Another, less serious problem is that the authors do not agree with Heady's classification of the national bureaucratic systems. However, this is, at least partly, a result of the time lapse from Heady's writing to the publication of this volume. A classification of the Latin American bureaucratic systems, using the Heady scheme, follows:

1. *Traditional-Autocratic:* Paraguay, Haiti, Nicaragua.

2. *Bureaucratic Elite:* Argentina, Brazil, Bolivia, Peru, Ecuador, Dominican Republic, Guatemala, Colombia, Panama, El Salvador, Honduras.

3. *Polyarchal-Competitive:* Costa Rica, Chile, Uruguay, Venezuela.

4. *Dominant-Party Semicompetitive:* Mexico.
5. *Dominant-Party Mobilization:* Cuba.

The justification for placing Haiti and Nicaragua in the traditional-autocratic category is simple. In the island republic, former President François Duvalier successfully, to this point at least, installed his son Jean Claude as chief of state for life—a hereditary presidency. The Somoza administration in Nicaragua, although new to this century, can be termed little other than a dynasty.

The justification for placing Colombia in the bureaucratic-elite category is more tenuous. For the past decade or so, there has been no party competition in that nation, and the public administration has received unbroken support from the political arena. If stability is achieved in Colombia, if violence does not break out with the renewal of party competition in 1974, then it will be because the civil and military administrative institutions have been able to assert themselves.

For reasons discussed above, we were not able to place Cuba in the final category, communist totalitarian. That the administrative system of that nation could drift in that direction is indisputable, but to argue that the nation is in an advanced state of totalitarianism at present is highly questionable. Hence we have situated Cuba in the dominant-party-mobilization category.

SUMMARY

The public bureaucracies are central decision-making institutions in practically all the Latin American countries. In fact, it seems possible that the larger and more economically developed the country, the more likely the bureaucracy exercises an important, if not dominant, role. Latin American bureaucracies are multifunctional; their functions include far more than the rule-application role normally associated with these institutions. Because of a number of advantages over other social groups and organizations and in the absence of aggregative parties, interest associations, or other similar mechanisms, the bureaucracies have important roles in making demands and providing supports for the systems. Perhaps equally important, public bureaucracies fulfill the function of maintaining system stability by providing jobs and income for the prestige class, those whose alienation could seriously threaten the systems. Furthermore, the bureaucracy acts as an effective control agent, providing the necessary goods, services, and special favors to its prestige-class clientele, while fulfill-ing a law-and-order role in relationships with the working classes, or providing symbolic outputs if the working-class demands are incon-sistent.

Most of the Latin American bureaucracies are fusions of the old and new. The differences among the countries in the degree of change in attitudes and behavior and in the roles of the bureaucracy vis-à-vis the rest of the political system are substantial. In the absence of more than a handful of empirical studies, however, it is difficult to generalize beyond the very tentative comments made above. It is certain, though, that the latent roles of the bureaucracy, as well as the more overt functions, must be examined if we are to understand the full impact of the bureaucratic institution in Latin America. This requires that we abandon approaches that examine public bureaucracy in artificial iso-lation from its political context.

NOTES

1. Outstanding exceptions are Daland (1967) and Graham (1968).

2. Graham (1968, pp. 6ff.). Daland (1967, Chap. 5) makes much the same argument for the Brazilian system.

3. Vernon's (1963) Chapter 5 contains his extended arguments.

4. Scott's general analysis is indicative of the findings of practically all of the admittedly scarce literature in this area.

5. For a perceptive analysis of pluralism, see Bachrach (1967).

SUGGESTED READINGS

Campos, Roberto de Oliveira. *Reflections on Latin American Development.* Austin: University of Texas Press, 1967.

Daland, Robert T. *Brazilian Planning.* Chapel Hill: University of North Carolina Press, 1967.

Daland, Robert T. "Development Administration and the Brazilian Political System." *Western Political Quarterly*, 21, No. 2 (June 1968), 325–339.

Denton, Charles F. "Bureaucracy in an Immobilist Society: The Case of Costa Rica." *Administrative Science Quarterly*, 14, No. 3 (September 1969), 418–425.

Gomez, Rudolph. *The Peruvian Administrative System.* Boulder: University of Colorado Press, 1969.

Graham, Lawrence S. *Civil Service Reform in Brazil: Principles versus Practice.* Austin: University of Texas Press, 1968.

Grimes, C. E., and Charles Simmons. "Bureaucracy and Political Control in Mexico: Towards an Assessment." *Public Administration Review*, 29 (January-February 1969), 72–79.

Groves, Roderick T. "Administrative Reform and the Politics of Reform: The Case of Venezuela." *Public Administration Review*, 27, No. 5 (December 1967), 436–445.

Henry, Laurin L. "Public Administration and Civil Service." In Harold E. Davis, ed., *Government and Politics in Latin America*. New York: Ronald Press, 1958. Pp. 477–495.

Kriesbert, Martin. *Public Administration in Developing Countries*. Washington, D.C.: Brookings Institution, 1965.

LaPalombara, Joseph, ed. *Bureaucracy and Political Development*. Princeton, N.J.: Princeton University Press, 1963.

Montgomery, John D., and William J. Siffin, eds. *Approaches to Development: Politics, Administration, and Change*. New York: McGraw-Hill, 1966.

Parrish, Charles J., and Jorge Tapia-Videla. "Welfare Policy and Administration in Chile." *Journal of Comparative Administration*, 1, No. 4 (February 1970), 455–476.

Poitras, Guy, and Charles F. Denton. "Bureaucratic Role Perceptions: Case Studies from Mexico and Costa Rica." *Journal of Comparative Administration*, 3, No. 2 (August 1971), 169–187.

Riggs, Fred W. *Administration in Developing Countries: The Theory of Prismatic Society*. Boston: Houghton Mifflin, 1964.

Scott, Robert E. "The Government Bureaucrats and Political Change in Latin America." *Journal of International Affairs*, 20, No. 2 (1965), 289–308.

OUTPUTS OF THE
POLITICAL PROCESS

The model presented in Chapter I emphasized politics as a system of interactions, involving a process whereby inputs of different types are converted by the authoritative decision-making agencies into policy outputs. These outputs in turn become part of the environment of the political system, conditioning and affecting political inputs either directly through the feedback process or more indirectly through other media. The process is, then, essentially without an end.

It has been argued that the political system is only a component of a much larger environment, the broader units being the national society and the international community of states. Attempts have been made to examine some of the more important ways in which the socioeconomic context conditions and patterns political interactions. An examination that omits environmental factors is incomplete at best. The economic context, another subunit of the general social system, has been given special attention because of its considerable direct impact on Latin American political systems.

The more immediately political environment was considered in the discussion of the legal and institutional context. The constitutional framework, the legal structure, and the dominant political institutional pattern of a system have considerable impact on how political interaction is patterned and on how conflicts are resolved.

The nature of the political-input process has been a recurrent theme of the volume. We have examined the major issues that dominate the Latin American political process, that is, the problems and issues that are fed into the political decision-making process as articulated interests or supports. Following this discussion was an examination of the interest-articulation process, with attention focused on those groups that generate the major inputs. The *process* of interest articulation has been emphasized—which groups and interests are represented, what types of issues are presented, how they are pursued, how strong the various groups are. Then the role of political parties was considered, especially in terms of what input functions are performed and how parties perform them. Thus, while the activities of various groups and institutions have been examined, the focus has been on what functions, especially input functions, are performed by these forces in their political roles.

The discussion of the authoritative decision-making activities and agencies included an examination of the institutions, such as the presidency and the bureaucracy. These are the agencies that produce the system's outputs, although the multifunctional character of these institutions in most of the countries should not be overlooked.

The analysis, to this point at least, has not explicitly focused on the content of policy output. A reasonably complete examination should include a clear and unified effort to investigate, and generalize from, the apparent patterns of the policy choices which present themselves in the Latin American countries. There will be some repetition of themes outlined either explicitly or, more likely, implicitly in previous chapters, but which must be reemphasized here in a different context. Thus, in this chapter we will be explicitly concerned with the actual outcomes of political interactions as different forces vie for the scarce resources of their societies.

As Litt (1969) and Lowi (1969), among others, have pointed out, policy output has long been the one subject most ignored by political scientists. Certainly the analyst with a social-science background and orientation approaches this topic with some trepidation where nations such as those of Latin America are involved—nations where relatively little is known even about inputs.

In view of the importance of policies actually pursued by decision makers, it is somewhat surprising and disappointing to discover that so few efforts have been made to describe and analyze the actual patterns of governmental policies, except in the broadest outlines. Data on expenditures are imprecise and often completely lacking. In important areas such as activities and control of government enterprises and corporations, virtually no reliable information is available. Even more important is the general lack of rigorous study of governmental regulation and subsidization of various economic activities.

THE EXTRACTION OF RESOURCES

In order for a system to be capable of allocating resources, it first must be capable of obtaining political values to distribute to the various groups which compete for them. Table XI-1 provides data on sources of the most formal and institutional of political resources—

TABLE XI-1. Government Revenue Sources (percentage of total current revenues), excluding Cuba.

Country	Nontax Revenues 1961	Nontax Revenues 1968	Indirect Taxes 1961	Indirect Taxes 1968	Income Taxes 1961	Income Taxes 1968
Argentina	10.6	16.1	70.3	65.4	19.1	18.5
Bolivia	3.1	7.7	81.1	68.1	15.8	24.2
Brazil	10.3	1.9	62.8	76.7	26.9	21.4
Chile	4.1	4.3	67.5	63.3	28.4	32.4
Colombia	7.0	4.2	44.4	49.5	48.6	46.3
Costa Rica	17.1	12.6	70.7	70.7	12.2	16.7
Dominican Republic	13.9	10.5	70.7	73.2	8.4	16.4
Ecuador	11.8	12.8	73.1	75.5	15.1	11.7
El Salvador	11.6	6.9	78.6	73.3	9.8	19.8
Guatemala	27.9	15.7	64.5	73.1	7.6	11.2
Haiti	31.0	44.1	61.6	49.0	7.4	6.9
Honduras	11.5	8.0	76.0	65.4	12.5	26.6
Mexico	12.7	10.1	52.1	44.3	35.2	45.6
Nicaragua	5.2	9.6	86.8	79.7	8.9	10.7
Panama	27.8	23.2	55.5	45.1	16.7	31.7
Paraguay	6.7	5.6	84.1	83.3	9.2	11.1
Peru	14.7	7.9	45.1	59.8	40.2	32.3
Uruguay	11.6	9.4	85.4	83.7	3.0	6.9
Venezuela	31.3	37.2	28.1	15.2	40.6	47.6
Average	15.0	12.7	56.4	55.8	28.6	31.5

Source: Socio-Economic Progress in Latin America: Social Progress Trust Fund Ninth Annual Report, 1969 (Washington, D.C.: Inter-American Development Bank, 1970), p. 74.

government revenues. These revenues are undoubtedly one of the
most important types of resources which are allocable and certainly
the most tangible. As can be seen from the data, the effects of taxes on
the distribution of wealth and more specifically income did not change
very much in the eight-year period which largely coincides with the
period of the Alliance for Progress. As a percentage of total governmental revenues, indirect taxes, which are usually regressive by nature, changed less than 1 per cent, declining from a level of 56.4 per
cent in 1961 to 55.8 per cent seven years later. While the revenue
structure of thirteen of the countries improved in terms of a more
progressive tax system, there was an actual deterioration in six, based
upon the fact that the relative proportion of income taxes declined.
Those nations experiencing significant income-tax increases tend to be
the small ones, such as El Salvador and Panama. Equally important,
those experiencing deterioration—Argentina, Brazil, Ecuador, Peru,
Colombia, and Haiti—account for almost 60 per cent of Latin America's population.

Income Taxes

Since income taxes are more likely to be levied primarily on members of the prestige classes, the fact that this source of income for
formal governmental institutions has increased in some countries may
be indicative of several factors. It could reveal a new attitude toward
paying taxes on the part of members of the prestige classes, that is, a
more favorable disposition toward contributing a greater portion of
their wealth. It might imply that enforcement techniques have been
improved by authoritative decision makers, or it may be that the prestige classes are obtaining a larger share of the resources allocated and
are willing to pay proportionally more. Probably the increase is the
result of a combination of all three factors.

However, the fact that only six of the nations receive more than 30
per cent of revenues from income taxes should be reemphasized. In
contrast, only two countries receive less than 45 per cent of revenues
from indirect taxation, and thirteen get 60 per cent or more of their
revenue from that source. The pattern of regressive taxation clearly
indicates that the political systems tend to extract proportionately
more from members of the lower social sectors, converting values into
benefits for the upper sectors, the latter receiving a disproportionately
large share.

Nontax Revenues

Of the nontax sources of revenue, most significant is the capital which originates from foreign sources. Between 1961 and 1968 nineteen of the governments (Cuban data are not available) received $7.8 billion in financing from abroad, of which $4.3 billion came from one country, the United States (Inter-American Development Bank, 1970, p. 80). The sums originating from abroad are so significant that it is difficult to envision the survival of a particular system in most of the countries without them. If the United States were to refuse any of the Latin American countries the resources upon which they have come to depend, a dysfunction would be quickly created not only within the political system itself but also in its socioeconomic environments. To be capable of extracting this public capital from the United States, it is usually necessary for the Latin American countries to meet conditions and to create systematic outputs favored by United States policy makers, and to provide protection for private investors. United States influence has not led to major changes in methods of extraction and allocation. On the whole, the interests of the United States as perceived by the State Department, the Department of Defense, and other relevant agencies converge nicely with those in positions of dominance in the Latin American countries. The United States bias toward political stability, privately capitalized economies, and the preservation of certain security interests in foreign-policy initiatives has not required significant changes in traditional patterns. The effects of United States private investment in the economies of the Latin American nations have been assessed in an earlier chapter.

Other nontax sources of revenue include the sale and production of commodities and services. This source can include everything from the manufacture of liquor and the operation of an airline to the sale of timber on publicly owned lands.

THE EXTRACTION OF COMPLIANCE

Equally important to the success of any system is the extraction of compliance from its environment. As Easton (1957) states, a steady flow of supports is maintained through a process of political socialization and through outputs that meet the demands of the members of the society. Lipset (1959b) asserts that legitimacy—political allegiance—involves the capacity of a political system to engender and maintain the belief that existing political institutions are the most appropriate ones for the society. The socialization process and the media of socialization are responsible for fulfilling this function. The political-socialization process has been discussed in a number of places throughout this volume. In the context of the discussion here, it is important only to note that the process is essentially a bifurcated one throughout the twenty nations. The people who matter politically, the small prestige class, are socialized to provide one type of support, while those who do not count politically, the large proportion of the working class, are socialized in such a fashion that the customary product is apathy. Apathy supports are similar to satisfaction supports because they allow authoritative decision makers more latitude in the decision-making process; the decision makers need consider fewer external pressures.

Members of the prestige class are socialized into believing that the system can be a legitimate one only if certain of their needs are met. The scarcity of resources and the inability of political systems to meet the demands of the prestige classes and the mobilized sectors of the working class result in a continuous change in certain kinds of formal institutions and in what appears to be instability. In fact, as Needler (1968) points out, it may be more apt to describe the situation in Latin America as one of "permanent instability," a subject discussed more completely at the end of this chapter. First, however, it is necessary to look more directly at the outputs of the Latin American authoritative decision-making process.

THE ALLOCATION OF RESOURCES

Central to this volume is the order of priorities placed on the expenditure of revenues and other resources by the Latin American authoritative decision makers. Table XI-2 provides an area overview and a country-by-country examination of revenue and expenditure patterns of the past decade. As related to gross national product, a very rough estimate of the resources available in a system, the areawide figures are interesting. They indicate that while GNP increased by 48 per cent from 1961 to 1969, revenues increased by 57 per cent, a point referred to in the previous section of this chapter. However, governmental expenditures kept pace with neither GNP nor revenue increases; in fact, they fell 22 per cent behind the more relevant figure for revenue increases.

The individual-country analysis indicates that the countries can be

TABLE XI-2. Government Revenue and Expenditure Patterns, excluding Cuba and Haiti.

Country	Index of Increase in GNP, 1961-1969[a]	Index of Domestic Revenue Increase, 1961-1969[a]	Index of Expenditure Increase, 1961-1969[a]	Tax Revenues as Per Cent of GNP, 1969[b]	Expenditures as Per Cent of GNP, 1969
Argentina	127	125	116	15.2	19.2
Bolivia	154	185	191	10.4	19.8
Brazil	143	178	107	15.1	15.5
Chile	136	169	155	21.3	27.1
Colombia	147	153	147	10.6	12.2
Costa Rica	167	194	183	15.3	18.9
Dominican Republic	143	142	127	16.8	18.2
Ecuador	149	159 (1968)	152 (1968)	20.8 (1968)	22.0 (1968)
El Salvador	162	155	162	12.4	14.9
Guatemala	149	172	169	9.3	10.2
Honduras	149	168	183	11.9	15.6
Mexico	176	205	185	8.3	12.8
Nicaragua	165	181	198	10.2	12.4
Panama	179	186	213	14.5	21.3
Paraguay	139	201	245	12.9	17.3
Peru	139	156	167	17.1	17.5
Uruguay	103	65	79	12.7	14.8
Venezuela	162	138	139	20.0	26.2
Average	148	157	135	13.9	17.0

a. 1961 = 100.
b. Tax revenues do not include all government revenues.

Source: Adapted from Office of Development Programs, Bureau for Latin America, Agency for International Development, *Summary Economic and Social Indicators 18 Latin American Countries: 1960-1970* (Washington, D.C.: Government Printing Office, April 1971), pp. 4, 22, 23, 33, 34.

roughly divided into three groups: (1) those with significant increases in revenue extraction relative to GNP; (2) those with approximately the same increases in both revenue extraction and GNP; and (3) those with significant declines in revenue extraction relative to GNP. Only five countries fit into this last category, Peru's decline is so slight that

Group 1
Chile
Paraguay
Bolivia
Argentina
Guatemala
Ecuador
Mexico
Honduras

Group 2
Nicaragua
Dominican Republic
El Salvador
Panama
Brazil
Peru

Group 3
Colombia
Costa Rica
Uruguay
Venezuela

it has been placed in the middle group, and two of these are the very small countries of Costa Rica and Uruguay. Although this pattern is mixed, it is encouraging in the sense that only four countries, and only two large ones showed sharp declines over the last decade.

Table XI-3 provides preliminary data demonstrating the priorities placed on three major categories of expenditures. In most of the countries, the military (defense) and education are principal competitors for resources. This situation in itself provides some reasons for the traditional antagonisms between the teachers and students on the one hand and the military on the other. (The reasons for the relatively large military expenditures were discussed in Chapter VIII.)

Since the basic patterns of political relations in Latin American systems have in general been stable over the past decade, it is probably

TABLE XI-3.   Resource Allocation in Selected Categories, excluding Cuba and Haiti, 1969.

Country	Defense		Agricultural Development		Education	
	Percentage of Total Expenditures	Index of Expenditures[a]	Percentage of Total Expenditures	Index of Expenditures[a]	Percentage of Total Expenditures	Index of Expenditures[a]
Argentina	11.4	101	1.4	105	11.4	178
Bolivia	8.8	103	3.9	313	16.7	194
Brazil	16.2	231	3.0	194	5.9	188
Chile	7.3	99	7.9	225	17.6	196
Colombia	10.5	125	8.2	221	15.7	198
Costa Rica	-	-	4.8	227	29.0	252
Dominican Republic	13.0	71	7.4	124	15.7	218
Ecuador	7.8	136	N.A.	N.A.	N.A.	N.A.
El Salvador	20.3	455	12.5	879	20.1	175
Guatemala	9.6	170	3.9	141	18.5	150
Honduras	14.3	225	4.7	142	17.2	191
Mexico	5.4	179	8.5	190	16.9	253
Nicaragua	11.8	148	8.4	316	19.6	290
Panama	0.7	259	5.2	850	24.1	233
Paraguay	11.2	190	3.2	272	10.2	204
Peru	19.5	213	6.4	301	24.0	189
Uruguay	12.9	119	4.4	168	27.7	157
Venezuela	7.6	156	8.8	131	12.7	217
Average	10.8	154	5.5	177	13.2	204

a. 1961 = 100.

Source: Adapted from Office of Development Programs, Bureau for Latin America, Agency for International Development, *Summary Economic and Social Indicators 18 Latin American Countries: 1960-1970* (Washington, D.C.: Government Printing Office, April 1971), pp. 40, 42, 44, 46, 62, 64.

safe to assume that resources are being allocated in such a way as to satisfy those groups or individuals in the political system capable of making demands and providing support to the polity. Clearly, the military in most of the countries must be placated with large shares of the resources, or it will move to take what it wants. The patterns of taxation and spending provide some illumination of this point. Because of the lack of information, the observer is sharply limited in the generalizations that can safely be made.

Defense

Of interest is the relationship between military expenditures and the existence of a polity dominated by military forces. At least ten countries in the region spend more than 10 per cent of their budgets on defense, for forces having little if any military defense function. Brazil and Peru spend 16 and 20 per cent respectively. No data are available for Cuba and Haiti. With the exception of Colombia and Uruguay, there is a clear relationship between military rule and the position of the military in the politics of the nation. Only Ecuador has a ruling military and does not appear on the list, and the decline in that country has only occurred since 1968, being 9.8 per cent in 1967. On the other hand, the countries spending least, in relative terms, on the military are those having the least "politicized" military establishments, these being Chile, Mexico, and Costa Rica, with Uruguay being a curious exception, even as far back as 1965. The situation in Colombia is not as deviant as it first appears, ranking third on the list. As late as 1957, Colombia was experiencing military rule, and the military acted as final arbiter of the civil war that raged in the country *(La Violencia)*. Since that time, the military has maintained itself in a threatening, potentially interventionist role.

It is only fair to note that the general recent pattern has been a definite decline in the amount of the budget consumed by the military in most of the countries. In only four—Brazil, Peru, Colombia, and Uruguay—has the share increased; but the increase has been considerably in Brazil and Peru, two large and populous states. Furthermore, in terms of their function of meeting external threats, the amount these organizations receive remains great. For example, for eighteen Latin American countries (excluding Haiti and Cuba), the average percentage of budget going for defense in 1969 was 11.0; in contrast, the percentage being allocated for the vast project of educating these large populations was 13.3, and even that represented a 4.5 per cent increase over the decade (Office of Development Programs, 1971).

Education

Although the allocations for education have risen dramatically over the past ten years, they are insufficient by many criteria. Between 1960 and 1969 the ratio of pupil to teacher in the schools actually deteriorated in the area as a whole (Inter-American Development Bank, 1970, p. 142). One of every four Latin Americans continues to be officially illiterate, while functional illiteracy raises the number to an incalculably higher ratio. Retention of students in school continues to be a major problem, although exact data are not available on this problem. Students dropping out, illiteracy, schools with abnormally high pupil-teacher ratios, all undoubtedly affect members of the lower social sectors of the Latin American countries much more severely than they do members of the prestige classes. Only 61 per cent of children in the 5–14 age group are even enrolled in the schools, and the ones who are not undoubtedly are those with fewest status and economic resources.

The increased emphasis on education in the allocations would lead to the impression that there would be more upward social mobility and certainly a larger pool of technology than there actually is in any of the countries. The fact that there is not more upward social mobility has at least partly been explained in the discussion of intraclass mobility, while the lack of technology in relation to investment in education can be attributed to a scale of values which assigns certain professions, such as business and the sciences, less prestige than is accorded in more economically developed societies. For the time being, the largest part of the Latin American educational establishment is dedicated to carrying out the function of political socialization and adapting the citizenry to the immobilist systems in which they are to live all their lives.

Agriculture

Expenditure for the agricultural sector, while still substantially lower in most of the countries than those for the military or education, has increased—dramatically in some countries—during the past decade. Only five of the eighteen countries for which we have adequate figures experienced less than a 50 per cent increase in expenditure from 1961 to 1969. Twelve of the eighteen countries have experienced increases of more than 200 per cent. The sharp increases are not confined to those countries experimenting with land reform.

Bureaucratic Salaries

The significance of the data in Table XI-3, however, is not only the story they tell but the one they do not tell. As noted in Chapter III, the most significant type of resource allocation in several of the countries is that of salaries to public administrators. Needless to say, even in the data in Table XI-3, salaries comprise a major proportion of the resources allocated to each area. As Felix (1961, p. 317) argues, it seems quite apparent that expansion of governmental activities, with the attendant expansion of payrolls, has been a goal of white-collar and professional groups, to stabilize and perhaps even improve their positions vis-à-vis lower-class groups.

> As the expansion of private employment slowed with the slackening growth of the economy, the white collar and professional classes used their political influence to expand government employment rolls, the largest increase in the salary share of government budget paralleling the drop in public capital expenditures.

Agronomists, economists, statisticians, planners, educational administrators—the list of prestige-class positions is endless—no doubt have managed to retain a sizable portion of the increases for themselves. These resources are allocated as much for the function of maintaining the legitimacy of the system as for the ostensible official function.

THE ECONOMIC ROLE OF GOVERNMENT

Aids to Private Business

The private business sector in most Latin American countries is one of the more important interest groups and one of the most effective in making demands on decision makers. Systemic outputs seem to reflect the favored position of the economic elites. One of the most important aids received by business is an advantageous corporate tax structure. Even though large-scale manufacturing and industrial enterprises represent some of the most significant concentrations of wealth in money-poor countries, the admittedly fragmentary data available indicate that taxes on these enterprises are quite low compared to the burden placed on other sectors.

Another indicator of the favored position given business, especially the large-scale enterprises, is the protection provided by high tariff barriers on goods competing with locally made products. These barriers—long present but especially raised since 1930, when import substitution was viewed as the cure-all or at least partial solution to economic underdevelopment—have been largely maintained at the insistence of the favored industries and manufacturers. The result has been the development of inefficient, noncompetitive enterprises that perpetuate underdevelopment, inflation, and general economic weakness. For the general consumer the result is high price for low-quality goods, with the greatest impact falling on those least able to manipulate their environment, the working classes.

Government Ownership or Subsidy

On an increasing scale Latin American governments are becoming directly involved in government-owned and -operated economic enterprises or at least partly governmentally financed projects. Almost without exception, these are activities that the private business sector refuses to undertake but which decision makers, including the economic elites, think desirable or necessary. Two components of elite attitudes are important in this context. First, in the period since 1930 and especially since World War II, there has been considerable importance attached to the concept of economic development. Second, a dominant theme in elite attitudes has been that economic activity and development should be largely, though not entirely, pursued in a framework of private enterprise, privately capitalized. This attitude has been reinforced by the position of the United States government and the often considerable pressures it can apply. Combined, these attitudes have meant that while government capital has been used to initiate projects for which (1) private capital was lacking in sufficient amounts (for example, steel mills, irrigation projects, power facilities) and/or (2) risks are so great as to deter private investment (for example, government subsidization of tourist facilities), the governmental role has been restricted and, more importantly, has been strongly influenced and even dominated by private interests. According to Petras, 35 per cent of the large firms and 14 per cent of the medium-sized firms in Chile were established with state aid as a major factor. In his study of managerial attitudes, Petras (1970, pp. 50–51) found that almost one-half the managers of large firms and one-third the managers of medium-sized firms expect state aid, while less than 10 per cent of small-firm managers entertain hope for aid.

It should come as no surprise, then, that government capitalization and subsidization of particular enterprises goes hand in hand with the desires of the economic elites that have themselves such a strong voice in decision making. Furthermore, state intervention provides an opportunity for the nonpropertied sectors of the prestige class to have a direct influence in the development process. This latter factor should not be underestimated. The importance for system stability of the government bureaucracies as a source of white-collar, prestige-class jobs for the ever growing number of well-educated youth with relatively high aspirations has been noted. Over the long run this development of a burgeoning bureaucracy staffed by well-trained and ambitious white-collar groups promises some reasonably important changes in Latin American systems, including ever increasing pressures for a larger governmental role in economic development and for more resources to build the bureaucracies themselves. This trend seems well developed in countries like Mexico, Chile, Uruguay, and Argentina.

Government Intervention and Regulation

It appears that only rarely in Latin America can governmental decision makers act to impede or curtail the interests of private capital, being especially aware of the interests of the large manufacturing and industrial enterprises upon which most of the economic-development hopes and possibilities are based. The Venezuelan industrial community's success in keeping that country out of the Andean Group in the face of President Caldera's open and strong endorsement of the integration movement is only a more obvious example of a widespread pattern of influence and activity. While government activity in so-called business ventures is increasing, such activity is not opposed by the private business sector but is in fact regularly supported. Not infrequently the initiative for government intervention comes from sectors of the business or agricultural community.

In this same context, it must be noted that government regulation of business activity, where it exists on any significant scale, has come into being to meet demands of the large-scale enterprises. Antitrust legislation is virtually nonexistent, regulation of business practices—such as that supposedly carried out by the Federal Trade Commission in the United States—is not provided for, and minimum-wage levels are subjects normally beyond the fringe of political discussion.

Restriction of Labor

At the same time, labor (urban and rural) is subjected to strong restrictions in a variety of ways. Where allowed to exist, unions can usually be organized only at the plant level, not on an industry-wide scale. Unionization figures verify the difficulty. No more than 15 per cent of Latin American industrial workers are organized at all; this percentage is almost surely an exaggeration of true membership numbers and includes even the most ineffective and company-dominated organizations. Virtually none of the rural working class has been organized; the only wide-scale effort has been made in Chile in the past five years under the leadership of the major political parties.

Similarly, labor has not been successful in wrenching rewards from the system in terms of social-security benefits, improvements in working conditions, health insurance, credit unions, minimum wages, or other similar outputs. It is true that hundreds of laws have been passed, and in some of the countries these laws rival those of practically any industrialized country in terms of providing for workers' welfare. The general conclusion of students of the Latin American labor movement, however, is that these laws are largely symbolic outputs and are usually nonimplemented (Alba, 1962).

In a few countries an elite of organized workers in crucial industries, usually the export-oriented enterprises, has been able to pressure the system for the same kinds of benefits given workers in the more economically advanced countries. In all of the Latin American states this group remains very small.

In virtually none of the countries can agricultural workers organize, and even where not illegal unionization is prohibited on anything larger than the individual unit of property. The poverty of the rural workers is such that even the *favelas, ranchos,* and *callampas* are perceived to be improvements, as is evidenced by the continued high emigration from rural areas. In other words, there are so few political goods and services provided the rural working man that he is willing to uproot his family and break personal bonds to enter an unfamiliar and forbidding environment. The correlations between rurality and lack of schools, housing, electricity, and similar goods and services are so striking as to demand attention and reemphasize the lack of input capabilities of the rural working class.

OUTPUT INEQUALITY AND SYSTEM STABILITY

In general, then, the outputs of the Latin American political process, insofar as the data allow for generalization, reflect the input process examined in previous chapters. Those groups that are organized, cohesive, and in control of social and economic resources—almost invariably members of the prestige classes—maintain, protect, and often reinforce their positions by controlling political outputs. The upper socioeconomic classes are relatively lightly taxed, their economic activities are relatively unregulated, governmental subsidies and other assistance are provided to major economic interests (including agriculture), government jobs are being provided on an increasing scale for the white-collar sectors (while in contrast the figures for unemployment and underemployment in the working classes are astronomical and may be rising, especially for underemployment). Social security and similar benefits, good schools, electricity, potable water, paved roads, subsidies, and so forth are all more widely available to the prestige class and the areas where they reside than to the workers and peasants. Such inequalities appear in all social systems to some degree; however, the degree of inequality in outputs in most Latin American countries is severe and is accented by the initial scarcity of resources.

Finally, it should be noted that the upper classes in any society have less need for governmental assistance than do lower-class groups. Their social and economic position enables them to provide well for themselves, relative to the rest of the population. It is the working classes that must look to political decision makers for betterment of their situation, usually through changing at least some of the social rules and institutions. Therefore, the lack of access to political decision makers and the subsequent failure of decision makers to consider working-class demands, except in terms of occasional symbolic rewards, are made even more significant.

In one of the most outstanding pieces of comparative research related to Latin America to appear in many years, Bwy (1968, p. 20) argues, with impressive data in support, that there is a close relationship between satisfaction and political instability in Latin America:

> While we may not be able to say that "dissatisfaction" then, is a sufficient condition for political instability, the available theoretical and empirical evidence presented thus far does strongly suggest that it comes close to being a necessary condition.

Satisfaction, dissatisfaction, change, nonchange—all depend on the criteria employed by a particular analyst. Needler (1968) discusses five different types of change which could occur in a Latin American system. The first involves an addition or subtraction in the set of groups participating in the polity. Such extreme instability happens only rarely in Latin America; the cases of Mexico, Cuba, and Bolivia (since partly reversed) come to mind. Argentina also may have experienced this type of change during the *peronista* period. The second type of change is in the way that groups act politically. Latin American groups have demonstrated an incredible versatility in this area and this is no doubt one of the reasons that basic social patterns have been so resilient. Needler talks of change in dominance relations, or revolution, which does require the use of violence. This has happened in Mexico, Cuba, and Bolivia in the Latin American area. Changes in elements of the polity, Needler's fourth category, have been quite rare; while change introduced deliberately by those in authority, the fifth category, has been the uncommon type of institutional change in Latin America. For members of the lower classes this has usually meant little or no significant change at all.

SUMMARY

The distribution of policy outputs of Latin American political systems reflects the patterns of inputs discussed in earlier chapters. While empirical analyses focusing on policy outputs are exceedingly rare, some generalizations seem warranted in the context of available data.

Resources are largely extracted from those least able to "pay" financially or otherwise, although the situation may be improving. Compliance is maintained by a socialization process that produces apathy within most of the working class. Furthermore, in terms of allocating the scarce resources available, most budgetary resources are apparently being allocated for essentially nonproductive purposes, such as for a military that has no external defense function and for salaries for prestige-class bureaucrats. Emphasis on economic development on a private-enterprise basis has reinforced the favored position of the business and propertied interests. Governmental elites have rarely intervened to oppose major economic interests. On the other hand, with the exception of a very thin stratum of workers in basic industries in a few countries, the working class, rural and urban, has received little more than symbolic rewards.

If accurately interpreted, these patterns clearly conform to expectations based on the analysis in previous chapters. The socioeconomic environment, the relative political influence of different groups, the methods of articulating political demands, and other features of the Latin American systems all point to the type of output pattern outlined here. While some changes are occurring that may modify these patterns, at the same time there is little reason to believe that basic alterations are imminent. In contrast, for most of the countries, present output patterns will apparently remain with only minor changes.

SUGGESTED READINGS

Anderson, Charles W. *Politics and Economic Change in Latin America: The Governing of Restless Nations*, Part II. Princeton, N.J.: Van Nostrand, 1967.

Cotler, Julio. "The Mechanics of Internal Domination and Social Change in Peru." *Studies in Comparative International Development*, 2, No. 3 (June 1966).

González Navarro, Moisés. "Mexico: The Lop-Sided Revolution." In Claudio Véliz, ed., *Obstacles to Change in Latin America*. New York: Oxford University Press, 1965. Pp. 206–229.

Gordon, Wendell C. *The Political Economy of Latin America*. New York: Columbia University Press, 1965.

Horowitz, Irving Louis. "Electoral Politics, Urbanization, and Social Development in Latin America." *Urban Affairs Quarterly*, 2, No. 3 (March 1967).

Sunkel, Osvaldo. "Change and Frustration in Chile." In Claudio Véliz, ed., *Obstacles to Change in Latin America*. New York: Oxford University Press, 1965. Pp. 116–144.

EPILOG: Toward a Theory of
Latin American Politics

There have been numerous attempts made in recent years, using varying types of criteria, to rank the nations of the Latin American area. Several of these attempts are particularly significant to the field of political science. Fitzgibbon has been ranking the nations for more than twenty years, reporting periodically on where each country stands in relation to others (see Fitzgibbon, 1967). He polls leading Latin Americanists from various fields both within the United States and from abroad, and on the basis of their expert opinions compiles his rank orderings. His indices have been institutional primarily, however, and there seems to be a decided bias in favor of polities of the type found in the United States and Western Europe. Bwy's (1968) variables are similar to those used by Fitzgibbon. Both Bwy and Fitzgibbon view "democracy" and "instability" as more or less juxtaposed or perhaps in opposition to each other. However, as discussed by Midlarsky and Tanter (1967), this may not always be the case.

Duff and McCamant (1968), concerned

221

with stability, base their assessments on such factors as the rates of economic growth in each country, on whether or not a nation has a broad-based political party or parties, income distribution, and political capabilities. Duff and McCamant's rank orderings differ considerably from Fitzgibbon's.

The failure among political scientists concerned with comparing a group of systems with another to agree on the variables to be used in the comparisons is a principal detriment to this sort of enterprise. To lend more weight to one type of electoral system or party than to another is as dangerous as it would be to attempt to allocate some comparative values or indices to a transistor radio and a *sarape*, an automobile and a *mola*, or a northern suburban home and a *piraqua*. As a result of the difficulties inherent in making this type of ranking, which inevitably contains personal or cultural biases, this volume does not contain a rank ordering of the countries. There are certainly sufficient data presented to permit the reader to set up his own rank orderings if he wishes. But it will also have to be up to the reader to weigh his own variables. It is suggested that a preferable course of action would be first to read the articles cited, and then to determine whether further action of this sort is desirable or needed. At minimum the reader will have to determine whether he desires to rank the countries according to stability, instability, potential for revolution, or degree of democratic content.

HYPOTHESES ABOUT THE POLITICAL PROCESS

Undoubtedly a more profitable type of comparison is to develop some preliminary hypotheses about Latin American political processes and then to test them in terms of data collected in each of the countries. The hypotheses can then be refined and revised as required until some fairly empirically testable generalizations can be tied into a general theory about politics in this particular area of the world. Six hypotheses are presented below, all of which can serve as starting points for further research on one, several, or all of the Latin American nations. The reader is encouraged to develop others, to modify those offered, or to restrict his attention to any single problem which they represent.

1. The scarcity of all types of resources has meant that members of these societies have looked to their political systems for arbitration in

disputes which could be settled without the use of authority in the more economically developed areas of the world.

2. Political systems have become so concerned with the distribution of resources that relatively little effort has been expended in attempting to expand the total amount of resources available.

3. The scarcity of resources has been so pronounced that even among the participant classes there has been little willingness to compromise, authoritative decisions are not often regarded as binding by the losers in a dispute, and the frequent change in decision makers is a consequence of this attitudinal pattern.

4. A consensus has arisen among the participant classes that the use of the latent strength of the nonparticipant masses to lend weight to one side in a dispute over resources does not extend participation to the masses except in the most formal sense.

5. The systematic exclusion of the masses from sharing in the resources has led not to alienation as much as to apathy.

6. International intervention, private and public, has led to a decrease in the number of resources available for allocation by authoritative decision makers.

SOURCES OF INFORMATION

Undoubtedly the greatest obstacle to the study of Latin American politics is the paucity of data and information sources on the subject. Regular inspection of most North American newspapers, news magazines, and other periodical publications gives the impression that Latin America either does not exist or is so quiescent as to be unworthy of attention. Of the major daily newspapers of the United States, the *Miami Herald* devotes more lineage to Latin American news than any other. The firm publishes an Air Express Edition which is available daily in the capital cities of all of the hemisphere nations and can be obtained within the United States by special arrangement. The *New York Times, Washington Post, St. Louis Post Dispatch*, and *New Orleans Picayune* carry Latin American political news on a fairly regular basis.

Also available to those particularly interested in the area are a weekly paper published in Washington, D.C., *The Times of the Americas*, and a monthly digest published at the University of Wisconsin entitled *Air Mail News from Latin America*.

There are several social-science journals which are devoted to reporting on research efforts in progress or completed in the Latin American area. The *Latin American Research Review*, published at the

University of Texas at Austin, is outstanding. The *Journal of Inter-American Studies* and *Inter-American Economic Affairs* contain articles of varying quality and in the case of the former not restricted to social science. Mexico's *Foro Internacional*, Chile's *Estudios Internacionales*, Argentina's *Revista Argentina*, and Brazil's *América Latina* carry a wide variety of articles written by Latin American scholars.

There is no substitute for field research in a country, an exercise which can provide a student with first-hand empirical data and an understanding of what makes the people of a country really tick. There has been a reduction in the amount of money available for scholarships and fellowships for study and travel in Latin America, but funds for outstanding students are always available. Much more difficult to obtain are grants for study in Cuba.

For those unable to make a trip to Latin America, statistical data are available from a number of sources. The United Nations Economic Commission for Latin America publishes an annual *Economic Survey of Latin America*. The *América en Cifras* series published by the Pan American Union is an excellent general source. The *Statistical Abstract of Latin America*, published by the University of California at Los Angeles, is improving with each yearly edition. For those who require more sophisticated material there are several Latin American data banks around the United States which will make their materials available for a modest price. The Demographic Institute of the University of Texas at Austin and the data banks at the University of Florida and at Stanford University are usually most cooperative.

Material on Individual Countries

There are some nations in the Latin American area which have never received an analysis of their whole political system. Other nations have experienced several. The list below is presented as a jumping-off point for the student rather than an extensive or comprehensive bibliography. New books are coming out all the time.

ARGENTINA

Blanksten, George I. *Peron's Argentina*. Chicago: University of Chicago Press, 1953.

Johnson, John J. *Political Change in Latin America*. Rev. ed.; Stanford, Calif.: Stanford University Press, 1965.

Snow, Peter G. *Political Forces in Argentina*. Boston: Allyn and Bacon, 1971.

Whitaker, Arthur P. *The United States and Argentina*. Cambridge: Harvard University Press, 1954.

BOLIVIA

Alexander, Robert J. "Bolivia: The National Revolution." In Martin C. Needler, ed., *The Political Systems of Latin America*. Princeton, N.J.: Van Nostrand, 1964.

Patch, Richard W. "Bolivia: United States Assistance in a Revolutionary Setting." In Richard N. Adams *et al.*, *Social Change in Latin America Today*. New York: Random House, 1960.

BRAZIL

Alexander, Robert J. *Labor Relations in Argentina, Brazil and Chile*. New York: McGraw-Hill, 1962.

Daland, Robert T. *Brazilian Planning*. Chapel Hill: University of North Carolina Press, 1967.

Furtado, Celso. *The Economic Growth of Brazil*. Berkeley: University of California Press, 1963.

Graham, Lawrence S. *Civil Service Reform in Brazil: Principles versus Practice*. Austin: University of Texas Press, 1968.

Hirschman, Albert O. *Journeys Toward Progress*. Garden City, N.Y.: Doubleday, 1965.

Schurz, William Lytle. *Brazil: The Infinite Country*. New York: Dutton, 1961.

Wagley, Charles. *An Introduction to Brazil*. New York: Macmillan, 1963.

CHILE

Gil, Federico. *The Political System of Chile*. Boston: Houghton Mifflin, 1966.

Gil, Federico, and Charles J. Parrish. *The Chilean Elections of 1964: An Analysis*. Washington, D.C.: Institute for the Comparative Study of Political Systems, 1964.

Hirschman, Albert O. *Journeys Toward Progress*. Garden City, N.Y.: Doubleday, 1965.

Johnson, John J. *Political Change in Latin America*. Rev. ed.; Stanford, Calif.: Stanford University Press, 1965.

Petras, James. *Politics and Social Forces in Chilean Development*. Berkeley: University of California Press, 1970.

Silvert, Kalman H. *The Conflict Society*. New York: American Universities Field Staff, 1966.

COLOMBIA

Fluharty, Vernon. *Dance of the Millions*. Pittsburgh: Pittsburgh University Press, 1957.

Hirschman, Albert O. *Journeys Toward Progress*. Garden City, N.Y.: Doubleday, 1965.

Martz, John D. *Colombia: A Contemporary Political Study*. Chapel Hill: University of North Carolina Press, 1962.

Payne, James L. *Patterns of Conflict in Colombia*. New Haven: Yale University Press, 1968.

Whitaker, Arthur P. *The United States and South America: The Northern Republics.* Cambridge: Harvard University Press, 1948.

COSTA RICA

Bussey, James L. *Notes on Costa Rican Democracy.* Boulder: University of Colorado Press, 1962.

Denton, Charles F. *Patterns of Costa Rican Politics.* Boston: Allyn and Bacon, 1971.

Goldrich, Daniel. *Sons of the Establishment.* Chicago: Rand McNally, 1966.

Martz, John D. *Central America.* Chapel Hill: University of North Carolina Press, 1959.

CUBA

Burks, David D. *Cuba under Castro.* New York: Foreign Policy Association, 1964.

Draper, Theodore. *Castro's Revolution.* New York: Praeger, 1962.

Goldenberg, Boris. *The Cuban Revolution and Latin America.* New York: Praeger, 1965.

Hansen, Joseph. *The Theory of the Cuban Revolution.* New York: Pioneer Publishers, 1962.

Huberman, Leo, and Paul Sweezy. *Cuba: Anatomy of a Revolution.* New York: Monthly Review Press, 1961.

Institute for International Social Research. *Attitudes of the Cuban People Toward the Castro Regime.* Princeton, N.J.: Princeton University Press, 1960.

Seers, Dudley, *et al. Cuba: The Economic and Social Revolution.* Chapel Hill: University of North Carolina Press, 1964.

DOMINICAN REPUBLIC

Bosch, Juan. *The Unfinished Experiment.* New York: Praeger, 1965.

de Galindez Suarez, Jesus. *La Era de Trujillo.* Santiago: Editorial del Pacifico, 1956.

Ornes, German E. *Trujillo: Little Caesar of the Caribbean.* New York: Thomas Nelson, 1958.

Szulc, Tad. *Dominican Diary.* New York: Delacorte Press, 1965.

ECUADOR

Blanksten, George I. "Ecuador: The Politics of Instability." In Martin C. Needler, ed., *The Political Systems of Latin America.* Princeton, N.J.: Van Nostrand, 1964.

Needler, Martin C. *Anatomy of a Coup d'Etat: Ecuador, 1963.* Washington, D.C.: Institute for the Comparative Study of Political Systems, 1964.

EL SALVADOR

Anderson, Charles W. "El Salvador." In Martin C. Needler, ed., *The Political Systems of Latin America.* Princeton, N.J.: Van Nostrand, 1964.

Martz, John D. *Central America.* Chapel Hill: University of North Carolina Press, 1959.

GUATEMALA
Adams, Richard N. "Social Change in Guatemala and United States Policy." In Richard N. Adams *et al., Social Change in Latin America Today.* New York: Random House, 1960.
Martz, John D. *Central America.* Chapel Hill: University of North Carolina Press, 1959.
Silvert, Kalman H. *The Conflict Society.* New York: American Universities Field Staff, 1966.
Whetten, Nathan L. *Guatemala: The Land and the People.* New Haven: Yale University Press, 1961.

HAITI
Logan, Rayford W., and Martin C. Needler. "Haiti." In Martin C. Needler, ed., *The Political Systems of Latin America.* Princeton, N.J.: Van Nostrand, 1964.
Rodman, Selden. *Haiti: The Black Republic.* New York: Devin-Adair, 1954.

HONDURAS
Anderson, Charles W. "Honduras: Problems of an Apprentice Democracy." In Martin C. Needler, ed., *The Political Systems of Latin America.* Princeton, N.J.: Van Nostrand, 1964.
Martz, John D. *Central America.* Chapel Hill: University of North Carolina Press, 1959.

MEXICO
Almond, Gabriel A., and Sidney Verba. *The Civic Culture.* Princeton, N.J.: Princeton University Press, 1963.
Cline, Howard F. *The United States and Mexico.* Cambridge: Harvard University Press, 1953.
Johnson, Kenneth F. *Mexican Democracy: A Critical View.* Boston: Allyn and Bacon, 1971.
Kling, Merle. *A Mexican Interest Group in Action.* Englewood Cliffs, N.J.: Prentice-Hall, 1961.
Lewis, Oscar. *The Children of Sanchez.* New York: Random House, 1961.
Padgett, L. Vincent. *The Mexican Political System.* Boston: Houghton Mifflin, 1966.
Schmitt, Karl. *Communism in Mexico.* Austin: University of Texas Press, 1965.
Scott, Robert E. *Mexican Government in Transition.* Urbana: University of Illinois Press, 1959.
Tannenbaum, Frank. *Mexico: The Struggle for Peace and Bread.* New York: Knopf, 1950.

NICARAGUA

Anderson, Charles W. "Nicaragua: The Somoza Dynasty." In Martin C. Needler, ed., *The Political Systems of Latin America*. Princeton, N.J.: Van Nostrand, 1964.

Martz, John D. *Central America*. Chapel Hill: University of North Carolina Press, 1959.

PANAMA

Biesanz, John, and Mavis Biesanz. *The People of Panama*. New York: Columbia University Press, 1955.

Dubois, Jules. *Danger Over Panama*. New York: Bobbs-Merrill, 1964.

Goldrich, Daniel. *Sons of the Establishment*. Chicago: Rand McNally, 1966.

Rodriguez, Mario. *Central America*. Englewood Cliffs, N.J.: Prentice-Hall, 1965.

PARAGUAY

Lott, Leo B. "Paraguay." In Martin C. Needler, ed., *The Political Systems of Latin America*. Princeton, N.J.: Van Nostrand, 1964.

Pendle, George. *Paraguay: A Riverside Nation*. London: Royal Institute of International Affairs, 1956.

Zook, David H., Jr. *The Conduct of the Chaco War*. New Haven: Bookman Associates, 1960.

PERU

Gomez, Rosendo A. "Peru: The Politics of Military Guardianship." In Martin C. Needler, ed., *The Political Systems of Latin America*. Princeton, N.J.: Van Nostrand, 1964.

Gomez, Rudolph. *The Peruvian Administrative System*. Boulder: University of Colorado Press, 1969.

Holmberg, Allan R. "Changing Community Attitudes and Values in Peru." In Richard N. Adams *et al.*, *Social Change in Latin America Today*. New York: Random House, 1960.

Kantor, Harry. *The Ideology and Program of the Peruvian APRISTA Movement*. Washington, D.C.: Saville Books, 1966.

URUGUAY

Fitzgibbon, Russell H. *Uruguay: Portrait of a Democracy*. New Brunswick, N.J.: Rutgers University Press, 1954.

Johnson, John J. *Political Change in Latin America*. Rev. ed.; Stanford, Calif.: Stanford University Press, 1965.

Pendle, George. *Uruguay*. London: Oxford University Press, 1963.

Taylor, Philip B., Jr. *Government and Politics of Uruguay*. New Orleans: Tulane University Press, 1960.

VENEZUELA

Bonilla, Frank, and José A. Silva Michelena. *A Strategy for Research on Social Policy.* Vol. 1 of *The Politics of Change in Venezuela.* Cambridge: M.I.T. Press, 1967.

Lieuwen, Edwin. *Venezuela.* New York: Oxford University Press, 1961.

Martz, John D. *Acción Democrática.* Princeton, N.J.: Princeton University Press, 1966.

References Cited

Adams, Richard N. 1967. *The Second Sowing*. Scranton: Chandler.

Alba, Victor. 1962. "Labor in America." *Dissent*, 9, No. 4 (Autumn), 387–392.
1969. *The Latin Americans*. New York: Praeger.

Almond, Gabriel A., and G. Bingham Powell, Jr. 1966. *Comparative Politics: A Developmental Approach*. Boston: Little, Brown.

Almond, Gabriel A., and Sidney Verba. 1963. *The Civic Culture*. Princeton, N.J.: Princeton University Press.

Andreski, Stanislav. 1969. *Parasitism and Subversion*. New York: Schocken Books.

Ayres, Robert. 1970. "Socio-Economic Correlates with Voting Behavior in Chile." Unpublished dissertation, University of North Carolina.

Bachrach, Peter, 1967. *The Theory of Democratic Elitism*. Boston: Little, Brown.

Barraclough, Solon. 1968–1969. "Agricultural Policy and Strategies of Land Reform." *Studies in Comparative International Development*, 4, No. 8, 167–201.

Blanksten, George I. 1959. "Political Groups in Latin America." *American Political Science Review*, 53, No. 1 (March), 106–127.

Bonilla, Frank. 1960. "The Student Federation of Chile: 50 Years of Political Action." *Journal of Inter-American Studies*, 2, No. 3 (July), 311–334.

Bonilla, Frank, and José A. Silva Michelena. 1967. *A Strategy for Research on Social Policy*. Vol. 1 of *The Politics of Change in Venezuela*. Cambridge: M.I.T. Press.

Braibanti, Ralph. 1968. "Comparative Political Analysis Reconsidered." *Journal of Politics*, 30, No. 1 (February), 25–65.

Bwy, D. P. 1968. "Political Instability in Latin America: The Cross-Cultural Test of a Causal Model." *Latin American Research Review*, 3, No. 2 (Spring), 17–66.

Campbell, Angus, *et al.* 1966. *Elections and the Political Order*. New York: Wiley.

Campos, Roberto de Oliveira. 1967. "Public Administration in Latin America." In Nimrod Raphaeli, ed., *Readings in Comparative Public Administration*. Boston: Allyn and Bacon. Pp. 283–294.

Charlesworth, James C., ed. 1968. *Theory and Practice of Public Administration: Scope, Objectives, and Methods*. Philadelphia: American Academy of Political and Social Science.

Chonchol, Jacques. 1964. *El Desarrollo de America Latina y La Reforma Agraria*. Santiago: Editorial del Pacifico.

——— 1970. "Eight Fundamental Conditions of Agrarian Reform in Latin America." In Rodolfo Stavenhagen, ed., *Agrarian Problems and Peasant Movements in Latin America*. Garden City, N.Y.: Doubleday. Pp. 159–172.

Cochrane, James D. 1970. *The Politics of Central American Regional Integration*. New Orleans: Tulane University Press.

Cornelius, William G. 1961. "The 'Latin American Bloc' in the United Nations." *Journal of Inter-American Studies*, 3, No. 3 (July), 419–435.

Daland, Robert T. 1967. *Brazilian Planning*. Chapel Hill: University of North Carolina Press.

Davis, Harold E., ed. 1963. *Latin American Social Thought*. Washington, D.C.: University Press.

Delgado, Oscar, 1962. "Revolution, Reform, Conservatism." *Dissent*, 9, No. 4 (Autumn), 350–363.

Denton, Charles F. 1969. "Bureaucracy in an Immobilist Society: The Case of Costa Rica." *Administrative Science Quarterly*, 14, No. 3 (September), 418–425.

——— 1971. *Patterns of Costa Rican Politics*. Boston: Allyn and Bacon.

Dinerstein, Herbert S. 1967. "Soviet Policy in Latin America." *American Political Science Review*, 61, No. 1 (March), 80–90.

Duff, Ernest A., and John F. McCamant. 1968. "Measuring Social and Political Requirements for System Stability in Latin America." *American Political Science Review*, 62, No. 4 (December), 1125–1143.

Duncan, W. Raymond. 1970. *Societ Policy in Developing Countries*. Waltham, Mass.: Ginn Blaisdell.

Duverger, Maurice. 1961. *Political Parties*. London: Methuen.

Dye, Thomas R., and L. Harmon Zeigler. 1970. *The Irony of Democracy: An Uncommon Introduction to American Politics*. Belmont, Calif.: Wadsworth.

Easton, David. 1957. "An Approach to the Analysis of Political Systems." *World Politics*, 9, No. 3 (April), 383–400.

Edelmann, Alexander T. 1965. *Latin American Government and Politics*. Homewood, Ill.: Dorsey Press.

Einaudi, Luigi R. 1970. *Peruvian Military Relations with the United States*. Santa Monica, Calif.: Rand Corporation.

Felix, David. 1961. "Chile." In Adamantios Pepelasis *et al.*, eds., *Economic Development*. New York: Harper.

Fitzgibbon, Russell H. 1957. "The Party Potpourri in Latin America." *Western Political Quarterly*, 10, No. 1 (March), 3–22.
——— 1967. "Measuring Democratic Change in Latin America." *Journal of Politics*, 29, No. 1 (February), 129–166.
Flores, Edmundo. 1963. *Land Reform and the Alliance for Progress*. Princeton, N.J.: Princeton University Press.
Fossum, Egil. 1967. "Factors Influencing the Occurrence of Military Coups d'Etat in Latin America." *Journal of Peace Research*, 4, No. 3, pp. 228–251.

Gale, Lawrence. 1969. *Education and Development in Latin America*. New York: Praeger.
García, Antonio. 1967. *Reforma Agraria y Economía Empresaria en América Latina*. Santiago: Editorial Universitario.
Glazer, Myron. 1966. "The Professional and Political Attitudes of Chilean University Students." *Comparative Education Review*, 10, No. 2 (June), pp. 293ff.
Goldrich, Daniel. 1966. *Sons of the Establishment*. Chicago: Rand McNally.
Gomez, Rudolph. 1969. *The Peruvian Administrative System*. Boulder: University of Colorado Press.
Graham, Lawrence S. 1968. *Civil Service Reform in Brazil: Principles versus Practice*. Austin: University of Texas Press.
Grimes, C. E., and Charles Simmons. 1969. "Bureaucracy and Political Control in Mexico: Towards an Assessment." *Public Administration Review*, 29 (January–February), 72–79.

Hamuy, Eduardo, *et al.* 1960. *Educación elemental, analfabetismo y desarrollo económico*. Santiago: Editorial Universitario.
Heady, Ferrel. 1966. *Public Administration: A Comparative Perspective*. Englewood Cliffs, N.J.: Prentice-Hall.
Heath, Dwight, and Richard N. Adams, eds. 1965. *Contemporary Cultures and Societies of Latin America*. New York: Random House.
Higgins, Benjamin. 1959. *Economic Development*. New York: Norton.
Hirschman, Albert O. 1965. *Journeys Toward Progress*. Garden City, N.Y.: Doubleday.
Hirschman, Albert O., ed. 1961. *Latin American Issues*. New York: Twentieth Century Fund.
Horowitz, Irving Louis, ed. 1970. *Masses in Latin America*. New York: Oxford University Press.
Houtart, François, and Émile Pin. 1965. *The Church and the Latin American Revolution*. New York: Sheed and Ward.

Inkeles, Alex. 1969. "Participant Citizenship in Six Developing Countries." *American Political Science Review*, 63, No. 4 (December), 1120–1141.
Inter-American Development Bank. 1970. *Socio-Economic Progress in Latin America: Social Progress Trust Fund Ninth Annual Report, 1969*. Washington, D.C.: Inter-American Development Bank.

Irish, Marian D., and James W. Prothro. 1965. *The Politics of American Democracy.* 3rd ed.; Englewood Cliff, N.J.: Prentice-Hall.

Johnson, John J. 1964. *The Military and Society in Latin America.* Stanford, Calif.: Stanford University Press.
　　1965. *Political Change in Latin America.* Rev. ed.; Stanford, Calif.: Stanford University Press.
Johnston, Bruce, and John Mellor. 1961. "The Role of Agriculture in Economic Development." *American Economic Review,* 51, No. 4 (September), 566–593.

Kantor, Harry. 1969. *Patterns of Politics and Political Systems in Latin America.* Chicago: Rand McNally.
Kling, Merle. 1956. "Toward a Theory of Power and Political Instability in Latin America." *Western Political Quarterly,* 9, No. 1 (March), 21–35.
　　1961. *A Mexican Interest Group in Action.* Englewood Cliffs, N.J.: Prentice-Hall.
　　1964. "The State of Research on Latin American Political Science." In Charles W. Wagley, ed., *Social Science Research on Latin America.* New York: Columbia University Press. Pp. 168–207.
Kolko, Gabriel. 1969. *The Roots of American Foreign Policy.* Boston: Beacon Press.

Lagos, Ricardo. 1965. *La concentración del poder económico.* Santiago: Editorial del Pacifico.
Lambert, Jacques. 1967. *Latin America: Social Structures and Political Institutions.* Berkeley: University of California Press.
Landsberger, Henry A. 1967. "The Labor Elite: Is It Revolutionary?" In Seymour Martin Lipset and Aldo Solari, eds., *Elites in Latin America.* New York: Oxford University Press. Pp. 256–300.
Langton, Kenneth P. 1969. *Political Socialization.* New York: Oxford University Press.
LaPalombara, Joseph, ed. 1963. *Bureaucracy and Political Development.* Princeton, N.J.: Princeton University Press.
Lauterbach, Albert. 1965. "Government and Development: Managerial Attitudes in Latin America." *Journal of Inter-American Studies,* 7, No. 2 (April), 201–226.
Leeds, Anthony. 1964. "Brazilian Careers and Social Structure: A Case History and Model." *American Anthropologist,* 66, No. 6, Part 1 (December), 1321–1347.
Lewis, Oscar. 1961. *The Children of Sanchez.* New York: Random House.
　　1965. *La Vida.* New York: Random House.
Lipset, Seymour Martin. 1959a. *Political Man.* Garden City, N.Y.: Doubleday.
　　1959b. "Some Social Requisites of Democracy: Economic Development and Political Legitimacy." *American Political Science Review,* 53, No. 1 (March), 90–91.

Litt, Edgar, ed. 1969. *The New Politics of American Policy.* New York: Holt, Rinehart, and Winston.

Lowi, Theodore. 1969. *The End of Liberalism.* New York: Norton.

McAlister, Lyle N. 1966. "Recent Research and Writings on the Role of the Military in Latin America." *Latin American Research Review,* 2, No. 1 (Fall), 5–36.

Mattelart, Armand, and Manuel Garreton. 1969. *Integración Nacional y Marginalidad.* 2nd ed.; Santiago: Instituto de Capacitación e Investigaciones Reforma Agraria.

Mecham, J. Lloyd. 1959. "Latin American Constitutions: Nominal or Real?" *Journal of Politics,* 21, No. 2 (May), 258–275.

Midlarsky, Manus, and Raymond Tanter. 1967. "Toward a Theory of Political Instability in Latin America." *Journal of Peace Research,* 4, No. 3, pp. 209–225.

Mitchell, Joyce N., and William C. Mitchell. 1969. *Political Analysis and Public Policy: An Introduction to Political Science.* Chicago: Rand McNally.

Myrdal, Gunnar. 1958. *Economic Theory and Underdeveloped Regions.* Mystic, Conn.: Lawrency Verry.

Navarette, Ifigenía. 1960. *La distribución del ingreso y el desarrollo económico de México.* Mexico City: Escuela Nacional de Economía.

Needler, Martin C. 1968. *Political Development in Latin America: Instability, Violence, and Evolutionary Change.* New York: Random House.

Neumann, Sigmund. 1956. *Modern Political Parties.* Chicago: University of Chicago Press.

Nun, José. 1965. "A Latin American Phenomenon: The Middle Class Military Coup." In Institute of International Studies, *Trends in Social Science Research in Latin American Studies: A Conference Report.* Berkeley: University of California Press. Pp. 55–99.

Nye, Joseph L. 1967. "Central American Regional Integration." *International Conciliation,* No. 562 (March), pp. 12–14.

Office of Development Programs, Bureau for Latin America, Agency for International Development. April 1971. *Summary Economic and Social Indicators 18 Latin American Countries: 1960–1970.*

Organization of American States. 1966. *Latin America: Problems and Perspectives of Economic Development.* Baltimore: Johns Hopkins Press.

Paredo, Inti. 1970. "Bolivian Communism, the Guerrilla 'Foco,' and the Death of Che Guevara." In Paul E. Sigmund, ed., *Models of Political Change in Latin America.* New York: Praeger. Pp. 64–68.

Parrish, Charles J., and Jorge Tapia-Videla. 1970. "Welfare Policy and Administration in Chile." *Journal of Comparative Administration,* 1, No. 4 (February), 455–476.

Payne, James L. 1968. *Patterns of Conflict in Colombia.* New Haven: Yale University Press.

Pearse, Andrew. 1966. "Agrarian Change Trends in Latin America." *Latin American Research Review,* 1, No. 3 (Summer), 45–69.

Petras, James. 1970. *Politics and Social Forces in Chilean Development.* Berkeley: University of California Press.

Petras, James, and Maurice Zeitlin, eds. 1968. *Latin America: Reform or Revolution?* Greenwich, Conn.: Fawcett.

Phelan, John Teddy. 1960. "Authority and Flexibility in the Spanish Imperial Bureaucracy." *Administrative Science Quarterly,* 5, No. 1 (June), 47–65.

Powell, John Duncan. 1965. "Military Assistance and Militarism in Latin America." *Western Political Quarterly,* 18, No. 2 (June), 382–392.

Putnam, Robert D. 1967. "Toward Explaining Intervention in Latin American Politics." *World Politics,* 20, No. 1 (October), 83–110.

Quijano Obregón, Aníbal. 1968. "Tendencies in Peruvian Development and in the Class Structure." In James Petras and Maurice Zeitlin, eds., *Latin America: Reform or Revolution?* Greenwich, Conn.: Fawcett. Pp. 323–328.

Radway, Laurence I. 1969. *Foreign Policy and National Defense.* Glenview, Ill.: Scott, Foresman.

Riggs, Fred W. 1964. *Administration in Developing Countries: The Theory of Prismatic Society.* Boston: Houghton Mifflin.

Rodó, José Enrique. 1929. *Ariel.* Portions have been reproduced in Harold E. Davis, ed., *Latin American Social Thought.* Washington, D.C.: University Press, 1963.

Rosenau, James N. 1966. "Pre-Theories of Foreign Policy." In R. Barry Farrell, ed., *Approaches to Comparative and International Politics.* Evanston: Northwestern University Press. Pp. 27–92.

Russet, Bruce, *et al.* 1964. *World Handbook of Social and Political Indicators.* New Haven: Yale University Press.

Sanders, Thomas G. 1968. "Andean Economic Integration." American Universities Field Staff, West Coast South America Series, 15, No. 2.

Sapin, Burton M. 1966. *The Making of United States Foreign Policy.* Washington, D.C.: Brookings Institution.

Schaedel, Robert P. 1965. "Land Reform Studies." *Latin American Research Review,* 1, No. 1 (Fall), 75–122.

Schmitt, Karl, and David Burks. 1963. *Evolution or Chaos?* New York: Praeger.

Scott, Robert E. 1965. "The Government Bureaucrats and Political Change in Latin America." *Journal of International Affairs,* 20, No. 2, 289–308.

    1967. "Political Elites and Political Modernization: The Crisis of Transition." In Seymour Martin Lipset and Aldo Solari, eds., *Elites in Latin America.* New York: Oxford University Press. Pp. 117–145.

Seers, Dudley, *et al.* 1964. *Cuba: The Economic and Social Revolution.* Chapel Hill: University of North Carolina Press.

Shively, W. Phillips. 1969. " 'Ecological' Inference: The Use of Aggregate Data to Study Individuals." *American Political Science Review*, 63, No. 4 (December), 1183–1196.

Sigmund, Paul E., ed. 1970. *Models of Political Change in Latin America.* New York: Praeger.

Silva Solar, Julio, and Jacques Chonchol. 1964. *Desarrollo sin Capitalismo: Hacía un mundo comunitario.* Caracas: Editorial Nuevo Orden.

Silvert, Kalman H. 1967a. "Nationalism in Latin America." In Peter G. Snow, ed., *The Government and Politics of Latin America.* New York: Holt, Rinehart, and Winston. Pp. 440–450.

    1967b. "The University Student." In Peter G. Snow, ed., *The Government and Politics of Latin America.* New York: Holt, Rhinehart, and Winston. Pp. 367–385.

Smith, Raymond T. 1956. *The Negro Family in British Guiana.* London: Routledge and Kegan Paul.

Statistical Abstract of Latin America. 1967, 1968. Los Angeles: University of California Press.

Stavenhagen, Rodolfo, ed. 1970. *Agrarian Problems and Peasant Movements in Latin America.* Garden City, N.Y.: Doubleday.

Stokes, William S. 1959. *Latin American Politics.* New York: Crowell.

Szulc, Tad. 1965. *The Winds of Revolution.* New York: Praeger.

United Nations. 1964. *The Economic Development of Latin America in the Post War Period.* New York: United Nations.

United Nations Economic Commission for Latin America. 1966, 1967, 1968. *Economic Survey of Latin America.* New York: United Nations.

    1970. *Development Problems in Latin America.* Austin: University of Texas Press.

Vallier, Ivan. 1967. "Religious Elites: Differentiations and Developments in Roman Catholicism." In Seymour Martin Lipset and Aldo Solari, eds., *Elites in Latin America.* New York: Oxford University Press. Pp. 190–232.

Véliz, Claudio, ed. 1965. *Obstacles to Change in Latin America.* London: Oxford University Press.

    1967. *The Politics of Conformity in Latin America.* New York: Oxford University Press.

Vernon, Raymond A. 1963. *The Dilemma of Mexico's Development.* Cambridge: Harvard University Press.

Wagner, H. Harrison. 1970. *United States Policy toward Latin America.* Stanford, Calif.: Stanford University Press.

Wheare, K. C. 1966. *Modern Constitutions.* 2nd ed.; New York: Oxford University Press.

Zeitlin, Maurice. 1967. *Revolutionary Politics and the Cuban Working Class.* Princeton, N.J.: Princeton University Press.

Index

239